BY STRANGE WAYS

By Strange Ways

Theologians and Their Paths to the Catholic Church

Edited by
Jonathan Fuqua and Daniel Strudwick

IGNATIUS PRESS   SAN FRANCISCO

Cover photo:
Mosaic of Christ, Pantocrator (detail)
Chapel of San Xeno
Basilica of Santa Prassede, Rome, Italy
Image in the public domain

Cover design by Enrique J. Aguilar

© 2022 by Ignatius Press, San Francisco
All rights reserved
ISBN 978-1-62164-363-0 (PB)
ISBN 978-1-64229-237-4 (eBook)
Library of Congress Control Number 2022935081
Printed in the United States of America ∞

CONTENTS

God knows what is my greatest happiness, but I do not. There is no rule about what is happy and good; what suits one would not suit another. And the ways by which perfection is reached vary very much; the medicines necessary for our souls are very different from each other. Thus God leads us **by strange ways**; we know He wills our happiness, but we neither know what our happiness is, nor the way. We are blind; left to ourselves we should take the wrong way; we must leave it to Him.

—John Henry Newman

FOREWORD

by

Matthew Levering

Reading about these Catholic conversions and thinking of my own story of conversion, I recall a time when such things hardly seemed possible. I grew up in the 1970s and early 1980s. Although I was not a Catholic, I had a number of Catholic friends, and the condition of their faith was generally abysmal. Many if not most of the children raised Catholic in my generation have now lapsed. The briefest glance at the 1970s bookshelf tells the tale regarding the struggles of that era: Richard McBrien's *Do We Need the Church?* and *The Remaking of the Church*; Peter Hebblethwaite's *Faith in Question*; Avery Dulles' *The Survival of Dogma*. The titles reflect the mood of the time.

Since the present volume contains the conversion stories of people who not only are converts but also are *theologians*, 1970s Catholic theology merits some attention in this foreword. McBrien's *The Remaking of the Church* was dedicated to Richard Cardinal Cushing and bore a preface by Leo Cardinal Suenens. In this book published only four years after the Second Vatican Council, McBrien asks: "Is there a point any longer to making proposals for institutional change within an organization [the Catholic Church!] whose long-term viability has been placed in fundamental question?"[1] He calls for a massive "reform", and he warns ominously about the resistance of the entrenched powers-that-be in the Vatican and elsewhere. Similar insistence that the Church must be entirely remade, and similar dire warnings about entrenched resistance to overthrowing fundamental teachings of Vatican II's own Dogmatic Constitution on the Church,

---

[1] Richard P. McBrien, *The Remaking of the Church: An Agenda for Reform* (New York: Harper & Row, 1973), 142.

Lumen Gentium, are everywhere among McBrien's fellow theologians after the council.

Much of the theological malaise of the era is summed up in Hans Küng's *Signposts for the Future*, a collection of essays written in the late 1960s and early 1970s. After proclaiming the good news that Jesus is alive, Küng goes on to explain that the first believers "regarded their faith as based on something that really happened to them", insofar as they were now "sustained, impelled, by the certainty that the man who was killed did not remain dead but is alive." He contends that at the Resurrection of Jesus, there was "no revival of a corpse". What then happened to the corpse? He does not say, but instead he offers the view that Jesus, having died, was "assumed into that incomprehensible and comprehensive last and first reality, by that most real reality which we designate with the name of God".[2]

Not surprisingly, such a less-than-robust account of Jesus' Resurrection fuels reductive understandings of the Church. In the 1970s and early 1980s, Karl Rahner proposed immediately uniting with the Protestants in order to form a new umbrella Church, unified by shared belief in Christ and the Trinity. Rahner deems that in the new unified Church, all "partner churches" must solely agree not to condemn the distinctive beliefs of the other "partner churches". He thinks this should be enough to ground full fellowship in Eucharistic communion and in ministry (whatever either would now mean)— with the pope as a figurehead, lacking authority to do anything other than to confirm the results of any future general councils of the partner churches.[3] In a 1977 essay, Rahner affirmed that "the history of faith and dogma will continue", but now in a new manner, as "the history of the new expression of the old basic substance of the faith confronting and assimilating the future horizons of understanding". He states that "many" or even "all" individual dogmas will be radically transposed; and many dogmas will be recognized as having been true only in an earlier horizon of understanding, now past.[4] It follows

[2] Hans Küng, *Signposts for the Future* (Garden City, N.Y.: Doubleday, 1978), 21–22.
[3] See Heinrich Fries and Karl Rahner, S.J., *Unity of the Churches: An Actual Possibility*, trans. Ruth C.L. Gritsch and Eric W. Gritsch (New York: Paulist Press, 1985).
[4] Karl Rahner, S.J., "Yesterday's History of Dogma and Theology for Tomorrow", in Rahner, *Theological Investigations*, vol. 18, *God and Revelation*, trans. Edward Quinn (New York: Crossroad, 1983), 34.

for Rahner that we cannot know today what Catholics will believe in the future, even if Catholic belief, he thinks, will retain a connection to Christ and the Trinity.

This was not exactly the heyday among Catholics of Saint John Henry Newman's dogmatic principle and sacramental principle. No wonder that the Yale professor Anthony Kronman began a lifelong process of conversion during the 1960s and 1970s, but to paganism rather than to Catholicism! In his *Confessions of a Born-Again Pagan*—surely a fitting mantra for the 1970s if there ever was one—Kronman discusses Augustine and Thomas Aquinas but takes the seventeenth-century skeptic Benedict Spinoza as his mentor and model, in arguing that "the world is both inherently *and* infinitely divine."[5] The divine, then, is nothing other than the unfolding cosmos, with its explosions, destruction, and (on Earth) death. He concludes on page 1074 that death is final, but that we will always be part of eternity because the world—the cosmos of which we are a part and always will be a part, materially speaking—is the immortal "divine" being. Some consolation!

Looking back on it, Catholicism in the 1970s seemed to be trying to convert *to* the world—and a dreary world at that. It is in this context that the conversions recorded in the present book should call us to rejoice, both in their fruitfulness and due to the amazing recovery executed by the Church in the final two decades of the twentieth century. As Newman remarks, "It is true, there have been seasons when, from the operation of external or internal causes, the Church has been thrown into what was almost a state of *deliquium*; but her wonderful revivals, while the world was triumphing over her, is a further evidence of the absence of corruption in the system of doctrine and worship into which she has developed."[6] In the fervid postconciliar years, the Catholic faith did not succeed in self-imploding, despite all the urgent demands that it do so, and despite all the requiems for the faith (many offered by theologians themselves!). "Where sin increased, grace abounded all the more" (Rom 5:20). Under the pontificates of Saint John Paul II and Benedict XVI, the contributors to this volume joyfully became Catholics. Many other theologians

---

[5] Anthony T. Kronman, *Confessions of a Born-Again Pagan* (New Haven, Conn.: Yale University Press, 2016), 585.

[6] John Henry Newman, *An Essay on the Development of Christian Doctrine*, 6th ed. (Notre Dame: University of Notre Dame Press, 1989), 444.

did as well: Thomas Joseph White, O.P., John Betz, Reinhard Hüt-
ter, Stephen Bullivant, Bruce Marshall, R.R. Reno, Richard John
Neuhaus, and many, many more. In this extraordinary volume, we
receive a taste of how this happened and why.

My colleague Melanie Barrett's conversion journey in the 1990s
took her from a secular Jewish upbringing influenced by New Age
spirituality, to a doctoral program at the University of Chicago under
the mentorship of Jean Bethke Elshstain, to friendship with Francis Cardinal George and then-Father Robert Barron and a profound
commitment to the Catholic moral life. Similarly, Lawrence Feingold began as a nonpracticing Jewish sculptor in Rome—a very tal-
ented sculptor, indeed. In Rome during the 1990s, Larry became a
Catholic and wrote a doctoral dissertation launching an entirely new
discussion of nature and grace that has continued to the present day.
Jeff Morrow was a third convert from secular Judaism, who became a
keen critic of Spinoza and who has greatly expanded our understanding of the earliest historical-critical scholars of Scripture.

Matthew Thomas was influenced by my friend Hans Boersma (who
has remained Evangelical—eventually becoming an Anglican—but
whose son, Gerald Boersma, is a Catholic convert currently on the
faculty of Ave Maria University). Matthew now teaches Scripture at
his hometown institution, the Dominican School of Philosophy and
Theology. Andrew Summerson, an expert on Maximus the Confessor, is doing inspiring work as a priest at his Byzantine Catholic parish
in northern Indiana and as a faculty member at the Sheptytsky Institute of Eastern Christian Studies. Paige Hochschild and her husband,
Joshua, both scholar-converts, made history at Wheaton College
when Joshua's conversion to Catholicism led to him being removed
from his teaching position in the philosophy department there. My
wife and I read Scott and Kimberly Hahn's conversion story, *Rome
Sweet Home*, when we were in the process of converting to Catholicism as young newlyweds. Scott has revitalized the Catholic biblical
movement, which, after the council, had been given up for dead.
Joshua Lim, a recent Notre Dame Ph.D. and now a tutor at Thomas
Aquinas College, is a brilliant Thomistic theologian and voracious
theological reader.

I have not had the privilege of meeting the other contributors to
this volume, but their stories are impressive. Barnabas Aspray is a

young Cambridge-trained Ph.D. whose concerns range from Paul Ricœur to care for refugees, and Petroc Willey has an extraordinary background as one of the leaders of the Maryvale Institute and now as a scholar of catechetics at the Franciscan University of Steubenville.

Surely the grace of God has been powerful in the lives of these theologians, as their stories invite us to perceive. In thanking God for their testimony, let us also thank God for raising up Saint John Paul II. A serious thinker, John Paul II embodied and articulated the best of the council's teachings on Jesus Christ, the Church, the moral life, religious freedom, the Virgin Mary, the Jewish people, and so on. His *Jeweler's Shop* and *Love and Responsibility* are so profound, creative, and moving. His decades of papal teaching are rich and courageous in their defense of the truth of the Catholic tradition. Joseph Ratzinger served as his closest theological advisor and added his profound insights into the liturgy and Scripture.

Saint John Paul II published *Crossing the Threshold of Hope* in 1994. Reading this book around the time of its publication, just as my wife and I were entering into the Church (which we did on Easter 1995), I was struck by the pope's answer to the question of why God, if he exists, is hidden from us. Far from hiding, says the pope, God in Christ *"has gone as far as possible. He could not go further.* In a certain sense God has gone too far!"[7] God has revealed himself to be such absolute humility, so intimately close to us in love, that we almost protest against it. Surely the living God would have no business becoming a mere man, let alone a man so lacking in worldly prestige or power—a mere man from Galilee, a backwater not only of the Roman Empire but of Israel itself. Surely the living God could do better than become an itinerant preacher and healer and die ignominiously, abandoned even by his disciples. He could have invented penicillin or computers! But instead he revealed the love and life of God; he healed the human race from sin and united us to his own life, through the path of humility, the path of the Cross as the antidote to pride and its consequences. In fact, our whole lives are governed by the Lord who died on a cross and rose from the grave, inaugurating the kingdom of God as a kingdom of self-surrendering love.

[7] John Paul II, *Crossing the Threshold of Hope*, trans. Jenny McPhee and Martha McPhee (New York: Alfred A. Knopf, 1994), 40.

Some of the contributors to this volume converted during the pontificate of Joseph Ratzinger/Pope Benedict XVI. My first encounter with Ratzinger's work was the 1985 *Ratzinger Report*, which I read in 1994. Surprisingly few of Ratzinger's writings had been published in English prior to that book-length interview. In the *Ratzinger Report*, one notices immediately that Ratzinger, even in off-the-cuff conversation, speaks in erudite and nuanced paragraphs. He shows Catholic faith to be reasonable, the fruit of divine *Logos* awakening human *logos* and drawing it upward into the realities of Christ and the Trinity. He calls the Church back to Sacred Scripture and, correspondingly, he calls scriptural study back to the Church. As he says, "a church without a credible biblical foundation is only a chance historical product, one organization among others, and the humanly constructed.... But the Bible without the Church is also no longer the powerfully effective Word of God, but an assemblage of various historical sources."[8] Likewise, he speaks about the liturgy along the lines of the preconciliar Liturgical Movement, with its delight in liturgical piety. He remarks, "Liturgy, for the Catholic, is his common homeland, the source of his identity. And another reason why it must be something 'given' and 'constant' is that, by means of the ritual, it manifests the holiness of God."[9]

Much more could be said about the graced impulse to conversion nourished by the work of these two pope-scholars. But of course no pope is the source and goal of conversion to Catholicism. Popes come and go, and no pope avoids mistakes, as distinct from solemn, definitive doctrinal error. Converts know that popes are sinners; and converts know that the Church, whether in the 1970s or today, is composed of sinners and will always face trials. What converts to Catholicism are seeking is something more than can be given by any human or by any merely human institution.

The present book directs us toward the real source of conversion, who is also the real source of the vocation of these theologians: Jesus Christ. Through the grace of the Holy Spirit, these converts yearned for the fullness of Christ in word and sacrament. They desired the

---

[8] Joseph Cardinal Ratzinger with Vittorio Messori, *The Ratzinger Report: An Exclusive Interview on the State of the Church*, trans. Salvator Attanasio and Graham Harrison (San Francisco: Ignatius Press, 1985), 75.

[9] Ibid., 126.

fullness of the salvation Christ brings; they thirsted for the fullness of faith in communion with Christ in his Church. Another convert, Paul, describes the charitable path that these theologians have followed: "Never flag in zeal, be aglow with the Spirit, serve the Lord" (Rom 12:11).

This book recounts the conversion stories of men and women who "serve the Lord" through study and teaching. With Paul, they testify to the "gospel of Christ" with all their minds and hearts (1 Cor 9:12). Like Paul, they are not strangers to controversies and troubles from inside and outside the Church. Having entered the Church and received a mission to teach theology, these convert-scholars "do it all for the sake of the gospel, that [they might] share in its blessings" (1 Cor 9:23). Aware of their own weakness and deficiencies, they implore the Lord's help for themselves, for their students, and for the whole Church and world. Let us listen to their testimonies to grace and rejoice that the Lord is so powerful in our day.

INTRODUCTION

by

Daniel Strudwick

When we began this project, we were inspired by the wave of excitement that was present as Saint John Henry Newman's canonization was quickly approaching. There was a good deal in the press that reminded Catholics of the heroic life of this saint and how he tenaciously pursued truth in the face of significant obstacles. Beginning with a profound experience of God in his youth, Newman set out on the quest to know God, and to know him in truth. His studies in the early Church Fathers led him initially to believe that his Anglican Church should return to some of its more ancient practices and devotions. This conviction disposed Newman to a more favorable view of Anglicanism's Catholic past. At this point, with Newman as a driving force of what is referred to as the Oxford Movement, he thought he could promote a *via media, a middle way* that might help to bridge the divide between Catholics and Protestants. Later, however, he resigned himself to the fact that his "middle way" was insufficient and that he must make the journey all the way to Rome. This move, for Newman, came at great personal cost.[1]

Following his conversion, he lost much in the way of position, security, prestige, close friends, and even family. Yet he emerged from this time with a great joy as he found his true home in the Catholic Church. In many varied ways, the path of Saint John Henry Newman exemplifies the quest shared by the contributors in this volume.

We found it providential that after we founded our project with Newman in mind, so many of our contributors made specific note of him in their essays. This, despite the fact that we did not specifically

---

[1] St. John Henry Newman, *Apologia Pro Vita Sua* (New York: W.W. Norton, 1968), 177.

mention Newman in our letter of invitation to potential contributors. We took this as an indication of his powerful influence among recent converts to Catholicism.

There is great variety found in the narratives offered by the contributors to this work. The stories come from priests and laity, men and women, Western and Eastern Catholics. For some, their study of theology led to their conversion to the Catholic Church; for others, their conversion to the Catholic faith led them to a life of study that developed into a theological vocation. In all cases, whether the study of theology was a cause or a consequence of conversion, they eventually found their home in Catholicism.

There have been many books published over the years that present the stories of individuals entering the Church.[2] This is the first that focuses exclusively on theologians. Our aim was to highlight the particular challenges faced by theologians as they consider the veracity of Catholicism. Having greater exposure to theological perspectives and divergent schools of thought, the theologian is likely to be more aware of arguments running counter to the claims of the Catholic Church. One's conversion and entrance into the Church must address these concerns, as for the theologian there are simply more questions on the intellectual front to be answered, and hence joining the Church is one, albeit momentous, step forward on the lifelong journey.

While Saint John Henry Newman emerged as an important source of inspiration for this project, not all of our contributors followed the course from Protestant to Catholic. A few contributors come from Judaism, and a number of our writers come from families where religious practice and belief had mostly died out. In these cases, their upbringing took place in the secularized atmosphere that has become pervasive in our time. The experience of this religious void inclined some to pursue fringe religious paths, or even to foray into the occult. The stories here are notably representative of our age. Yet, however unique the narratives in this project are, common themes emerge that unite the essays.

One theme that unites the authors of these chapters is that of the journey. If this verges on overuse, it does so because it is so apt a

---

[2] Patrick Madrid, ed., *Surprised by Truth: 11 Converts Give the Biblical and Historical Reasons for Becoming Catholic* (Gastonia, N.C.: Basilica Press, 2016); Brian Besong and Jonathan Fuqua, eds., *Faith and Reason: Philosophers Explain Their Turn to Catholicism* (San Francisco: Ignatius Press, 2019); Charles Connor, *Classic Catholic Converts* (San Francisco: Ignatius Press, 2001).

theme. It reaches far back into the universal human practice of telling our stories. Once, in conversation with a great contemporary Thomist, Father Norris Clarke, I asked for advice concerning fruitful venues of philosophical and theological projects for the future. Without hesitation, he directed me to the theme of "the journey". For Father Clarke, the notion of journey was synonymous with the grand philosophical account of human life as an *exitus* and a *reditus*, a going forth from God and a journey back to him—an understanding of human existence that goes at least as far back as Plato and that is taken up by many significant Christian thinkers. According to Father Clarke, this meant that the human story has a beginning, a middle, and—most especially—an end. And this end is more than simply a conclusion or finale. It is a *finis* in the philosophical sense of a goal toward which the human person strives, one that gives purpose and meaning to the whole of human life. For good measure, Father Clarke contrasted this notion of life as a journey with the plot lines of contemporary soap operas, which were, as far as he could tell, "full of sound and fury, signifying nothing".[3] In these chapters, we see how our authors, coming from very diverse backgrounds and following very different paths, are led to discern and pursue a common end. Even so, their shared arrival at the Catholic Church in no way amounts to the final end of their journey. It amounts, instead, to a new beginning with more chapters to come.

The title of the book, *By Strange Ways*, rightly describes the stories found in this collection. It speaks to the wide-ranging and surprising paths traveled by these authors as they followed the voice of God, leading them where they would have never thought they would find themselves. This phrase comes from a lengthier quote by Saint John Henry Newman that can be found at the beginning of the book in recognition of God's mysterious leadings.

Another notable commonality is that the contributors assembled here make clear that their entrance into the Catholic Church was a broadening and deepening of elements of truth that they had received earlier. To a person, each contributor expresses a deep appreciation for his past. The parents, pastors, and teachers who formed them, and were instrumental in their journeys, are held in esteem. The truths

[3] See W. Norris Clarke, *The One and the Many: A Contemporary Thomistic Metaphysics* (South Bend, Ind.: University of Notre Dame Press, 2001), 303–13.

they imparted are not forgotten, but treasured; the wisdom garnered is built upon rather than discarded. Some aspects of that earlier theology and practice make for a more robust Catholicism, as they incorporate appropriate elements into their Catholic faith.

From the time of the Reformation, the particular contours of each fractured ecclesial and theological tradition have taken on particular shapes. These unique elements of belief have at times become stumbling blocks for unity, as each group is strongly invested in its own peculiarities, and any movement away from them seems a betrayal. This does not have to be the case. In *Ut Unum Sint*, Pope Saint John Paul II notes that although the fullness resides in the Catholic Church, in other communities "certain features of the Christian mystery have at times been more effectively emphasized."[4] Converts to the Catholic Church bring with them the strengths of their traditions, and these strengths are often the leaven needed for advancing Catholic fullness. These sentiments were well stated by Dr. Peter Kreeft, a convert to Catholicism, when he said in an interview that if the churches were ever to reunite, they should do so while retaining the good and true elements of their varied Christian traditions.[5]

We see, too, that even as these converts bring into the Church the treasures gathered up in the course of their personal journeys, they relate to us their wonder at the riches they discover within the Church. Many Protestants, for example, note the difficulty posed to them by the Church's traditional devotion to Mary. However, many converts come to find that the influence and aid of the Mother of God become a greater source of blessing in their spiritual lives than they could have ever imagined. Their discovery of the beauty and inspiration of the Blessed Virgin seems to confirm the observation of Vladimir Lossky,

---

[4] Pope St. John Paul II, encyclical letter *Ut Unum Sint* (May 25, 1995), no. 14.

[5] As Kreeft put it in an interview with Jedd Medifind, "If the churches ever did reunite, it would have to be into something that was as sacramental and liturgical and authoritative as the Roman Catholic Church and as protesting against abuses and as much focused on the individual in his direct relationship with Christ as the Evangelicals, as charismatic as the Pentecostals, as missionary-minded as the old line mainline denominations, as focused on holiness as the Methodists or the Quakers, as committed to the social aspects of the Gospel as the social activists, as Biblical as the fundamentalists, as mystical as the Eastern Orthodox, etc." See Jedd Medifind, "A Conversation with Peter Kreeft about C.S. Lewis", Catholic Education Resource Center, October 2003, https://www.catholiceducation.org/en/religion-and-philosophy/apologetics/a-conversation-with-peter-kreeft-about-c-s-lewis.html.

who regarded an intimate association with the Mother of God to be the treasure awaiting those who make their way into the inner life of the household of God. "While Christ was preached on the house-tops ... the mystery of the Mother of God was revealed only to those within the Church."[6] The same might be said for countless other features of Catholic life—the Eucharist, liturgical worship, traditional devotions, papal authority, the communion of saints, and an integral moral theology. The writers featured in this book describe their surprising encounter with many of these elements of the Catholic faith. In nearly all cases, these were unsought and unasked for, and often were originally stumbling blocks to our pilgrims. But in the end, these traditional features of Catholic life came to be seen by them as great helps to achieving a greater knowledge and intimacy with God. Now, as Catholics, these authors find new strength, sink their roots more deeply, and take advantage of the rich soil of the Catholic Church that has been tilled for two millennia.

A final uniting theme for this work is that our writers see their journey not only as a theological quest but as a spiritual pilgrimage incorporating mind, heart, and soul in pursuit of God. A move into the Catholic Church is not merely the solving of a theological puzzle, but the movement of the entire person into ecclesial life. The tradition of the ancient Church speaks of the vocation of the theologian as intimately tied to prayer as well as study. In the words of Evagrius, "If you are a theologian you truly pray. If you truly pray you are a theologian."[7] This often-neglected truth is not lost to the writers here.

On October 3, 2019, we witnessed the canonization of Saint John Henry Newman. This marked the successful, long, ponderous journey of Newman as he entered the Catholic Church. The final leg of this journey would end with him making it all the way back to the Triune God and resting in the company of the angels and saints. We hope that this book inspires and edifies readers as they make their own paths in search of a God who often leads us by strange ways.

Glory to Jesus Christ!

---

[6] Vladimir Lossky, "Panagia", in *The Mother of God*, ed. E. L. Mascall (London: Dacre Press, 1949), 35.

[7] Evagrius of Pontus, "Chapters on Prayer", in *Evagrius of Pontus: The Greek Ascetic Corpus*, trans. Robert Sinkewicz (Oxford: Oxford University Press, 2003), 199.

Chapter 1

A GREATER HOPE

by

Barney Aspray

If I had to put my reason for becoming Catholic in one sentence, then I would say that it was because I felt the need for a standard outside of myself by which to discern truth from falsehood. I became convinced that God must have provided such a standard, because we human beings need to be saved from the tendency to set ourselves up as our own standard. As to why I felt that this salvation was only available in the Catholic Church, that is what I shall try to explain—although I feel a little like Sam in *The Lord of the Rings*, for whom a question "needed a week's answer, or none".[1] In what follows I shall limit myself to showing why the three main alternatives I tried—Scripture (biblical studies), reason (academic theology), and tradition—were insufficient to dislodge me from the center of my theological world. I shall then show why Catholicism ceased to seem like one denomination among many, and how I was compelled to take its claims seriously, and why it offered for me a hope greater than anything I could find elsewhere.

Disunity as a Practical Problem

I grew up in a Charismatic Evangelical free church in the south of England, which belonged to one of the many networks of churches

---

[1] J. R. R. Tolkien, *Lord of the Rings*, vol. 3, *The Return of the King* (London: HarperCollins, 2005), 1008.

born out of the 1960s renewal movement. When I left home and went to university, I befriended many Christians from other traditions, whose beliefs and practices were often quite different from my own. Worse, I discovered that many of these differences were incompatible with each other. For example, some of my friends loved liturgical worship, while others considered it a harmful constraint on the authenticity of free self-expression. Both could not be correct.

In short, I encountered the problem of disunity in the church. Ever since then, I have been convinced that this disunity is a scandal and a disgrace from which all Christians suffer and for which all Christians share responsibility. That the Gospel of peace should be in conflict, that the ministry of reconciliation should not be reconciled, that the servants of the One God should not be one—these things undermine our faith. Christians from all traditions need to take seriously the call to unity that we find in Jesus' climactic prayer, echoed everywhere in the apostle Paul's writings,[2] "that they may all be one".[3]

But disunity is not just a scandal, it is also a practical problem. And it was the practical problem, more than the longing for unity in itself, that troubled me as a young Protestant. The absence of unity makes the search for truth more difficult. When more than one community claims to know best what Christian discipleship looks like, how can one judge between them?

One sometimes hears that "it doesn't matter which denomination you're a part of, as long as you love Jesus and follow him with all your heart." This is a wonderful thing to say and really mean. It is one of those foundational insights that we must always return to and remember, preventing us from losing perspective and showing un-Christlike behavior toward fellow brothers and sisters.

---

[2] "I have come to the conclusion that the central symbol of Paul's worldview is the united community: Jew-Greek, slave-free, male-female: the one family of Abraham, the family for the world, the single family created anew in Jesus Christ from people of every kind" (N. T. Wright, "Whence and Whither Pauline Studies in the Life of the Church?", in *Jesus, Paul and the People of God: A Theological Dialogue with N. T. Wright*, ed. Nicholas Perrin and Richard Hays [Downers Grove, Ill.: InterVarsity Press, 2011], 265).

[3] John 17:21. Every Christian ought to read the first two chapters of Hans Urs von Balthasar's brilliant work *The Theology of Karl Barth: Exposition and Interpretation*, trans. Edward T. Oakes (Communio Books; San Francisco: Ignatius Press, 1992), which are about ecumenical dialogue. They show why church unity should be a priority for us all.

But as anyone following Jesus will have found out, that is only the starting point of the journey of discipleship. At some stage, you will reach forks in the road where you must make choices. Questions arise about what following Jesus looks like in practice. Does it mean supporting or opposing same-sex marriage? Contraception? Transgenderism? Abortion? Divorce? Euthanasia? I have chosen these practical issues as examples instead of doctrinal issues (predestination, transubstantiation, *sola scriptura*, immaculate conception, etc.), because I often hear people saying that we cannot be certain about doctrinal questions, and we do not need to know the answers to live our lives as Christians, nor should we try to impose a single viewpoint on everyone; we should be comfortable with a certain ambiguity and diversity of opinions in the church. The practical questions show, however, that what is at stake is not merely an intellectual exercise in getting one's doctrines in a line (although doctrines all have practical implications, too). Nor is it about getting final and certain black-and-white answers. Even if there is always a grey area of uncertainty or ambiguity in theory, sometimes in practice no such grey area exists when it is about how to live one's life as a Christian. For example, a pregnant teenager has a short space of time in which to decide either to have an abortion or not; there is no third option, no room for agnosticism or postponing the question to a later date. And if you are not a pregnant teenager, same-sex attracted, or wrestling with divorce, you still need to know how to love with Christlike love those who are, and that starts with knowing how to think about these things as a Christian. As for celebrating the diversity of opinions: the more important one considers an issue, the less one will tolerate diversity; even the most liberal of Christians can be staunchly dogmatic on things that they think matter. Nor are they necessarily wrong: these questions clearly involve major decisions that affect a person's whole life and may require significant levels of self-sacrifice, depending on the conclusion reached. The way you live your life and treat other people involves an (at least implicit and provisional) answer to them.

Most Christians find their answers to such questions by asking the advice of people they trust, perhaps their pastor, priest, or a wise older person. To that degree, they are submitting to a standard of authority higher than themselves, and that in itself is spiritually healthy

regardless of what they are taught. But as a budding theologian, I felt
called to *become* such a trusted source of guidance, so I felt the weight
of responsibility for what I would teach; teaching the wrong thing
could be catastrophically damaging to a person's well-being.[4]

This is not to suggest that all Christians ought to live and worship in an identical way. The diversity of spiritual expressions can
be wonderfully enriching. One community emphasizes fasting,
another social justice, another Bible reading, and another the Charismatic gifts; one loves exuberant singing, another quiet meditation, another ancient Latin rites. Every Christian group has its own
unique insight into God's glory, like the explosion of colors in a
garden of flowers or the delicious array of flavors in an ice-cream
shop. Likewise, every Christian group has its unique function in
the overall Body of Christ. Diversity is both necessary and beautiful.
Nor do I mean that Christians must be united institutionally before
they can achieve great things together in the world. The ecumenical movement in the twentieth century may not have helped many
institutional churches to reunite, but it has had this wonderful side-
effect, that today we are seeing more collaborations across denominations than ever before: conferences, worship events, social action,
and more. When Christians of all kinds work together to alleviate
poverty, preach the good news, and promote a just society, what else
can we do but celebrate? The friendly relationships that have sprung
up between different Christian groups are a necessary first step to
doctrinal reunification.

It is a blessing that Christians no longer burn one another at the
stake or declare one another the Antichrist. But this renewed friendship across borders can lead us to forget the original reason that different denominations exist. They are not a consequence of the flowering
diversity of spiritualities. They are not even the result of disagreement
on nonessentials. The origin of disunity is a particular kind of fundamental disagreement: a breaking of fellowship due to a failure to
agree on *the process by which agreement might be reached*. And although
love for one another is an essential first step to reconciliation, it must
not be used to decrease the importance of the doctrinal issues that led

---

[4] "Let not many of you become teachers, my brethren, for you know that we who teach
shall be judged with greater strictness" (Jas 3:1).

to disunity: instead, it should stimulate us to renewed dialogue in an effort to resolve those issues.

The Bible: Necessary but Not Sufficient

In the face of the disunity of the church, I sought just such a process by which agreement might be reached. You might call this a "meta-doctrine", a standard by which to determine the truth of other doctrines. Faced with any theological controversy, I wanted a method that would help me find the right answer. As an Evangelical committed to the Bible as the source of all my beliefs, I thought the right method was obvious: biblical exegesis. So at the age of twenty-seven, after saving money for many years, I left my software engineering job at the BBC and signed up to an Evangelical theological college. For three years, I studied the art and science of exegesis, learned Greek and Hebrew, and read the works of great biblical scholars.

I have never regretted doing this, but one thing rapidly became clear: biblical scholars do not agree on very much. Walter Brueggemann describes biblical studies as being in a "competitive, conflictual situation" from which "there seems to be no way out."[5] Dale Allison puts it this way:

> The biblical guild is not a group-mind thinking the same thoughts. Nor are the experts a single company producing a single product, "history".... The unification of academic opinion would be almost as miraculous as the union of the churches. If you are holding your breath waiting for the consensus of the specialists, you will pass out. So if we are to do something with the historical Jesus, it will have to be someone's particular historical Jesus—Wright's Jesus or Crossan's Jesus or Sanders's Jesus; it can no longer be the Jesus of the guild or the Jesus of the scholars, because they, in their writings and at their academic conferences, argue with each other over almost everything.[6]

[5] Walter Brueggemann, *Theology of the Old Testament: Testimony, Dispute, Advocacy* (Minneapolis: Fortress Press, 1997), 63.

[6] Dale Allison, *The Historical Christ and the Theological Jesus* (Grand Rapids, Mich.: Eerdmans, 2009), 11.

I do not wish to exaggerate the problem. Biblical scholars also disagree about how much disagreement there is in biblical studies. Some insist, contrary to Brueggemann and Allison, that there is a broad consensus on a large body of knowledge that can be trusted as a sure foundation. I do not wish to take sides in that debate, yet even if such a consensus exists, it is limited to the things biblical scholarship is concerned with, i.e., historical particulars about what a Bible passage meant in its original context. The question of how to "apply" the Bible to contemporary issues is beyond the expertise of biblical studies.

Let me illustrate this last point with an example. One of the *prima facie* simplest Bible verses to understand is "thou shalt not kill" (Ex 20:13 KJV). But exegesis reveals that the word "kill" is translated from the Hebrew *ratsach*, which is not identical to the English "kill". Peter Craigie suggests that *ratsach* "is normally used in the context of one Hebrew killing another Hebrew.... Thus the preliminary meaning of the commandment seems to be: 'you shall not kill a fellow Hebrew.' "[7] What, then, is today's equivalent of the "fellow Hebrew"? Does this command mean that we should not kill people who hold the same passport as we do, or come from the same ethnic group, or live in the same nation-state? Perhaps, as André LaCocque suggests, we should take this more broadly to include "killing 'out of enmity, deceit, or hatred' ", in other words, "murder".[8] Still, this does not solve the problem. Does this category include abortion and euthanasia? Does it include killing in a time of war, meaning that we should all be pacifists? Does it prohibit capital punishment, a legal killing by a state authority? Does it prohibit killing animals as well as humans, as Paul Ricœur suggests?[9] Every attempt to give meaning to this commandment requires using a contemporary category of thought, which is out of scope for the discipline of exegesis.[10] That is why two exegetes may agree on what a Bible passage meant in its original context, yet disagree on its contemporary application.

---

[7] Peter Craigie, *The Problem of War in the Old Testament* (Grand Rapids, Mich.: Eerdmans, 1978), 58.

[8] André LaCocque and Paul Ricœur, *Thinking Biblically: Exegetical and Hermeneutical Studies*, trans. David Pellauer (Chicago: University of Chicago Press, 2003), 89.

[9] Ibid., 137.

[10] As James Barr says, "The use of concepts and categories taken from 'without' the Bible is both natural and necessary" (cited in Anthony C. Thiselton, *Two Horizons: New Testament Hermeneutics and Philosophical Description* [Grand Rapids, Mich.: Eerdmans, 1980], 9).

And today's situation is not new. There have always been disputes on points of doctrine and practice throughout church history, and on each occasion, Christians have used the Bible to support opposing views. In the second century, the question was Marcionism and the status of the Old Testament. In the fourth century, the question was the divinity of Christ. In the eighth century, it was the legitimacy of icons. In the sixteenth century, it was any number of things— the Eucharist, justification, baptism, predestination, and so on. If there was no ambiguity in Scripture about a topic, then why would Christians—sincere, devout Christians—be disagreeing? Would the answer not be obvious to all? I do not mean that the Bible is useless for solving such debates: it is indispensable. I only mean that it is clearly *insufficient* to settle doctrinal disputes. Some may reply that we do not need to settle all doctrinal disputes, as long as we agree on the essentials, and that the Bible is clear on these. But this is begging the question, an assertion and not an argument. How do we know what the essentials are if not by deciding in advance that anything we disagree on must be nonessential? And even supposing it were true, do nonessentials have no importance for the Christian walk? If they have any importance at all, then getting them right is also part of following Jesus, and we should tirelessly seek the path by which to grow in wisdom and the truth. What, then, is that path?

Independent Reason: Necessary but Not Sufficient

The Bible, then, is necessary but not sufficient to resolve disagreements in the church, and to guide the believer in progressing down the path of wisdom.[11] How should I proceed? People told me that there was no other way than humbly and prayerfully to apply your intellect to a particular problem, evaluating the arguments on all sides

[11] One common objection to this conclusion is that the problem is not with the Bible, but with us. In other words, the Bible is sufficient *in itself*, and it is only *our* sinful inability to understand it that prevents us from agreeing about what it says. My response is that, if this were true, it would be cold comfort. Those who say this do not seem to see what a despairing option it is. It implies that our sin is more powerful than the Gospel of salvation, at least in regard to reconciliation and unity. I want to live in hope that there is something more. I suspect, although I cannot prove, that if the medicine does not cure the patient, it is a mistake to blame the patient. Perhaps other medicine is also needed?

impartially, and come to a provisional judgment. This is, essentially, what we mean by the study of theology. But if this is what everyone is already doing, and coming to opposite conclusions, then how can it be a solution? Theology is no more united than biblical studies. I could only be satisfied with this option if I believed my own intellect were superior to those with whom I disagreed or if I were being more prayerful (i.e., more devout or virtuous) than they. I suspect that this is what many of us theologians really think, even if we never admit it to ourselves. I am fascinated by Kathryn Schulz's analysis of the three reasons we think other people are wrong and we are right: either (1) they lack some information I have, (2) they have not thought it through as carefully as I have, or (3) they are maliciously twisting the truth for their own ends.[12] In each case, I am making a judgment about other people that implies my own superiority. Either (1) I know more than you do, (2) I understand it more clearly than you, or (3) I am less blinded by prejudice than you.

Looking back, I wonder why I thought that I could find the silver bullet that would give me the right answer in all doctrinal disputes. Had enough people not been trying to do that for long enough already? Did I imagine I was more intelligent than every other theologian and could, with penetrating insight, get to the heart of all disagreements? Did I think I could build the tower of Babel all by myself and, with the raw power of my own mind, reach into the heavens and access the mind of God? I never consciously thought such things, or I would have repudiated them immediately. But I was part of a culture that quietly encouraged such an attitude. That culture, of which theology and biblical studies are card-carrying members, is called modern academia.

The academic world is geared toward the cultivation of independent minds. If you want to succeed as an academic, i.e., to obtain long-term employment, you need to publish a lot of research. But as everyone knows, your research has to be original, or it cannot be published. Therefore, you are under pressure to find creative new solutions, to express them confidently and boldly, and to show why former solutions were misguided and flawed. Linn Tonstad observes:

---

[12] See her TED talk, "On Being Wrong" (https://www.ted.com/talks/kathryn_schulz_on _being_wrong).

Theology cannot but be affected by its position inside the modern
university: it comes to value what the modern university rewards....
The university values what is new and groundbreaking; it values the
originality ascribed to a single scholar; it values radical programs or
critiques of existing structures, discipline-shifting paradigms; and it
values productivity of a measurable sort (publications), especially in
prestigious venues. The more radical and counterintuitive the program, the more it may be rewarded. These values therefore affect not
only the shape theology takes as a profession, but also the influence
and attention granted certain kinds of theological projects.[13]

This helped me to understand why so many biblical scholars and
theologians are untroubled by the level of disagreement in their disciplines, cheerfully declaring that everyone before them has been
wrong about a particular question, everyone today is still missing the
point, and—thank God—he or she (usually he) has come along to set
things straight and put the church on the right track. This attitude is
simply part of academic culture, the air you breathe. When biblical
studies and theology are practiced within academia, they are fash-
ioned according to its likeness, not only because they are influenced
by the culture, but for more down-to-earth economic reasons that
concern who gets the jobs and the publishing contracts. Academia
rewards people who have new ideas and are able to defend them
from all kinds of critique. Therefore, the theologians who win their
way to renown more often than not are the ones who have the highest degree of confidence in the correctness of their own opinions.
Listening to some biblical scholars and theologians, I have at times
received the impression that they really believed they were themselves the meta-doctrine that could resolve all theological disputes;
that if only the church would listen to them, we could all be reunited
around the paradigm of truth that they teach.

Anyone who knows the world of academic theology will recognize
that what I have just said is a caricature in that it contains some truth
but is also an oversimplification. The wheat and the tares are very hard
to separate. Not all theologians are arrogant and self-assured. Indeed,
no one is simply one thing or the other: someone may write profound

---

[13] Linn Marie Tonstad, "(Un)Wise Theologians: Systematic Theology in the University",
International Journal of Systematic Theology 22, no. 4 (2020): 505.

wisdom that inspires greater love of God and, at the same time, be a little over-confident that his or her picture of things is the only correct one. Other theologians are detail-oriented in personality, satisfied to become experts in a narrow area of knowledge, never daring to venture a bolder judgment on larger substantial questions. But I am particularly sensitive to the self-assured type of theologian because it is my own strongest temptation. Theologians like me, of whom there are many, want to have the final answer to every question. We long to have total mastery over all knowledge and truth, to survey the world from the heights of heaven with a perfect theological system that has no inconsistencies, no flaws, and leaves nothing unexplained. In short, we want to be like God. It sounds trite to say that we human beings are not God. But the truth is that we often act as if we had God-like certainty and objectivity in our opinions, imagining that we understand the world with transparent clarity compared to those with whom we disagree. The Serpent's temptation is something we all experience—to become dissatisfied with our humanity and to attempt to "be like God, knowing good and evil" (Gen 3:5). *Knowing* does not mean *recognizing* here, else Adam and Eve would not have understood the prohibition, nor is such knowledge especially divine. No: their temptation was to become independent agents who *judge* good and evil, right and wrong for themselves, submitting to no higher standard—a truly divine quality. I want to be clear that this is not an attack on independent reasoning, any more than the preceding section was an attack on the Bible. I shall say more later about the right place of independent reason for finite creatures. Independent thought is not problematic within the domain of academia—indeed, it is essential for academia to function at all. But academia does not need a unified set of beliefs beyond the bare minimum required to keep academics talking with one another. What independent reasoning cannot do *by itself and unaided* is bring about a church-wide consensus even on the essentials of what to believe and how to live as a Christian. Like the Bible, it is necessary but not sufficient.

Tradition: Necessary but Not Sufficient

Why can independent reasoning not unify people? Because however brilliantly intelligent an individual might be, he only sees the world from a contingent and limited perspective. Every person is situated in one and only one point of history, one culture, one gender, one social situation. It is no coincidence that most Muslims are born in Muslim-majority nations, most Catholics are born in Catholic countries, most gay-rights activists are gay, and most feminists are women. Our value judgments, emphases, questions, and concerns are contingent, a consequence of the time and place in which we live, the DNA we were given, and the culture in which we were raised. We are human, and that means we are finite.

Few paragraphs have had a greater impact on my self-understanding than this one by C. S. Lewis:

> Every age has its own outlook. It is specially good at seeing certain truths and specially liable to make certain mistakes.... All contemporary writers share to some extent the contemporary outlook—even those, like myself, who seem most opposed to it. Nothing strikes me more when I read the controversies of past ages than the fact that both sides were usually assuming without question a good deal which we should now absolutely deny. They thought that they were as completely opposed as two sides could be, but in fact they were all the time secretly united—united with each other and against earlier and later ages—by a great mass of common assumptions. We may be sure that the characteristic blindness of the twentieth century—the blindness about which posterity will ask, "But how could they have thought that?"—lies where we have never suspected it, and concerns something about which there is untroubled agreement between Hitler and President Roosevelt or between Mr. H. G. Wells and Karl Barth. None of us can fully escape this blindness, but we shall certainly increase it, and weaken our guard against it, if we read only modern books. Where they are true they will give us truths which we half knew already. Where they are false they will aggravate the error with which we are already dangerously ill.[14]

It is easy to laugh at the foolish mistakes of people in other ages and cultures. It is obvious to us that we should not be anti-Semitic, that slavery is wrong, that women should be given the vote. How could former generations not have seen this? They were children of their

---

[14] C. S. Lewis, "Introduction", in *On the Incarnation*, by Athanasius (New York: St. Vladimir's Seminary Press, 1953), 4–5.

era, blinded by assumptions and prejudices. What is much harder to accept is that we are also children of our era, that we too have blind spots, moral failures of which we are not aware, flaws in our reasoning that neither we nor our contemporaries have spotted.

This realization should not plunge us into a despairing relativism, even though in the first shock of impact that can feel inevitable. But accepting our finitude as an important truth can lead, instead, to two positive results. The first is a proper humility about our own understanding; we may have political and religious opinions, but we must always hold them lightly, recognizing that we cannot see the whole picture and might always be wrong. The second is to seek a remedy, however incomplete, that might free us from total captivity to the spirit of our age. "The only palliative", continues Lewis,

> is to keep the clean sea breeze of the centuries blowing through our minds, and this can be done only by reading old books. Not, of course, that there is any magic about the past. People were no cleverer then than they are now; they made as many mistakes as we. But not the same mistakes. They will not flatter us in the errors we are already committing; and their own errors, being now open and palpable, will not endanger us. Two heads are better than one, not because either is infallible, but because they are unlikely to go wrong in the same direction. To be sure, the books of the future would be just as good a corrective as the books of the past, but unfortunately we cannot get at them.[15]

In other words, we need tradition. Only the deep roots of tradition can prevent us from being "tossed back and forth and carried about with every wind of doctrine" (Eph 4:14). We need to drink deep of the insights of theologians throughout history to provide some ballast to our otherwise fickle and changeable views, easily swayed by the pressure of the surrounding culture. This is a very counterintuitive insight for anyone who has grown up in the Western world, in a culture steeped in the narrative of progress, according to which each generation has better and keener understanding than the generation before. We borrow the paradigm of science and technology and apply it uncritically to moral and theological truth, calling an

[15] Ibid., 5.

idea "outdated", like an old computer or phone, meaning it is false without need for further argument. But the narrative of progress is itself one of the assumptions of our culture that needs to be exposed and questioned. "Things that change", writes Hans-Georg Gadamer, "force themselves on our attention far more than those that remain the same."[16] In the midst of a rapidly changing world, we can easily lose sight of what does not change. We may now be able to fly, freeze our food, and chat with people on the other side of the world. But we are still human beings, with the same needs, longings, desires, hopes, dreams, vanities, foolish pursuits, and need for wisdom as all human beings in all ages. And wisdom, like wine, is proven by longevity, by its power to appeal to many generations of people as an anchor of truth in the midst of a sea of change.

In fact, no Christians, even the most anti-traditional, ever fully rejected tradition. Why else would they depend on the Bible for their faith? Who told them that the Bible is the revealed Word of God? Where did they even get the Bible from, with its precise list of ancient books, a selection from a much greater number of texts? This argument from the canon of Scripture is rehearsed regularly in Catholic apologetics, and I need not dwell on it. Suffice it to say that I began to see that Scripture and tradition cannot be separated, because Scripture has its basis in tradition. This was the first step that moved me to be more favorably disposed toward Catholicism. Yet it was by no means sufficient reason to become Catholic. While it is impossible to be Catholic and anti-traditional, it is quite possible to be Protestant and have deep respect for The Great Tradition, the rich repository of theological wisdom from every denomination throughout history. Why put limits on the places you can go to learn? If Luther said something true, if Jacob Spener has wisdom to offer, if Calvin's insights are valuable, then their treasures must also be harvested. Indeed, the first book I read that argued in favor of tradition was by a Reformed Protestant theologian. When I had the honor of meeting him face to face, I asked him why, if tradition was so great, he was not a Catholic. He responded that he saw the Reformation as a legitimate development of the tradition.

---

[16] Hans-Georg Gadamer, *Truth and Method*, trans. Joel Weinsheimer and Donald G. Marshall (London: Continuum, 2004), xxii.

Furthermore, at that time Catholicism seemed to me to be a slav-ish copying of tradition rather than a creative application to the needs of the present day. In 2011, I wrote an article in my college maga-zine titled "A Better Way of Honouring Tradition". I argued that: "there are times when imitating the form of the past may eventually contradict its spirit" and that it is better to engage our forefathers critically than to feel obliged to agree with them on everything. "If we dialogue with the past, this may mean dissenting from it, not because we don't respect or honour our historical heroes, but pre-cisely because we do. It is what they themselves would have done if they were here." This critical appropriation of the past seemed to me more respectful than the progress narrative that exalts us to a posi-tion of greater insight than every previous generation, and also more sensible and exciting than giving up your brain and blindly accepting whatever The Tradition told you was true.

But there was still a problem, which it took me a couple more years to grasp. Among those who critically engage tradition, who accept some bits and reject others—surprise, surprise—not everyone agrees about *which* bits to accept as a valuable treasure and *which* bits to reject as a mistake. Is Orthodox veneration of icons or Calvinist iconoclasm the greater treasure to retrieve? What about purgatory? Transubstantiation? Infant baptism? Mary's perpetual virginity? 1 and 2 Maccabees? Not to speak of the more controversial issues men-tioned at the start of this essay, on which traditionalist Protestants have a wide variety of views. How was I to distinguish between legitimate and illegitimate developments of the tradition?

Tradition may be necessary, but it is not sufficient to arbitrate between opposing views in a contemporary dispute. Tradition is by definition a matter of the past and can only be brought to bear on the present by living representatives. If those disagree on the most faithful representation of tradition, who is to arbitrate between them? Who, if not a living authority, trusted by all parties to have the final word?[17]

---

[17] This is the conclusion I reached in the last article I published before becoming Catholic: "'Scripture Grows with Its Readers': Doctrinal Development from a Ricœurian Perspec-tive", *Modern Theology* 35, no. 4 (2019): 746–59. I called this article a "Protestant-ecumenical" proposal because it started from a *sola scriptura* presupposition. But near the end, I argue that there needs to be an authoritative arbitrator to discern between true and false developments of the tradition, to whom all parties in the dispute will submit even if the verdict is not in their favor.

Copernican Revolution

I saw no way to avoid making private judgments about everything. Tradition alone could not prevent me from using myself as the standard of judgment. I was still the final authority who decided whether an element of tradition was right or wrong. I was still the judge, and tradition was the thing judged. But did I trust myself to be an adequate judge? What other choice did I have?

None at all, unless there was something else in the Christian faith that I had not yet discovered. Up until now, I had been assuming *sola scriptura* as the foundation for all my thinking—not the poor caricature often made of this doctrine by its opponents, but the real thing that includes a high view of reason, tradition, and the guidance of the Holy Spirit. According to *sola scriptura*, the early Church handed to us a bag called the "deposit of faith" containing one item and one item only: the Bible. I had never seriously questioned this doctrine. Or, to put it more positively, I did not have sufficient reason to believe that anything else had been put in the bag, precisely because Christians disagreed over whether it had.

But then, to my astonishment, I found something about which Christians did not disagree. Everyone who studied early Church history gave the same report: that the early Christians were episcopalian, i.e., that they believed that the first apostles had appointed successors to govern the Church after they had died.[18] These successors were called bishops, and—this was the crucial issue—these bishops were the final authority to settle matters of dispute. When a controversy threatened to divide the Church, the bishops would gather together and debate until they came to an agreement, which they believed was guided by the Holy Spirit. They would then establish an agreed upon, precisely formulated doctrine that every Christian ought to believe from then on.[19] The first of these gatherings is recorded in

[18] I was deeply impacted by this blog post by Brantly Millegan: "How Quickly Did Catholic 'Heresy' Take Over the Early Church? Immediately", Church POP, September 22, 2015 (https://churchpop.com/2015/09/22/how-quickly-did-catholic-heresy-take-over-the-early-church-immediately).

[19] This model for resolving disagreement helps explain something it is very hard for *sola scriptura* Protestants to understand: why it took so long (almost four hundred years) for the list of canonical Bible books to be finalized. If the early Church had been *sola scriptura*, surely the question of which books had canonical status would have had more urgency?

Acts 15, concerning whether Gentiles should live by Jewish customs. The next was called the Council of Nicaea and concerned whether Jesus was divine. And so on.

Nobody disagreed over the facts about the early Church in this respect. The disagreement was whether this model was in continuity with the Gospel or a corruption of it. As a free-church Evangelical, I had been taught that the early Church got a lot of things wrong soon after the end of the New Testament period and that it was only at the Reformation that "we" started to understand the Gospel more adequately. But who was "we"? It had never occurred to me that not every Christian held this view, that it was inflected by confessional interests or agendas. Nobody can approach the question neutrally. Protestants need the early Church to have been wrong on several doctrinal points, because they are in discontinuity with it on those points. Catholics need it to have been right, because they are in continuity with it not only on the particular doctrinal points but on the meta-doctrine, the method for resolving doctrinal disputes. By *continuity*, I do not simply mean that the Catholic Church happens to have the same method as the early Church, like two people might say "we are wearing the same hat!" That would imply that the Catholic Church had merely copied the early Church. I mean it is *the same method*, like two photographs, one of an old man and one of a boy, yet who are the same person, however altered with age.[20] I had to face the fact that the early/Catholic Church's episcopal model for resolving disputes, whether it was God-given or not, at least worked.[21] Not only that: most Protestants depend on some of its

---

[20] This analogy allows me to add the nuance that Catholic ecclesial structures are not the spitting image of those in the early Church—they have undergone certain developments, just as a human being undergoes developments while having a constant identity. This assertion of common identity is controversial. Some suggest that the Catholic Church has undergone significant enough changes to place her in discontinuity with the early Church (see, e.g., Jerry L. Walls and Kenneth J. Collins, *Roman but Not Catholic: What Remains at Stake 500 Years after the Reformation* [Grand Rapids, Mich.: Baker Academic, 2017], 27–31). There is no neutral or objective way to determine what counts as illegitimate change vs. legitimate development; either way, an element of faith is required that will have other reasons and motivations than the issues themselves.

[21] To be sure, heretical groups (Marcionites, Montanists, Arians, Nestorians, etc.) have kept breaking off from the main trunk and asserting their version of Christianity as the true one. Nobody can prove beyond doubt that they were all wrong. But if one of them was right, it would mean that the whole of what we now call the church—Catholic, Protestant, and

results, like the acceptance of the Old Testament against Marcionism, the twenty-seven-book New Testament,[22] and the Trinity. Viewed this way, Protestantism began to look arbitrary, accepting some early Church doctrines and rejecting others (including the meta-doctrine for resolving disputes) for inconsistent reasons. But I do not wish to make unfair generalizations about Protestantism. Some Protestants pursue consistency by making the canon of Scripture and the Trinity open questions like everything else.[23] Other Christian groups, such as the Anglican Communion and the Orthodox Church, are consistent in accepting apostolic succession along with the canon and the creeds and only reject the papacy (about whose role in the early Church there is less agreement, we must admit).[24] Still others argue that there are consistent reasons to accept the canon and reject apostolic succession. I do not pretend to settle these questions here. What mattered

---

Orthodox—has dramatically misunderstood the Gospel since that time, and the truth was lost with the death of the last member of the breakaway group we had wrongly called heretical. What would this mean about how God works in history?

[22] Some object that the early Church did not *determine* the NT canon, but only *recognized* it as we recognize it today (see, e.g., Walls and Collins, *Roman but Not Catholic*, 66–70). This means that we can accept the canon as authoritative without submitting to the early Church authorities that first decided/articulated it But even if true, it leaves the same problem. Why should we blindly trust the early Church's powers of recognition? If the determination of the canon has no binding authority, then it is open to question and possible revision among Christians today. To be consistent, every individual Christian would be obliged to examine the evidence to see whether he recognizes the same canon of Scripture as the early Church. Famously, Martin Luther did not.

[23] See, e.g., William Wrede, who said that anyone who gives special status to twenty-seven historical documents "places himself under the authority of the bishops and theologians of [the first four] centuries. Anyone who does not recognize their authority in other matters— and no Protestant theologian does—is being consistent if he questions it here, too" (William Wrede, "The Tasks and Methods of New Testament Theology", in *The Nature of New Testament Theology: The Contribution of William Wrede and Adolf Schlatter*, trans. Robert Morgan [London: SCM Press, 1973], 71).

[24] I cannot pretend to have mastered the vast volume of literature about the early papacy or to know better than all the experts on both sides of this debate. I have been greatly helped by Collins and Walls' discussion in chapters 6 and 11 of *Roman but Not Catholic* and by Markus Bockmuehl's balanced and scholarly book *Simon Peter in Scripture and Memory: The New Testament Apostle in the Early Church* (Grand Rapids, Mich.: Baker Academic, 2012). In addition, I will only say this: if the Catholic position could be proven historically, there would be no respected scholars who deny it. If it could not be defended historically, there would be no respected scholars who affirm it. Both exist; therefore, both positions can be held without *sacrificium intellectus*. We must find other reasons than the historical evidence to believe or disbelieve it, of which mine have to do with the need for a centralized unifying authority.

to me was that I had found a candidate meta-doctrine, a standard for distinguishing truth from error, that was not my own subjective point of view—and, more importantly, that claimed to have been established by Jesus himself.

There is no knock-down proof that it was. If there were, then the only people denying it would be either stupid or wicked, and they are neither. But for me, it came down to a simple question: Do I trust my own understanding of the Gospel more than that of the early Church? How likely was it that they failed to grasp what Jesus wanted when they put more than one item in the "deposit of faith" bag, and that I (or anyone living today) understand better than they did what belongs and does not belong in that bag? Did I think I understood Jesus better than the entire early Church?[25]

I began to experience a "Copernican revolution", a reversal of perspective. With myself as the judge of theological truth, I had placed myself in the center of my world, and the stars and the planets revolved around me. I had the authority to decide what I believed, based on what made sense to my mind. But I began to feel a gentle invitation to another way of thinking. I felt summoned to surrender my private judgment, to relinquish my place at the center of my universe, and to submit to a community that was far bigger and longer-lasting than anything I could have constructed and from which emanated whatever light I already possessed. Was this summons from the Holy Spirit? I cannot prove that it was. I can only say that it felt like a milestone in my spiritual journey: a step away from pride and self-centeredness and a step toward humility and submission. As such, it felt continuous with everything I already knew about the Christian walk: the call to die to my own will, to give up trying to control my life and surrender to Jesus. It was also continuous with my Evangelical heritage, which had taught me to relinquish my private judgment when it contradicts the message of Scripture, because

[25] I could try to make this sound humbler by saying that it was the whole of Protestantism, not just myself, who understood Jesus better than the early Church (and the Catholic and Orthodox Churches today). But within Protestantism, there is very little agreement on anything except that these are wrong. If I were to take a stand on any other doctrine, I would be implicitly claiming to understand Jesus better than all other Protestants who disagree, as well as the early Church and the Catholic and Orthodox Churches today. I would still be putting myself, and only myself, in the center.

Scripture is a higher authority than my personal opinion. Yet as an Evangelical I found that my private judgment still had too prominent a place: Scripture alone was not enough to tame it. I needed to go farther along the same path and to submit not only to Scripture but to the church's interpretation of Scripture.

I had come to realize that one does not become Catholic by reaching independent agreement with each and every Catholic doctrine. The church will never be united if it waits for everyone to agree on everything. If we have learned anything from the last two thousand years, it is that there will always be disputes in the church and theological debate will not resolve all of them. If the church is to remain united, some disagreements will need an authority to step in and make a judgment, putting an end to the debate. If everyone were happy with the judgment, it would not be necessary to make it in the first place. Therefore, there will always be people on the wrong side of the judge's decision. These are then left with a choice: either to reassert their own judgment and leave the church (presumably to start a new denomination), or to submit and relinquish their opinion despite their dislike of the decision made. The truth is that I am not always on the right side of every decision made by the Magisterium. I do not "like" every Catholic doctrine. There are some that I would not have invented myself and that I wish were not there. Yet I treasure these very doctrines, because they refute the Feuerbachian in me who would create God in my own image. They are proof that the Catholic Church is not a projection of my own ego, but something real that I did not invent and cannot control, to which I must submit even when it costs.

Yet this submission is not the same as a Buddhist self-annihilation, leaving nothing at all of the will or of independent reason. (Following the "Copernican revolution" metaphor, the earth may not be the center of the entire solar system, but it has its own satellites that revolve around it. Following the Genesis narrative, Adam is given the authority to name the animals, implying a limited degree of freedom to judge.) The precise role of the Magisterium is not to pass judgment on every doctrine, but to pass judgment on *which doctrines are essential and which are not.* When there is a doctrinal dispute, one of the judgments the Church authority may make is precisely *not* to make a judgment in favor of either side. This is itself a positive decision, encouraging ongoing debate and dialogue, and "forbidding the contending parties from calling each other heretics".[26] Catholics are required to embrace each other as brothers and sisters, however strongly they disagree on matters the Church in her wisdom has left open. The Catholic Church is not a sect, demanding blind obedience to an endless list of rigid and inflexible doctrines. She does not demand that you destroy your independence altogether, but only that you restore it to its rightful place where sin had swollen it to unhealthy proportions.[27] The Church has room for diversity of viewpoints on a wide range of issues—sometimes more than I am comfortable with, e.g., when it comes to metaphysics or politics! A simple proof of this is the vigorous theological activity in the Catholic Church over the last century, every bit as lively as in the Protestant churches. Think of names like Hans Urs von Balthasar, Karl Rahner, Henri de Lubac, Bernard Lonergan, Edward Schillebeeckx, Yves Congar, Erich Przywara, Edith Stein—each of whom alone has no small volume of published work! We have plenty to talk about.

No Need to Say Goodbye

Jesus said that those who give up their lives for his sake will find them again. Following this principle, wise people also say that if your relationship to something (e.g., alcohol) has become unhealthy, you may have to let go of it before you can receive it back restored to its rightful place in your life. This was true for my independent judgment, as

---

[26] Walls and Collins, *Roman but Not Catholic*, 135.

[27] This is an important point often forgotten by Catholic apologists, as Walls and Collins insightfully point out in *Roman but Not Catholic*, chapter 8, "You Are Your Own Pope". Both Catholics and Protestants require submission to authority, and both leave some space for individual judgment, but the amount is different for each. I used my individual judgment when I judged that the space given in Protestantism for individual judgment was too big for the health of my soul. This is not remotely paradoxical, as some people have made it seem (e.g., Onsi A. Kamel, "Catholicism Made Me Protestant", *First Things*, October 2019, https://www.first things.com/article/2019/10/catholicism-made-me-protestant). Everything, of course, starts with individual judgment. But one of the things the individual must judge is whether his own judgment is superior to another's on a concrete question. If I am sick, I go to the doctor and do whatever the doctor tells me, because, in my judgment, the doctor's judgment *on medicine* is superior to mine.

I have shown. But it was an unexpected gift to find that it was also true of my Charismatic Evangelical faith.

In September 2015, I began attending a Catholic church in Cambridge, where I had just moved to begin my doctoral studies. On my third Sunday there, I was touched in a profound way by the Holy Spirit. What else can I say? It was unmistakably the same Spirit who had touched me many times before. I ran home after the service and burst into tears at the beauty of what I had experienced, both overjoyed and unhappy at the same time. I longed to be part of this beautiful tradition, to belong to the same Church to which Aquinas, Augustine, and Tolkien belonged, the same Church that held the Council of Nicaea and was already old by then. But I was also afraid of what it would mean to become Catholic. Would my family think I had gone crazy? I was teaching at my church network's Bible college: Would they cast me out of their midst? I had helped plant a church in London nine years ago that contained most of my closest friends: Would they view this as a betrayal and insult to all we had done together?

Yet I no longer saw any way to remain outside the Catholic Church that would not be fatal for my spiritual health. I did, however, feel the call of wisdom to move slowly, burning no bridges. Over the next few years, I gradually introduced my friends and family to Catholicism and my convictions about it. I did not do this perfectly. Some of my earliest conversations were unpleasant, because I felt the need to condemn the failures of Protestantism in order to justify my actions. My heart was still in turmoil, and those years were necessary for me too, to purify my attitude and intentions and to restore some stability after the vertigo that accompanies a conversion. But over time, my family and friends recognized that I still loved Jesus, loved them, and—what they were more likely to doubt—that I still loved the church tradition of which we were all part. Graciously, the Bible college allowed me to continue teaching (provided I not use it as a platform for Catholic apologetics), and the church in London continued to ask me to preach there a few times a year, the only difference being that I no longer take communion there. I would have become Catholic without these concessions, since by then I felt powerfully that it was a necessary step of obedience on my spiritual journey. But these gifts of continuity were greatly comforting and made me glad I had progressed slowly.

Finally, in 2018, I approached my priest, who knew me well by then, and began to receive instruction. At the 2019 Easter Vigil, I was confirmed into full communion with the Catholic Church. My mother and many of my Protestant friends were present, a sign of their support that meant a lot to me.

Why was I able to retain such continuity with my past? First and foremost, it was the generosity of the communities of which I was a part. But I was able to ask for that continuity because of the example of converts who had gone before me. On my journey to Catholicism, few things helped me emotionally more than the tone taken by Louis Bouyer in his book *The Spirit and Forms of Protestantism*.[28] Until then, every conversion story I had encountered was full of bitter criticisms of the belief system that the convert had abandoned (it is a hard temptation to avoid, as I discovered). Bouyer astonished me by the absence of any such thing. His ardent praise of Protestantism was ten times more compelling than any of the attacks I had heard. They showed that his conversion did not require him to tear down his former faith, only to fulfill it by taking it up into something bigger. Since then, I have encountered many Catholic converts who retained all that was positive in their former faith. I think in particular of deacon Alex Jones, who remained a fiery Pentecostal and thereby found a unique ministry to his fellow Catholics,[29] and of Jean-Marie Lustiger, who "always insisted that he had remained a Jew after his conversion".[30] These showed me a way of converting that performatively lived out the Catholic principle that *grace fulfills and perfects; it does not destroy and replace.*

With great joy I have found myself able to keep all that I treasure about the faith in which I was raised, adding Catholic elements to it but subtracting nothing. Both the Evangelical emphasis on Scripture's crucial importance and the Charismatic focus on the transforming power and gifts of the Holy Spirit are as strong in me as ever before. I continue to learn much from non-Catholic theologians and

---

[28] Louis Bouyer, *The Spirit and Forms of Protestantism*, trans. A.V. Littledale (1956; San Francisco: Ignatius Press, 2017).

[29] Alex Jones, *No Price Too High: A Pentecostal Preacher Becomes Catholic* (San Francisco: Ignatius Press, 2006).

[30] John Tagliabue, "Jean-Marie Lustiger, French Cardinal, Dies at 80", *The New York Times*, August 6, 2007, https://www.nytimes.com/2007/08/06/world/europe/06lustiger.html.

speakers. Why should I not? There is much there that is good and valuable. What matters is that I no longer have to depend on myself to distinguish what is good and valuable from what is not. I now have a standard higher than myself or any individual theologian that can help me discern.

Catholicism is not helped by its over-zealous apologists who incessantly point to the flaws in Protestantism or Orthodoxy. Apart from being uncharitable, it is appalling psychology. Nobody ever converted after hearing someone pour scorn on his current beliefs. Why? Because a denomination or religion is not merely a set of intellectual opinions, but a familiar home with its own culture and customs. It is loved before it is thought correct, and "what defines us is what we love."[31] Blaise Pascal taught us long ago that we must first be drawn by the beauty of something before we will listen to arguments in favor of it.[32] A generous spirit that represents all opponents in their best light is far more attractive than a critical spirit that condemns them for their failures. There may come a time to criticize something, but that will only be after we have shown that we understand why good people love, respect, and draw strength from it. We must show by our actions that *Catholicism fulfills and perfects Protestantism; it does not destroy and replace it.*

Conclusion

Scot McKnight has identified four needs that Evangelicals frequently give as reasons for crossing the Tiber: "certainty, history, unity, and authority".[33] I resonate with all of these except certainty. I do not pretend that anything I have said amounts to a proof for the truth of Catholicism. I do not even claim that it is the most rational—such

[31] James K. A. Smith, *Desiring the Kingdom: Worship, Worldview, and Cultural Formation* (Grand Rapids, Mich.: Baker Academic, 2009), 25. Emphasis removed.

[32] "Men despise religion. They hate it and are afraid it may be true. The cure for this is first to show that religion is not contrary to reason, but worthy of reverence and respect. Next make it attractive, make good men wish it were true, and then show that it is" (Blaise Pascal, *Pensées*, trans. A. J. Krailsheimer [London: Penguin, 1995], 12 [187]).

[33] Scot McKnight, "From Wheaton to Rome: Why Evangelicals Become Roman Catholic", *Journal of the Evangelical Theological Society* 45, no. 3 (2002): 460.

a claim would still imply a transcendent perspective from which to measure the rationality of all options. I do claim, however, that Catholicism is rationally defensible at every level, which is the most anyone can say about any belief.

No, I am not certain. But I became Catholic because it gives me a hope far greater than anything I could find elsewhere. A hope that I do not need to depend on my own flawed judgment to find the path to Christian maturity. A hope that God had a solution to our divisive tendencies right from the start and that he provided a way to keep his Church united throughout history for any who choose to submit to it. A hope that the past, present, and future of the Church is in his hands and is being guided by those he has ordained. On this hope I have wagered.

Chapter 2

FROM NEW AGE SYNCRETIST
TO CATHOLIC MORAL THEOLOGIAN

by

Melanie Susan Barrett

My Mother's Spiritual Journey

My conversion story begins with my mother, Cheryl, who was born into a Jewish family in Brooklyn, New York, on the very same day that the State of Israel was born (May 14, 1948). When she was eight years old, her family moved from its safe haven in Brooklyn to a new home in Orange County, California. Suddenly, she found herself alone: as the only Jewish student not only in the third grade but in the entire K–6 elementary school. Her Jewish identity was obvious, as her last name was "Goldstein". Her sense of being different, alone, even isolated from others, extended to her home life as well. Her family kept kosher—including separate dishes for meat and dairy—and they decorated their living-room window with elaborate Hanukkah decorations, for all their non-Jewish neighbors to see.

Her sense of isolation was deepened in junior high, when she began to encounter explicit anti-Semitism. Several of her classmates said things like "the Jews killed our Savior", "the Jews killed Jesus", and "the Jews are Christ-killers." Such comments caused her internal pain, but she said nothing; she resolved, instead, to keep to herself and suffered in silence. Another classmate, supposedly a close friend, complained once after purchasing an item that the seller had "Jewed"

47

her down. My mother was shocked, and she felt embarrassed about being Jewish.

Rejection and abandonment, on account of religious differences, would rear its ugly head again six years later. In 1968, when Cheryl was twenty years old, her older brother Mick announced his engagement to their parents. To their great dismay, they learned that Mick's intended fiancée was not Jewish but a Protestant Christian, and the bride's father was an Episcopalian minister. A heated conversation ensued later in an alley outside Mick's work. Mick's stepmother did all the talking, while his father just stood there. They threatened Mick that if he married his intended bride, then he would be "disowned" by them. He would no longer be their son. Instead, he would be a mere stranger to them. Despite the threat, Mick went ahead and married his fiancée, Penny, and her father performed the ceremony in their church. (Notably, Mick and Penny recently celebrated their fifty-second wedding anniversary.) At the time of their wedding, Cheryl still was living at home with her parents. Her stepmother explicitly forbade her from attending her brother's wedding or from having any contact with him whatsoever. If Cheryl disobeyed, then she would be disowned as well.

Six months later, Cheryl's father died tragically in a car accident. Her brother Mick was informed by their stepmother that he was "allowed" to attend his father's funeral, but that the penalty of disownment—for having married outside the family's religion—would not be revoked. About two years later, Cheryl secretly began seeing Mick and Penny behind their stepmother's back. Such meetings had to occur in secret because their stepmother swore that *she* could never forgive her stepson because his own father had died without forgiving him.

In 1970, Cheryl married Myles: my future father. Myles was culturally Jewish (though not practicing), so he was deemed acceptable by her family. Cheryl and Myles were married in a Jewish ceremony. They subsequently spent time with Cheryl's extended family during religious holidays and attended synagogue services with them during the High Holy Days (Rosh Hashanah through Yom Kippur).[1]

[1] Rosh Hashanah celebrates the Jewish New Year and Yom Kippur celebrates the Day of Atonement.

In 1973, I was born. My parents hosted a naming ceremony for me in which my godfather and godmother were appointed, and I formally received my Jewish name. Two and a half years later, when my younger brother David was born, another large family gathering would take place: David's bris (his ritual circumcision) and Jewish naming ceremony. Also in 1973, Cheryl's best friend (Susan) and her husband (Marty) both left Judaism and became Jehovah's Witnesses. They strongly encouraged Cheryl and Myles to convert as well. When my parents subsequently declined, Susan and Marty ended their friendship with them: yet another rejection, due to religion, to add to her list.

While living in Southern California in the late 1960s and early '70s, Cheryl encountered people from a wide variety of backgrounds, who introduced her to some nontraditional alternatives to Judaism. In the fall of 1968, Cheryl took a world religions class at a local community college, which expanded her horizons and whet her appetite to think more deeply about the meaning of life. She briefly attended a Science of Mind church, considered joining a Karl Jung group, read about Scientology, researched Mormonism, read some Ralph Waldo Emerson, and started visiting New Age bookstores. Intrigued by the newspaper horoscopes, she began studying astrology. She also visited a psychic, who predicted that Cheryl and her family would relocate somewhere with trees and mountains—like Colorado—where eventually they did move, just a few years later.

In 1978, Cheryl and Myles moved with their children (my brother David and myself) to Colorado Springs, a small city located at the foot of Pikes Peak. Even though Cheryl had been pulling away from Judaism for a while—due to some intellectual disagreements and a lack of emotional satisfaction—she initially intended to educate her children in the Jewish faith, for their own moral and spiritual benefit.

She visited the one Conservative synagogue in the city, intending to enroll me in religious education there. (I was five years old at the time.) She was told that she and her husband needed to become official members of the synagogue—and pay the relevant fee—in order for me to be schooled in the faith. Aside from her lack of interest in Jewish religious practice—now that she no longer was living near extended family—the fee was regarded as a financial hardship. At the time, neither of my parents had a job, only savings from my father's

California teacher's retirement fund he had taken out before moving
to Colorado Springs. Not only was there a hiring freeze on teachers'
jobs, but my father was burnt out from his earlier career teaching in
an inner-city school and unsure of what to do next. My mother thus
asked the synagogue to waive the fee. They refused, even though
they waived the fee for military members who did not have a Jewish
Sunday school program on base.

Cheryl was frustrated. She already had misgivings about "organized" religion rooted in a personal history of rejection: her Christian
schoolmates using anti-Semitic slurs; her Jewish parents disowning
her brother for marrying a Christian; her best friend Susan severing
their friendship over Cheryl's refusal to convert; and now, the Jewish
synagogue demanding a commitment from her that she was psycho-
logically and financially unable to provide.

The latter event was the proverbial straw that broke the camel's
back. Perhaps because of her personal experiences of exclusion, my
mother resolved that she did not want to embrace organized religion.
She still believed in God, but she disliked the separateness, alienation,
hatred, and perpetual conflict that seemed to be caused by religion. In
its place, she sought a positive vision that affirmed our shared humanity as brothers and sisters in this world. She found solace for her worldview in the lyrics of "Imagine", released by John Lennon in 1971:

> Imagine there's no countries.
> It isn't hard to do.
> Nothing to kill or die for,
> And no religion too.
> Imagine all the people, living life in peace.
> You may say I'm a dreamer,
> But I'm not the only one.
> I hope someday you'll join us,
> And the world will be as one.

In search of peace, unity, and brotherhood, she began to delve
more deeply into New Age spirituality and practice, while continuing to study the great world religions as well, especially Buddhism,
Hinduism, and Christianity. She also studied some of the Jewish Kab-
balah, the mystical side of Judaism. She regarded all the religions

metaphorically as spokes on a wagon wheel, each one leading to God in the center, but by means of a different path. Because each held that only *its* path was the way to God, she sought to appropriate their important insights from a safe distance, where she consciously could leave behind anything that conflicted with her humanism.

Although she had been raised to believe that God would punish her if she did not behave correctly, she felt that in reality God was not vengeful but loving, and this became her central focus. Studying the Old and the New Testaments, she found herself especially drawn to the teachings of Jesus. She embraced Jesus' Sermon on the Mount as a moral guide in her life. She concluded that Jesus was a great prophet who embodied God's unconditional love in his own life, who viewed all men as children of God, and who sought to raise human consciousness from fear to love. She also admired Catholic Christianity: for its explicit rejection of anti-Semitism (in the Vatican II document *Nostra Aetate*) and its consistent position against the taking of human life. However, because she did not accept Jesus as God (the eternal Word made flesh), she never seriously considered becoming a Christian.

Growing Up in a "Spiritual, but Not Religious" Household

Once my family moved to Colorado and was freed from the religious-observance expectations of my mother's relatives, our practice of Judaism evaporated almost completely. We did not belong to a synagogue. We did not attend Jewish religious services during the High Holy Days. We did not commemorate the beginning of Passover with a *seder* or even acknowledge it on the calendar. We did not gather for a *Shabbat* meal on Friday nights or recognize Saturdays as a day of rest. In contrast to my mother's family, we did not keep a kosher home: all foods were permitted (except those deemed physically unhealthy because they contained too much sugar or artificial ingredients). Occasionally, my mother cooked some traditional Jewish foods (like potato pancakes with applesauce, or fried Matzoh), but their appearance on our table was never correlated to anything on the Jewish liturgical calendar. My brother and I did not attend Jewish Sunday school (religious education), Jewish summer camp, or any other structured occasions for inculcating Jewish identity within a communal context.

The one exception (of Jewish practice) was Hanukkah, but even that family celebration was minimal. We lit one candle on the *menorah* every night for eight nights and recited the traditional prayer in Hebrew, which I eventually learned by heart ("Baruch atah Adonai Eloheinu melech ha'olam, shehecheyanu, v'kiyimanu, v'higiyanu lazman hazeh") but never knew what it actually meant ("Praised are you, our God, ruler of the universe, who has given us life and sustained us and enabled us to reach this season"). Next, my brother and I opened presents: one each per night. Because my family did not have much money, they were wrapped in colored newspaper (either the Sunday comics or the grocery store ads) rather than gift wrap, but we tore them open with gusto and joyful expectation without concern for their humble exterior. Entirely disconnected from Jewish tradition, I had no idea why we celebrated Hanukkah, but I did not really care. To me, it was a worthwhile family tradition because it was fun to strike a match and light candles; saying words in Hebrew that I did not understand felt like incanting a magic spell, which was thrilling and mysterious; and what child does not enjoy opening presents?

This family tradition persisted until I was about fourteen, when my brother and I petitioned our parents to celebrate Christmas instead of Hanukkah. We had wanted to invite friends to our home during the holiday season, but always felt embarrassed about not having a Christmas tree. My parents agreed, and they permanently retired our menorah to a high bookshelf in the den. An artificial Christmas tree was purchased for our sunroom, and we decorated it with lots of tinsel and silver icicles. My brother and I were excited, but not nearly as much as our two cats. Endlessly fascinated by the sunlight shining on the icicles, the cats batted at, chewed on, and swallowed many of them. The end result? Random piles of cat vomit appeared on the carpet, and then reappeared once again: not once, but multiple times over the next several weeks.

Our enthusiasm was dampened, yet David and I were not deterred. We awaited the big day with great anticipation. At long last, Christmas morning arrived. But when we proceeded to open our gifts, we were shocked by the scarcity. Instead of the eight gifts to which we were accustomed, we only had three gifts each. Where were all our missing presents? Cheryl and Myles replied that because we had dispensed with Hanukkah, eights gifts were no longer necessary. David and I felt like the rug had been pulled out from under us, and from that day forward we regretted our decision to replace the menorah with a Christmas tree.

Aside from our annual family Hanukkah tradition, nothing else made me "feel" Jewish in a positive way. But I did experience my Jewish cultural identity in a negative way: as being different from the other children and their families. Like my mother's experience when her family first moved to Orange County, I grew up in a non-Jewish neighborhood and was the only Jewish child in my school. Most of my schoolmates were Christians: either Evangelicals or mainline Protestants. A few were Catholics. None were Jewish, at least none of whom I was aware.

I remember one day in elementary school when my teacher conducted a survey. She called out different religions and asked us to raise our hand when ours was mentioned. To my recollection, I was the only student who raised my hand when she said "Jewish". I felt everyone's eyes on me. No one made any disparaging remarks, but no one said anything supportive either. All I could think of was: *Now they know that I'm not one of them*. But I did not feel a part of the Jewish community either, since I did not know anyone else who was Jewish. Consequently, I felt very much alone.

On occasion, my sense of aloneness deepened into a sense of rejection. In the 1980s, Colorado Springs had a strong military presence in town, was politically conservative (most people were Republican or at least Libertarian), and was predominantly Evangelical. The primary message that I heard from Christians while growing up was simple and straightforward: "Accept Jesus Christ as your personal Savior, or you're going to hell." That was it. No one ever said anything like, "Hey, you're Jewish; that's great. Did you know that Jesus was a Jew? And so was his mother? And all his disciples? We have a lot in common." Or even, "We believe in the Ten Commandments too." And certainly not, "You're God's chosen people and part of a special covenant." All I knew was that in the eyes of others—whether they knew me to be Jewish or not—my entire family was destined for hell.

Once, during high school, a friend invited me to her church service. I do not recall much except the main event: an altar call.

Everyone who was ready to "accept Jesus Christ into their heart" was invited to come forward and proclaim it publicly. I was completely terrified. My teenage self—always anxious about pleasing others and fitting in—felt an incredible amount of social pressure to make a proclamation. I thought, *They all know each other, they all know that I don't belong, and they're watching me to see what I do.* I wanted so much to be accepted by them—to belong to the group—but I had been raised by my parents to be a person of integrity, so I could not justify proclaiming something externally that I did not believe internally. So I did nothing and felt not only rejected but also angry. *How could they demand I make such an important, life-changing decision after just a few minutes of reflection?* But my anger was overshadowed by a stronger sense of fear, even terror.

A milder sense of being separate, of not fitting in with other people, took place in the Unity church. My father took no interest in—and refused to discuss—either religion or politics. But my mother was searching actively for answers to ultimate questions, and one stop on her journey was the Unity Church of the Rockies. Incorporating wisdom from many faith traditions, they emphasized unconditional love—seeing good everywhere and in everyone—turning within to the Spirit (for guidance and active communication), celebrating life's unlimited possibilities, and embracing all people as expressions of God.[2] We attended services there a few times, and I experienced them as strange (completely unfamiliar) and boring. We sang uplifting hymns like "Let There Be Peace on Earth" and "Kumbaya", and we had fellowship with juice and cookies. The experience was inoffensive, but it also lacked spiritual nourishment, so we ceased going after a few visits, for which I was grateful.

Two decades later, my mother would visit the Unity church again on her own, to give it a second try. On one occasion, she was invited to share publicly an "inspirational" piece of literature with the congregation, and she chose a passage from the New Testament that had inspired her. Afterward, she was privately criticized by church

---

[2] The spiritual movement called Unity was founded in the 1890s by Charles and Myrtle Fillmore. For contemporary statements of Unity belief and practice, see, for example, https://unityrockies.org/home (Unity Spiritual Center in the Rockies), https://www.unityofnashville.org/about-us (Unity of Nashville), and https://www.ucop.org/vision-mission-and-values (Unity Church of Overland Park).

leadership for having selected a biblical passage, on account of the fact that her selection might have offended some of the non-Christians (or former Christians) present. As a non-Christian herself, my mother was not only surprised; she was incensed. One more experience of exclusion to add to her list—though ironically in the name of inclusiveness—so she never set foot there again.

Growing up, the one place I did feel at home was in the New Age community. My mother became adept at both astrology and numerology, and virtually every question I had—about future career paths, potential boyfriends, why I excelled in some areas and struggled in others—was addressed by examining my personal astrology chart (or the numbers that comprised my name and birthday) to discern what past-life karmic lessons I was here on earth to learn, who would best assist me on my journey, and what measures I needed to undertake in order to grow spiritually. We frequented so-called "metaphysical" bookstores, where I flipped through New Age literature, examined crystals, imagined myself wearing flowing long skirts and tie-dyed natural fabrics, felt transported by the aroma of burning incense, and enjoyed opening countless bottles of essential oils to compare their unique scents.

We also visited health stores, where I found myself mesmerized by the array of pristine fruits, vegetables, juices, herbs, and other concoctions largely in their natural, unprocessed state: along with the dramatic health benefits promised to those who adhere to such a pure lifestyle. (I was less impressed by the treats made with carob— a popular chocolate-alternative in the '80s—which tasted nothing like chocolate whatsoever.)

My firm belief in the inherent goodness of creation was cultivated by these trips, along with the camping trips into Colorado forests that my family frequented during the summers. Spending time in nature made me feel profoundly connected to God. I was awed not only by starry night skies but also by the immense variety of grasses, flowers, trees, and animals that we encountered on our family hikes. The beautiful array of colors; the diversity of shapes; the refreshing aroma of pine trees; and the distinct sounds of snapping twigs, chirping crickets, squawking birds, and small creatures scurrying underfoot all pointed to God as their source. I regularly praised him for it all, imbued with joy and peaceful contentment.

My New Age formation was deepened by regular trips to "holistic" practitioners—such as herbal-focused nutritionists, chiropractors, Rolfers, and acupuncturists—who offered viable alternatives to traditional Western medicine; this greatly improved my mother's health, and healed the rest of us from various illnesses and injuries as well. On occasion, we also attended "psychic fairs", where I would have tarot card readings, crystal readings, progressive/predictive interpretations of my astrology chart, aura photographs, and generic psychic readings. I even had a past-life regression once, which I undertook in an effort to understand why I was struggling in a bad romantic relationship. Sometimes events that the psychics had predicted—but could not have known—came true, which fascinated me and deepened my faith in all that the New Age movement had to offer.

Despite these affirming experiences, I found myself searching for more. I always had believed in God—I never doubted his existence—and had prayed to God as a loving father. I also possessed an unshakable faith in God's essential goodness; after all, the logic of reincarnation (from the New Age perspective) meant that *everyone* would be saved eventually: even if it took hundreds or thousands of lifetimes for certain individuals to learn all the spiritual lessons necessary for their advancement.

My mother possessed what could be categorized as an Arian view of Jesus—he was the greatest of all creatures, but not divine—but she coupled this with her study of Buddhism, concluding that Jesus was a bodhisattva: a human being who already had attained enlightenment and, thus, no longer needed to reincarnate, but chose to do so out of compassion, to help the rest of humanity still trapped in suffering. Having also read the contemporary Hindu author Paramahansa Yogananda—who correlated many of Jesus' parables, and key images from the Book of Revelation, with the chakras (spiritual energy centers of the human body) in Hinduism—my mother summarized Jesus' spiritual instruction as the means to connect with God through the heart chakra in particular.[3]

I found this syncretistic Christian/Buddhist/Hindu/New Age worldview to be both coherent and compelling. However, it did not

---

[3] For a fuller exposition of this position, see R. Kevin Hennelly, "The Heart Chakra and the Kingdom of God", Christianity and the Chakras, July 5, 2015, http://www.christianity andthechakras.com/heart-chakra-kingdom-god-jesus-revelation/.

satisfy my restless heart and mind. It merely whet my appetite to go deeper. But where should I go for answers? If every religion possesses only a partial grasp of universal truth, then choosing any *one* of them necessarily would hinder my search rather than expand it.

My Own Brief Religious Adventures

I went to college at Northwestern University and received an excellent liberal arts education there. However, despite taking courses in philosophy, classics, world history, art history, and music, I never took a single religion course. I did dabble in a few things outside of the classroom, however.

First, in 1990, just prior to starting college, I took a summer job in my hometown working for our family chiropractor. Several of his adult daughters worked in the office as well. Everyone there was personable, kind, generous, and warm, and they seemed very close as a family. All of this attracted me, and I wanted to learn more about them. The daughters invited me to begin studying Mormonism with them, and I accepted. I began reading their key scriptural texts—*The Book of Mormon, Doctrine and Covenants*, and *The Pearl of Great Price*—and then meeting with them afterward to discuss what I had read. I also attended a few religious services with them.

Some of the things I learned about both surprised and concerned me. One was their view of heaven. Everyone residing there was pure, and purity seemed synonymous with "whiteness". Although I was not yet attentive to social justice issues concerning racism, this depiction struck me as incomplete. What about all the people on earth with different skin colors? Were they included as well?[4]

A second issue regarded the differential treatment of men and women in marriage. Even though polygamy no longer was

---

[4] Although Joseph Smith (the founder of the Church of Jesus Christ of Latter-Day Saints) ordained some black men of African descent, beginning in 1852, the LDS Church prohibited such ordinations and also disallowed such men (and women) from participating in certain temple services. The priesthood ban was lifted in 1978, based upon a new revelation. In 2013, the LDS Church officially denounced racism (both past and present) more thoroughly. See "Race and the Priesthood", The Church of Jesus Christ of Latter-Day Saints, December 2013, https://www.churchofjesuschrist.org/study/manual/gospel-topics-essays/race-and-the-priesthood?lang=eng.

practiced in the United States, it still was considered to be a spiritual law. This spiritual law had tangible earthly consequences, however. If a Mormon couple chooses to be married in the church, I was told, then their marriage lasts until death, so either party is free to remarry if their spouse dies. By contrast, if they choose to marry in the temple, then their marriage is considered binding for eternity. Consequently, if the husband dies, then his wife is not free to remarry, because her one husband awaits her in heaven. If the wife dies, however, then her husband is free to remarry, because he can possess multiple wives in heaven. Although I did not classify myself as a feminist, the lack of fairness in this scenario—coupled with the idea of being part of a spiritual harem in heaven—greatly troubled me. The first issue was a red flag for me, but this one was a deal breaker, so I walked away.

Second, during college I was accosted by some Christians who were proselytizing passersby in the student union building. Out of curiosity, I met with them and began studying their faith. Initially, I was intrigued, but then I learned about one of their unique practices: confessing their sins to one another, publicly, in a group. I reasoned that if my "sin" involved someone else in the group, then I would be required to announce it to everyone—including the person in question—which would be awkward and embarrassing (at least) or hurtful (at worst). Another deal breaker.

A third excursion involved Buddhism. During my teenage years, I had read several books authored by a Tibetan Buddhist monk. I was impressed by his compassion for all living beings, his mental self-discipline, and his contemplative practices. While in college, I learned about a Buddhist meditation workshop being offered by the Shambala Meditation Center, located just a few train stops away. I signed up and tried it out. I found their meditative techniques practically useful; the leaders taught us to meditate with our eyes open but slightly downcast—while either sitting or walking—so that we could cultivate inner peace in the midst of light and noise. Less appealing: we were instructed to meditate on the universe itself, which felt empty to me. I had believed in God my entire life; I had prayed to God during good times and bad; and I had felt God's consoling presence. My interest in meditation stemmed from my heartfelt desire to connect with God more deeply. But in Buddhism, I realized, there is no personal God with whom to connect; God does not even exist. Another deal breaker.

By the end of college, I resolved to continue along my mother's path. I would remain on the lookout for discrete spiritual insights—wherever I might find them—but I would forgo organized religion altogether.

Encountering Christian Theology in Graduate School

In 1994, I graduated from Northwestern with a double major in political science and international studies. At the time, I intended to take a year off to work, study for the GRE, and apply to graduate programs in political science. My research focus would be nonviolent conflict resolution, as a moral and practical alternative to armed conflict. My long-term plan was to work either for the State Department or the United Nations. When subsequently I was not accepted into any of the graduate programs for which I had applied, I contacted one of the schools for constructive feedback. They informed me that my research interests did not dovetail closely enough with any of their faculty members and recommended that I target a *person* with whom I wanted to work, rather than a *program*.

Of the authors I had read in college, the one who had most impressed me—especially in her writings on just war theory—was the political philosopher Jean Bethke Elshtain. Unfortunately, Elshtain had recently left her position in the political science department at Vanderbilt University to teach political ethics at the University of Chicago Divinity School. That seemed considerably outside my area of expertise, as I neither practiced religion nor had studied it in college. Nevertheless, I decided to meet with Elshtain in person. To my surprise, I enjoyed talking to her immensely, and she strongly encouraged me to apply to their M.A. program in divinity, with the intention of continuing on to pursue the Ph.D. in religious ethics. She assured me that if I worked with her as an advisor, then I could write my dissertation on just war theory (or a related topic).

Later on, I reviewed the list of required courses for the M.A. degree, which focused heavily (though not exclusively) on Christian theology. I thought to myself, *I haven't studied any of this before, but I've*

always been interested in spirituality and religion, so why not? It would be fun.
I decided to apply and subsequently was accepted into the program.

My first year of graduate study was a whirlwind: exciting but very challenging intellectually. In contrast to my classmates, the majority of whom had been religion majors in college—and also had attended religious services growing up—I struggled to keep up. The terminology and the core concepts of the disciplines of religious studies and theology were completely foreign to me. Yet much of what I read utterly captivated me.

The first book to inspire me was Augustine's *City of God*. Augustine's emphasis on Jesus' rich emotional life, in contrast to the Stoic ideal that stressed *apatheia*, enabled me to see Jesus' humanity and relate to him as a person (rather than as an abstract, esoteric ideal). Augustine also acknowledged God's existence (which I appreciated, given my disagreement with Buddhism), but he further maintained that God's very essence is love. I began reflecting on this core Christian doctrine. I recalled that sometimes during prayer, I had felt loved by God. But this radical assertion not only that *God loves* but also that *God is love* completely stunned me. It struck a profoundly deep chord in the very depths of my being, and I *knew* it to be true.

How do I account for making such a cognitive leap? A compelling analysis is provided by the theologian Hans Urs von Balthasar, in the course of explaining how aesthetic contemplation of the person of Christ enables the perceiver to recognize the truth that he is divine. As I explain in my book on Balthasar (published in 2009),

> The beauty of God's love in Christ is so far beyond what the person commonly understands as love that it is "too beautiful to be true." And yet, this love is *so* beautiful that it shakes the person at [his] foundations and [he knows] that it *must* be true. The person is ultimately persuaded by what Balthasar calls the "evidential power of love," the fact that when all other things are in disarray, only love can be believed.[5]

I would not read the writings of Balthasar until years later, after my conversion was complete. But his claim that an experience of sublime

[5] Melanie Susan Barrett, *Love's Beauty at the Heart of the Christian Moral Life: The Ethics of Catholic Theologian Hans Urs von Balthasar* (Lewiston, N.Y.: Edwin Mellen Press, 2009), 143–44. See also Balthasar, *Love Alone: The Way of Revelation*, ed. Alexander Dru (London: Burns & Oates, 1968), 83 and 68.

beauty can help us to grasp objective truth resonates strongly with what happened to me upon reading Augustine and contemplating the idea that God's very essence is love.

A second theologian who inspired me was Thomas Aquinas, when I read his treatises on virtue and law (in the *Summa Theologiae*). Aquinas' account of morality painted a stark contrast with that of the later Protestant Reformation theologians Martin Luther and John Calvin, whom I also read around the same time. For both Luther and Calvin, man is so fallen—due to original sin—that lacking explicit faith in Jesus Christ, he tends to perform wretched deeds. Calvin writes, for example:

> Those who have defined original sin as the lack of the original righteousness with which we should have been endowed ... have not fully expressed the positive energy of this sin. For our nature is not merely bereft of good, but is so productive of every kind of evil that it cannot be inactive.... Whatever is in man from intellect to will, from the soul to the flesh, is all defiled and crammed with concupiscence.... The whole man is in himself nothing but concupiscence.[6]

Even justification, rooted in faith, does not substantially heal this depravity; it merely covers it over, so that God judges Christ in our stead. Luther thus characterizes any good that faithful Christians accomplish as an "alien righteousness", which is Christ's righteousness operating within them rather than their own.[7] The dismal account of human nature provided by Luther and Calvin did not correspond at all to my positive experience growing up in a loving family. My parents not only taught us strong moral values; they also modeled such values through their own good conduct. Yet no one in my family had professed a faith in Jesus Christ as our Savior.

Aquinas, by contrast, set forth a theory of natural law in which those lacking Christian faith still can *know* the good and *do* the good, albeit imperfectly. Though faith in Christ and baptism (at least by desire) is necessary to accomplish salvific good, the absence of them

---

[6] John Calvin, *Institutes of the Christian Religion*, ed. John T. McNeill (Philadelphia: Westminster Press, 1967), bk. 2, chap. 1, as quoted by Margaret L. King, *A Short History of the Renaissance in Europe* (Toronto: University of Toronto Press, 2016), 314.

[7] Martin Luther, "Two Kinds of Righteousness", in *Martin Luther: Selections from His Writings*, ed. John Dillenberger (New York: Anchor Books, 1962), 86–98.

does not imply utter depravity in one's actions.[8] Rather, without the healing grace of Christ, men are "corrupted" insofar as they "cannot fulfill all the Divine commandments" both in substance and motivated by love for God (and for one's neighbor in God).[9] Put differently, the lack of grace does not condemn men to perpetual sin; it merely prevents them from abstaining from sin completely.[10] Compared to the Protestant Reformers, this more positive account of human nature (without the supplementary assistance of grace) better corresponded to the experience of morality both in my family and in my personal life.

A third source of intellectual inspiration arose from my reading of the contemporary Catholic social tradition, beginning with Pope Leo XIII's 1891 document *Rerum Novarum*. The core teaching about human dignity—the intrinsic value of all mankind, created in God's own image and likeness, for whom Christ died even while they still were sinners—not only affirmed but also extended the humanistic vision that I had been taught as a child. Catholic social teaching emphasized not only human rights but also the corresponding moral responsibility (which obliges us all) to protect and promote those rights: especially among the vulnerable, such as the poor, the sick, the unborn, the elderly, and those with disabilities. Moreover, the principle of subsidiarity, which provided a practical framework for how best to organize a society, struck me as eminently practical. The vision as a whole satisfied both my heart's yearning for justice and my intellect's aspiration to evaluate serious moral issues logically and systematically.

Continuing the Exploration: Liturgical Experiences

Intellectually persuaded that the Catholic tradition contained great riches, I decided next to explore its practices. I consulted with one of my professors, Paul Griffiths, a philosopher of religion (and specialist

---

[8] For example, Aquinas contends that the general principles of the natural law "can nowise be blotted out from men's hearts" even though reason can be impeded from applying such principles to particular cases (if unduly influenced by concupiscence or some other passion); or secondary precepts can be blotted out "by evil persuasions ... or by vicious customs and corrupt habits". *Summa Theologica* I-II, q. 94, art. 6 (from the translation of the English Dominican Fathers, New York: Benziger, 1911–1929).

[9] *Summa Theologica* I-II, q. 109, art. 4.

[10] *Summa Theologica* I-II, q. 109, art. 8.

in Buddhism) who recently had converted from Anglicanism to Catholicism. He invited me to participate in a contemplative prayer group run by Lumen Christi, a Catholic intellectual center on campus that he had cofounded (along with Thomas Levergood).

I arrived on a weekday evening and sat near the back. At the beginning, someone read aloud a psalm from the Old Testament, followed by Augustine's commentary on the psalm. Then all were quiet, praying and reflecting on their own for six or seven minutes. Next, we recited the psalm together, followed by more quiet time. This continued on for about forty-five minutes. Unlike my previous experiences with public worship, I felt neither excluded nor bored. Rather, I felt peaceful and reflective—like I did when praying alone—except this time I was not alone. I was part of a small community. Rather than replacing my private spirituality, this form of worship expanded it.

I was intrigued, so I decided to try out a Catholic Mass as well. While spending the summer of 1998 back in Colorado Springs with my parents, I attended Saint Francis of Assisi Catholic Church on Sunday mornings. This mission parish, located on pristine grounds in a mountainous area, is home to the Sisters of Saint Francis of Perpetual Adoration. The experience of attending a Catholic Mass was foreign to me, and I did not understand much of the ritual. But I had a palpable sense of God there: the same mysterious, powerful, and consoling presence that I had occasionally felt during private prayer. I could not fathom why I was feeling it there. *Was it the beauty of the stained glass, the vestments, the choreographed gestures and movements? I didn't feel this when visiting my friends' Protestant churches*, I thought to myself. *Could it be this Eucharist thing?*

The latter possibility perplexed me the most. My Jewish background, coupled with my mother's conscious rejection of Jesus' divinity, had formed in me a sense of God as utterly transcendent. From childhood on, I had imaged God as a loving Father, fierce protector, and awe-inspiring source of all creation. I struggled to imagine this God taking on a human nature and living among us. As I had not yet wrapped my head around the Incarnation, the idea of God being present in the simple objects of bread and wine seemed beyond the pale. As a non-Catholic attending Mass, I was not yet receiving the Eucharist. But as I watched other people receiving it, I thought *maybe ... but there's no way to know for sure.*

The Final Piece of the Puzzle: Existential Aspects

Alongside the intellectual and liturgical pieces of the puzzle was an existential one. While studying for my M.A. in divinity, I was married to a man named Kevin. The marriage was fairly new, and I enjoyed the companionship aspect immensely; I considered my husband my best friend. Outside the bedroom, we spent countless hours in deep conversations about serious topics, ranging from music, culture, and politics to philosophy, spirituality, and the meaning of life. Our time together inside the bedroom, by contrast, always left me feeling empty.

At the age of thirty-two, Kevin had spent the past twenty years of his life habitually consuming pornography, and this long tutelage had shaped both his attitude toward sex in general (as something only for physical pleasure) and his preferences: the particular images, words, and activities that aroused him. Whereas I was a woman in her early twenties who desired romance, love, and deeper emotional connection from sex, he was a man who objectified sex and became obsessed with pornography. Rather than relating to me as a whole person, comprised of both body and soul, Kevin treated me as a mere physical object in one of his preexisting mental fantasies. The end result was physical "intimacy" that was anything but intimate. Instead of being personal, it was profoundly impersonal. As a consequence, sex never was fulfilling for me: either emotionally or physically. When I challenged him on his unhealthy attitudes, he responded by abandoning our sex life altogether—turning exclusively to pornography to fulfill all his sexual needs.

As a consequence, our marriage went into crisis. I confided in the wife of one of his buddies from AA. (Kevin had been clean and sober for eight years, since before we first met, but he still attended AA meetings regularly.) She listened sympathetically and provided me with a diagnosis of his problem: sexual addiction. Many men in recovery from alcohol/drug addiction struggle with sexual addiction as well, she explained, and she referred me to a book on the topic (by author Patrick Carnes) as well as a twelve-step recovery program (SA).

When subsequently I read the book and discussed it with Kevin, our conversation did not have the desired result. Kevin oscillated between (1) admitting that he had a sexual addiction, while maintaining that all of his AA friends had transferred their addictions from alcohol to something else, so better to be addicted to sex than something worse, like heroin, and (2) claiming that he did not have a problem, that I was the one with the problem due to my unrealistic expectations (which failed to correspond with what men actually are like in reality). He thus refused to attend SA meetings. He did agree initially (when asked by our marriage counselor) to take a two-month break from porn, but sadly was unable to break his slavery.

We briefly separated, but then reconciled. I was disheartened, but I did not know what to do next. I confided in a second friend: this one a peer in my graduate program, who happened to be Catholic. She recommended the book *Love and Responsibility* by Karol Wojtyła (Pope John Paul II), and she gave me her copy to keep. I had studied Catholic sexual ethics in one of my academic courses, but we had focused more on liberal and feminist critiques of the Church's teaching on contraception. Neither this philosophical text nor John Paul II's later lectures on the theology of the body had been included, so this was completely new.

I took the book home and read the first forty pages. Against the commonly held view that "problems of sex are above all problems of the body", Wojtyła declares that "sexual morality is within the domain of the *person*."[11] Furthermore, the person is not merely an object of action, but is also a subject: one who possesses free will and whose inner self is free. Wojtyła explains, "*No one else can want for me. No one can substitute his act of will for mine.... I may not want that which he wants me to want—and in this precisely I am incommunicabilis. I am, and I must be, independent in my actions. All human relationships are posited on this fact.*"[12]

He then draws a contrast between "using"—employing some object as a means to an end—and "loving": seeking a good together with other people and subordinating oneself "to that good for the sake of others, or to others for the sake of that good".[13] Because human beings are not things but persons, he reasons, they always ought to be loved rather than used. "Using" a person (in the sexual realm) is to treat him as a mere means to the end of attaining sexual pleasure.[14]

---

[11] Karol Wojtyła, "Author's Introduction to the First Edition (1960)", in *Love and Responsibility*, trans. H. T. Willetts (San Francisco: Ignatius Press, 1981), 18.

[12] Wojtyła, *Love and Responsibility*, 24.

[13] Ibid., 25 and 29.

[14] Ibid., 34.

Wojtyła then sets forth his foundational moral principle: *the person-alistic norm*, the norm guiding how to treat persons. This norm tells us, first and foremost, what not to do: *Don't use persons.* Why not? Because "the person is the kind of good which does not admit of use and cannot be treated as an object of use and as such the means to an end."[15] (Wojtyła adapts this idea from the philosopher Immanuel Kant). Secondly, the norm instructs us what to do instead: *Love persons.* Why? Because "the person is the kind of good towards which the only proper and adequate attitude is love."[16] (He bases this latter idea upon the commandment to love found in the New Testament.)[17]

After reading all of this, I put the book down, and I sobbed uncontrollably for a very long time. I sobbed because the light of truth finally had broken through the darkness of my mind. I knew it to be true because it was so utterly beautiful amidst the ugliness of what I had endured. I realized that I had been used—repeatedly and without remorse—rather than loved by the man who had vowed to love me until death, the man whom I had trusted completely.

Wojtyła's words gave voice to the deep yearnings of my heart, longings I had tried to express but failed to because I lacked both the overarching Catholic vision and the interlocking concepts that held it all together. I had known that something was wrong, deeply wrong, in the depths of my being; but I had been written off by my husband as an idealist who expected something of men that was unrealistic. But now I knew the truth. The truth had been laid out systematically and elegantly: and not by a woman driven by romantic longings, but by a man. A man who asserted that loving rather than using other people not only is *possible*; it is *morally obligatory*. Rather than asking too much of my husband, I had demanded too little. I thus resolved to demand more. I issued Kevin an ultimatum. I told him that I was willing to be patient, that I would stand by him, but only if he were willing to go to SA meetings and work hard to fix his problem. Sadly, faced with a choice between me and porn, he ultimately chose porn. I filed for divorce, and I never looked back.

Armed with the truth, and captivated by the beauty of the truth—intellectually, liturgically, and existentially—I decided to begin RCIA

[15] Ibid., 41.
[16] Ibid.
[17] Ibid., 40–41.

(the Rite of Christian Initiation for Adults) that fall; at the same time I was beginning my first year of Ph.D. studies. The following Easter (of 1999), at Holy Name Cathedral in Chicago, Francis Cardinal George baptized me, confirmed me, and gave me First Communion.

Becoming a Catholic Moral Theologian

Fully received into the Catholic Church, I began attending Mass regularly and delving more deeply into Catholic theology. Instead of just war theory, I decided to write my Ph.D. dissertation on the theologian Hans Urs von Balthasar: on how the *beauty* of the truth—especially the truth about the good—enables us both to recognize the good and to be motivated to pursue it.

At the end of graduate school, I began interviewing for academic teaching positions. Still on fire with the faith, I hoped to teach at a Catholic university. But then I recalled the Catholic seminary I had visited during my RCIA retreat: University of Saint Mary of the Lake (Mundelein Seminary), located in the suburbs of Chicago. I wondered, *Would they have any interest in a lay-woman-convert from Judaism/ New Age teaching their seminarians?*

The answer turned out to be yes, and I joined their faculty in 2004. Sixteen years later, I continue to teach there and could not be happier. I especially appreciate the opportunity to teach our seminary's required course on the ethics of sexuality and marriage, so that our future priests might be enlightened and emboldened with the truth as well. My present ability to bring great good out of the terrible evil that I suffered in the past makes it all worthwhile. It also gives me great confidence in God's providential design.

My Family's Reaction to My Conversion

Unsurprisingly, my mother struggled initially with my decision to become Catholic. Although she preferred Catholicism to Protestantism, and even enrolled in a course on Catholic mysticism and spiritual direction (taught by Benedictine religious Sisters) around the same time I was baptized, she lacked confidence that I had chosen wisely. She also felt concern for my spiritual well-being. After all, I had joined an *organized religion*, a path that she had explicitly rejected as an inferior (and often oppressive) path to truth. For the first year, she kept sending me articles (typically written by liberal Catholics) that critiqued official Catholic positions on various issues. Her stated goal was simple: to ensure that I was sufficiently informed about important topics.

I asked, "Why do you choose to read only those things that are critical of the Catholic Church? If it's important to be open-minded in seeking the truth, then why not read things from the other side as well?" With generosity of heart, she suggested that I send her something positive (rather than critical) and promised to read it with an open mind. We both did as agreed upon, yet the tension between us continued unabated.

One day, about a year after my conversion, we were engaged in yet another religious quarrel concerning Catholicism. I was feeling increasingly frustrated. I could not understand why she seemed to be taking our intellectual disagreement so personally. Suddenly, a light bulb went off in my head. I asked, "Mom, do you feel that by becoming Catholic I rejected you?" She considered my question briefly and then replied in the affirmative. She had taught me many things, and leaving her ideas behind felt like leaving her behind as well.

I replied, "No, it's not that way that all. Your passionate interest in spirituality, your lifelong search for God and the meaning of life: all of that inspired me as well, both personally and in my chosen career path."

"So you didn't reject me?" she asked again. "No, I didn't reject you. I appreciate everything you gave me. I remained on the spiritual journey that you began. I just added on something new at the end, my own path." She finally understood, and we reconciled. Many tears were shed that day, by both of us.

Later that same year, for Christmas, she and my father gave me a very special gift: a gold cross necklace. They told me that it signified their acceptance of my decision to convert. It was such an unexpected surprise, and I was overjoyed.

To this day, I remain so grateful to God: for the gift of a loving family, for healing my personal wounds, for healing my relationship with my mother, for leading me to the truth, and for giving me many unique opportunities to bear fruit for his kingdom. "Great is the LORD, and greatly to be praised, and his greatness is unsearchable" (Ps 145:3).

Chapter 3

THE BEAUTY OF HER VARIED FACE

by

Lawrence Feingold

My conversion story is bound up with that of my wife because, thanks be to God, it happened to us together. There are two great themes in it: art and beauty, on the one hand, and marriage and spousal love, on the other, and the two are naturally intertwined. At first I focused on beauty in nature and art; through marriage I discovered the higher beauty of the human person and the human heart with its great need for love. These were a preparation for the discovery of the supernatural beauty of the face of Christ and of his Bride, the Church.

I was brought up with no religious beliefs, although I had a great interest in comparative religion. My father was Jewish and my mother Protestant, but neither practiced any faith, although very occasionally we attended Unitarian services. My father had renounced belief in Judaism after his bar mitzvah, but I grew up with some sense of Jewish identity through my family on my father's side. Growing up, I was not aware of anyone among family or friends who had religious faith, although doubtless there were some who did.

As an early teenager I remember thinking, Why am I me? I had the thought that I had a calling to preach love. Perhaps that is how an atheist can express an implicit baptism of desire. As an older teenager I had a passion for nature, environmentalism, and recycling; I loved to read outside in nature and feel its peace; I got involved in yoga and transcendental meditation for a time.

Art History

The principal focus of my idealism as a teenager was art and beauty. During those years, I spent seven summers at a wonderful art and music camp (Lighthouse) in the Appalachians. I wanted to be an artist (a sculptor), and I was immersed in the ideology of modern art; I was interested in abstract art, such as the sculpture of Henry Moore, and abstract expressionism.

In college I had the great good fortune to study art history with Norris K. Smith, a truly remarkable professor at Washington University in Saint Louis. In my freshman year I took his survey course, Art and Civilization. Professor Smith loved to have us examine works of art from different periods to compare their distinct view of the human person. He started the course by showing us two portraits— one by Rembrandt, and the other by an abstract expressionist painter named Willem de Kooning, called *Woman IV*. Smith then asked us which of these images we would prefer to have in our room to contemplate on our deathbed. Like the other hundred freshmen in the lecture hall, I imagine, I had never thought of being on a deathbed before. His point was that art is not just about shapes and colors, but about the nature of man and human society and, ultimately, about God and man's relationship to him. Smith taught us to see art primarily as the sensible expression of convictions and beliefs concerning God, man, the world, and their beauty. Every great work of art expresses, in sensible and artistic form, a certain worldview, and our preference and admiration for works of art should not be divorced from the worldview that animates them. The greatest works of art are sustained by a true and profound view of the nature of reality and the human person.

Imagining contemplating a painting on one's deathbed provokes the question: Is it true as well as beautiful? Does it manifest a foundation for hope? Although at the time I was deeply influenced by abstract expressionism and I was making artworks somewhat like *Woman IV*, I knew that I preferred to have a Rembrandt or Van Eyck over my bed, let alone a deathbed.

This course set in motion an ambivalence and interior conflict that took me ten years to fully resolve. Part of the ideology of modern art that I had imbibed was the idea that art and beauty are values that are distinct from truth and moral goodness. One professor had defined art simply as what an artist does. This ended up untying beauty from truth and goodness and emphasizing only its subjective side: art for art's sake, and for the sake of self-expression. Smith challenged that again and again, showing that it was foreign to the concerns of artists in cultures before modernity.[1] What demands expression is not the pure self, but *convictions* about what is true and good and, therefore, beautiful. And what is the source of these convictions? If the self is not the source, is there a first source—a First Beauty, Truth, and Goodness? For medieval, Renaissance, and Baroque art, it was clear that faith in Christian revelation was the source.

A closely related thesis of Prof. Smith was that many currents of modern art were marked by a pervasive dehumanization that no longer manifested the truth of the dignity of the human person made in the image of God. Often they manifested the alienation of that image, coming from a loss of faith and resulting in a cry of pain or boredom. Most of us did not entirely agree with him at the time, but his teaching worked as a leaven in me for years. I came to see that a key part of the beauty of the great works of art is the profound truth of the vision of the world that they portray. Beauty is intrinsically joined with truth. The falsehood of an artist's view of the world produces ugliness, whether it is the ugliness of an overly sentimental and shallow view or a jaded and cynical vision.

At this time I met my future wife, Marsha, at Washington University. She was Jewish. She enjoyed attending a Conservative synagogue in high school, but lost her faith in college. Her mother was a Holocaust survivor and both her parents, above all because of the problem of evil, were Jewish atheists.

We both took our junior year abroad in Germany in an exchange program. That art history course at Washington University led us to visit countless museums and churches throughout Europe that year and constantly to compare the dominant trends of modern art with Renaissance and classical art.

I was more and more struck by how Renaissance art especially captured the dignity of the human person, seen not just as a

---

[1] See Ananda K. Coomaraswamy, *Christian and Oriental Philosophy of Art* (New York: Dover, 1956), 10–12, 36–40.

universal—Apollo or Venus—as in classical art, but also as a particular individual. And I was no less struck by how the dignity of the human person seemed so often to be trampled on in the dominant trends in twentieth-century art. What happened? Although I was an atheist, I could not help drawing the conclusion that the change had to do with the place of Christianity in society, which was changing from a Christian society to a "post-Christian" one. How different their images are!

It became increasingly apparent to me that the dehumanization of modern art and architecture was absolutely tied to the progressive loss of Christian faith in society and its resulting secularization. The great works of the Middle Ages, the Renaissance, and the Baroque were obviously based on Catholic faith, from which they drew their inspiration, in whose service they humbly placed themselves, and apart from which they cannot be understood. The interiority of a Rembrandt portrait, for example, was unthinkable without the Christian view of the immortal soul, made in the image of God, lost in Adam's Fall, and redeemed by the blood of Christ.

I also was struck by how medieval art—the Gothic cathedrals—captured the aspiration of the human heart for transcendence. In 1979, we found ourselves in Chartres Cathedral on a Christmas afternoon; the cathedral was entirely empty except for some monks chanting the Divine Office. God was knocking on our hearts through that beauty, but we were not yet ready to open to him.

Marsha and I were married in 1981 after graduating from college. While studying art history in a master's degree program at Columbia University in New York, I took a class in stone sculpture and fell in love with that medium. In 1985, we moved to Pietrasanta, Italy, where I could do stone sculpture surrounded by craftsmen, marble, and the tools of the trade. Living in Tuscany enabled us to visit many more churches throughout Italy. I made several statues of my wife that were attempts to manifest the depth, mystery, and beauty of an individual person.

I remember being in the Sistine Chapel, seeing hundreds of tourists take pictures of *The Last Judgment*, and it hit me that no one—myself included—was asking whether it was true. Is there a Last Judgment? And where will I stand in that Judgment? I knew that the whole reason that Michelangelo painted it was to represent its truth in the most powerful way so as to remind the viewers—especially the cardinal electors—of their deathbed and what was to follow after it. It hit me that Michelangelo would have been appalled by our aestheticism, which is an aesthetic appreciation indifferent to the truth of what is portrayed.

Marriage, Pregnancy, and a Crisis

Art took us a long way toward an appreciation for Christianity, but I needed a still more profound encounter with a different kind of beauty: the beauty of the human heart. When my wife and I were married the summer after graduation from college in 1981, we chose a Unitarian minister to conduct the ceremony, who acquiesced to our request not to mention God. We substituted some Shakespeare sonnets for biblical readings. Now, after seven years of marriage, in 1988 (a Marian year), while I was doing sculpture in Pietrasanta, Marsha was pregnant with our son.

The fact of my finally being open to have a child was a kind of miracle, which came about when we were staying at the house of Saint Catherine of Siena. My wife's pregnancy confronted me first with the question of what I was to teach our child about the purpose of life. It hit me that I did not have a conviction about the meaning of life to pass on to him. More importantly, Marsha was experiencing unreasonable and severe anxiety about the pregnancy. At a certain point, about seven months into the pregnancy, she said that she did not want to live. This was actually the moment of grace. I experienced my lack of inner solidarity with her anxiety, how I wanted to run away from it, and that I was not able to love her as she needed to be loved. I could see that she was made to be loved absolutely and unconditionally, but that I could not do it.

Like many in our culture, I had assumed that we could give meaning to the world through art, culture, and beauty, as if we human beings were the source of that meaning and value and could fulfill ourselves through it. As a teenager I used to love books about self-realization, self-actualization, and creativity.

In a similar way, I had assumed that we could fulfill each other through our relationship. True friendship goes a long way, but this incident led me to see that there was a need to be loved in her immensely bigger and more noble and fundamental than any power of my own could fulfill.

In the face of my wife saying that she did not want to live, it was obvious that she was made for a greater love than I could give her. But how could she be "made" to be loved unconditionally if there were no God the Father who alone could love her in that way? How could she have such a desire and need for this love, I thought, if there is no God? If there is no God to love us as a Father, then this thirst of the human soul to love and be loved would ultimately be subject to frustration and absurdity. But that could not be. That would be the victory of *Woman IV* over Rembrandt.

The aspirations of the atheist humanism on which I had been brought up could not address the pain of the human heart. Spousal love gives us a direct experience of the human person for who he or she is: tremendously vulnerable, tremendously worthy of love, holding a secret identity that only love can see and discover. What I saw on this particular day in 1988 was that the human person—my wife—is immensely more worthy of love than I, or any human being, is capable of giving. Therefore, the thought came to me with great force that a God of love—God the Father—must exist who can love the human person as he or she is worthy of being loved. Otherwise, life would be absurd. *Woman IV* would be the truth about the human person and the world. But an absurd answer rules itself out and is repugnant to the heart, and I had come to see that and chosen to invest my life in the non-absurdity of the human person, and particularly of my wife.

If God did not exist, then there would be no loving providence at the very basis of my wife's existence, as the ultimate reason for her coming into the world. She and I would be nothing more than products of blind chance and freak accidents of an intrinsically meaningless world, as Sartre and many images of contemporary art would have it. But love tells us that this cannot be so, that the human person cannot fail to be the product of a love greater than the stars, in which we are made to share.

This is an example of what theologians call the "reasons of the heart". The French philosopher Blaise Pascal observed that the most effective arguments for convincing people of the existence of God and the truths of religion are reasons of the *heart*, rather than rigorous and abstract philosophical or apologetical demonstrations.[2] It should not be inferred that the heart's reasons are not truly reasons. The point is that reason informed by love has a power that cold "Cartesian" reason cannot attain. The heart must give the proper disposition to the quest for understanding in all matters that touch on the meaning and end of human life.

We often say that love is blind. But in matters of faith, real love sees *more intuitively and concretely* what reason struggles to see. True love takes us out of ourselves to marvel at the beauty, fragility, and mystery of another person, precisely as a person capable of love, and it greatly enhances our ability to see that the person we love transcends the material and temporal world. This also happens with regard to sexual morality. We may fail to grasp a moral norm considered abstractly but be profoundly convinced of it with regard to the lives of our children or spouse. Our parents, for example, did not like *us* living together but could not articulate why. In the same way, love for other persons, especially in proximity to death, can better dispose us to grasp the arguments for God's existence and to recognize his revelation, in which he makes known his infinite love for those whom we love.

Saint John Henry Newman, whom I would shortly discover, speaks about the difference between notional and real apprehension.[3] It is one thing to understand something abstractly as true in general of other beings; it is another to see something as true in someone that one loves and in oneself. So much of conversion consists in making the transition from the notional or abstract to the real and personal.

First Prayer

I somehow also realized not only that there is a God who loves in a divine way but that the ability to love is God's gift, which must

---

[2] See Pascal, *Pensées*, trans. A.J. Krailsheimer (New York: Penguin Books, 1966), 154: "The heart has its reasons of which reason knows nothing: we know this in countless ways.... It is the heart which perceives God and not the reason. That is what faith is: God perceived by the heart, not by the reason."

[3] See John Henry Newman, *An Essay in Aid of a Grammar of Assent* (Notre Dame, Ind.: University of Notre Dame Press, 1979), 85–92. See p. 89: "Persons influence us, voices melt us, looks subdue us, deeds inflame us. Many a man will live and die upon a dogma: no man will be a martyr for a conclusion.... No one, I say, will die for his own calculations: he dies for realities. This is why a literary religion is so little to be depended upon."

be asked for through prayer. So the next day I set out to pray for the first time in my life. I decided to take the train to Florence (we lived about an hour away) to pray in the Duomo built by Brunelleschi. I was not definitively thinking of Christianity, but neither was I opposed to it. I was thinking only of God the Father, and not of Jesus Christ. The question of public revelation was absent from my mind. On the train to Florence, I was moved to make this prayer: Teach me to love; teach me to be a light unto others. The first part of the prayer was prompted by the realization of the previous day. I was praying to be able to love my wife better. I do not know what, humanly speaking, prompted me to pray the second part, but to this day I know of no better prayer than these two petitions.

It is obvious that God had been calling me to pray for many years. This was over ten years after that art history course. He waits for us; he knows our times and places. Conversion stories show how personally God deals with us. He uses all the particulars of our life to find a unique opening to enter, almost always a cross, and then he waits for our cooperation.

And when we allow him to enter, he pours his grace upon us. After making this prayer, I thought of the words said by the Father in the baptism of Christ: "You are my Son in whom I am well pleased." This went together in my mind with Psalm 2: "You are my son; this day I have begotten you." Although an atheist, I knew the Bible from studying art history and comparative religion. As graduate students studying Renaissance art, we were required to read the New Testament. Of course, I only knew it from a third-person or cultural perspective. This was the first time I heard it in the first and second person (applied to myself): *You* are my son.... Conversion happens when we allow ourselves to hear God speak to us personally, and not just in a third-person or abstract way.

In this moment of grace I understood that these words were addressed by God the Father to Jesus Christ his Son and also to Marsha and me (and all other human beings) in Christ the Son. I understood that this was the answer to her need to be loved unconditionally. She is loved as a daughter, and, although I had not been thinking about myself, *I* am loved as a son in him. That is, I understood in that moment something of the mystery of divine filiation, a mystery at the center of the Catholic faith. We were created in order to become sons of God the Father in the eternal Son and to have God for our inheritance. This was a first glimpse of the third level of beauty: that of Christ and the divine plan of which he is the capstone.

I did not know it at the time, but this is, in fact, the most profound meaning of baptism, for it is through baptism that we are adopted as sons and daughters of God. There followed an emotional experience of rebirth, joy, and recovered innocence. It was April in Tuscany and new life was blossoming. I did then go to the Duomo and knelt to pray for the first time. I remember being concerned about being seen kneeling. We take for granted the power of simple signs of faith like that.

People later asked me why I "decided" to become Christian rather than practice Judaism. The question was not rightly posed. It was not experienced as a choice. I was initially attracted to the Church by her art and beauty. That is why I was going to pray in the Duomo in Florence. I was not thinking of Christ, but he made himself known to me. As he said to the apostles, "You did not choose me, but I chose you" (Jn 15:16). This happens in every conversion. He calls all, but we are not usually ready to hear. Interestingly, other Jewish converts who had become atheists or agnostics have had a similar experience. They prayed to know God and were shown Jesus at the same time. Good examples are Alphonse Ratisbonne[4] and my friends David Moss,[5] president of the Association of Hebrew Catholics, and Roy Schoeman.[6]

The arguments of the heart are efficacious not only for leading to belief in God's existence, but especially for recognizing the fullness of revelation in Jesus Christ and for recognizing his Church. In his *Essay in Aid of a Grammar of Assent*, John Henry Newman speaks about how the transition between natural religiosity and revealed religion proceeds not by way of opposition or contradiction, but as development and completion; for faith in revealed religion presupposes natural

---

[4] See *The Conversion of Ratisbonne, Narratives of Alphonse Ratisbonne and Baron Theodore de Bussiere* (Fort Collins, Colo.: Roman Catholic Books, 2000); and Roy Schoeman, ed., *Honey from the Rock* (San Francisco: Ignatius Press, 2007), 1–32. Many of the conversion stories in *Honey from the Rock* also show this supernatural illumination about the divinity of Christ, such as that of Charlie Rich (pp. 84–86) and Judith Cabaud (p. 193).

[5] See David Moss, "Called to Fulfillment", in Schoeman, *Honey from the Rock*, 140–41.

[6] See Roy Schoeman, "Surprised by Grace", in *Honey from the Rock*, 271–89.

religiosity as its proper predisposition, while elevating and perfecting it.[7] By natural religion he means the God known through conscience and the reasons of the human heart. Revealed religion picks up from natural religion and carries it to Christ and his Church. The God sought in the experience of conscience and human love and dimly glimpsed shows himself in the face of Jesus Christ and his relation to the Father. The same line of thought that leads people to recognize the existence of a loving and personal God disposes them to recognize the God of Abraham, Isaac, and Jacob,[8] the divine identity of Jesus Christ, and the truth of his Gospel that we have been loved *to the death*. In the words of John 3:16: "God so loved the world that he gave his only-begotten Son, that whoever believes in him should not perish but have eternal life." Or John 12:32: "And I, when I am lifted up from the earth, will draw all men to myself." In other words, the Gospel confirms our noblest intuitions about human dignity and promises to fulfill our wildest aspirations for unlimited love, goodness, truth, beauty, and communion.

As an atheist, I loved the great images of the crucifixion of Christ in art, and I saw the Cross as the greatest symbol in art—a symbol of suffering not closed into itself, but opening out to the four directions and to the whole world. But that was a completely abstract appreciation. Conversion happens when we see Christ on the Cross in personal terms, as in Galatians 2:20: "[Christ] loved me and gave himself for me."

So after that prayer I knew that we had to be Catholic, but I did not understand the difference between Catholic and Protestant and what to think or believe about that. God does not reveal everything at once.

Catholic or Protestant?

When I got back home I spoke with my wife about this epiphany experience. She wanted to believe, but did not want to believe

---

[7] See Newman, *An Essay in Aid of a Grammar of Assent*, 302–3.

[8] See Pascal, *Pensées*, 285: "Fire. 'God of Abraham, God of Isaac, God of Jacob,' not of philosophers and scholars."

unreasonably. There started a kind of tug of war that lasted for a couple of months in both of us. The following Sunday we went to church for the first time. We lived near a beautiful although modest Romanesque Catholic church. We planned to pray before Mass and then leave before it started, because we were still very suspicious of "organized religion". But as we were just going out the door, our landlady, who was very dear to us, came in and invited us to stay, and so we stayed for Mass. It was the fourth Sunday of Easter, which is Vocation Sunday, and the Gospel reading was the parable of the Good Shepherd. Both of us were deeply moved.

I was moved in particular by seeing an elderly woman sitting next to me receive Holy Communion. Although we did not receive—we were not yet baptized—somehow I felt that I was brought into communion with her, through her faith. (I later found out that she had a very deep faith and had experienced a miracle at Lourdes, which cured her of being a hunchback.) With regard to the Eucharist, I had another special grace. I took a trip to Rome and was in Saint Peter's Basilica. As I was walking down the nave of the church, I saw to my right a side chapel with two bronze angels sculpted by Bernini that I had studied in art history. So I went into the chapel to see the statues. As I entered, my breath seemed physically taken out of me. I looked around and people were kneeling before the Blessed Sacrament exposed. It was the Blessed Sacrament chapel. Although I did not understand anything about the Real Presence, I was profoundly moved and drawn to pray.

We also received some special graces with regard to Mary. Shortly after our first participation in Mass, our parish held a novena in honor of Mary. This was 1988, a Marian year, during May, the month of Mary, and our parish had a painting of Mary held to be miraculous and to have protected the city from the plague in 1629–1631. The archbishop of Pisa had this painting carried with honor during a rosary procession, and he also offered a novena of Masses with homilies on Mary's place in salvation history. The first homily (the only one I remember) was on Mary as the "new Eve". This was a great introduction to the Catholic understanding of Mary's role and the importance of public displays of faith and devotion. Growing up in America, we shared many Protestant prejudices against her, but, on the other hand, after Jesus, she is the most painted and sculpted

person in the history of art. Every admirer of medieval and Renaissance art has encountered her thousands of times among the greatest
works of painting and sculpture.

However, we were also drawn to Protestantism. Part of it was
cultural and human. I found an Anglican priest in Florence who
was very excited about bringing an atheist family into the Anglican
Church. He gave us a stack of good books to read, many of which
were from the Oxford Movement. I also came from a very liberal
family, and the Anglican position (or non-position) was much easier on many social issues that I had rather passively assimilated from
my upbringing. It seemed like a "middle way". In addition, I was
feeling called to leave aside sculpture and to study theology. I knew
that Anglican priests could marry, and I thought of studying for the
priesthood down the road.

One of the books that the Anglican priest gave me was actually a
classic of Catholic spirituality: *The Sacrament of the Present Moment* by
the eighteenth-century French Jesuit, Father Jean-Pierre de Caussade. It also goes by the title *Abandonment to Divine Providence*.[9] Much
of the book went over my head, but it still had a great impact on us
and changed the way that I looked at the world and everyday life. An
atheist has no choice but to see the events of everyday life and history
as mere accidents or chance events. Coming to faith in God means
believing in divine providence that extends to everything. The "sacrament of the present moment", or "abandonment to divine providence", consists in seeing the events and circumstances of everyday
life as part of a providential plan arranged by God from eternity so
that we encounter his will in all of them, in both the positive and
the negative, in trials and consolations. It was liberating to be able to
leave behind a view of the world that ultimately left all to chance.

Another book the Anglican priest gave me was a history of the
Reformation written by his former professor. This was not at all
appealing to me because of the iconoclasm of the Reformation. I had
fallen in love with the Catholic culture of the Middle Ages and the
Renaissance. At the same time, I spoke with some Catholic priests
in Pietrasanta. They happened to be less excited and less persuasive.

---

[9] Jean-Pierre de Caussade, *Abandonment to Divine Providence*, trans. Algar Thorold, ed. John
Joyce (Rockford, Ill.: TAN Books, 1987).

While Marsha was oscillating between a despairing atheism and a beginning of belief in God, I was wrestling with the question of the church. For several months I was going interiorly back and forth between Protestantism and Catholicism, and I would notice that when I thought that we should be Protestant, I felt a certain sadness about it, and when I leaned in the opposite direction, I encountered a joy. I could not articulate the reasons for this, and we were baptized in the Anglican Church that September. However, I came to see that the joy was caused by a recognition of the beauty of the Church as she lived in popular culture through the centuries and as she was expressed in the works of Christian art and in the lives of the saints, such as Saint Francis of Assisi, whom we had come to know a little through the history of art. The sadness came from the idea that we had to reject as a kind of human seduction that beauty of Christ working in human history and through the communion of the Church.

This is an example of what the Catholic tradition refers to as discernment of spirits. Saint Ignatius of Loyola describes this in his *Spiritual Exercises*, and he first observed it in himself in his own conversion. Discernment of spirits means being attentive to the movement of our desires and praying that God will help us to know whether these desires are actually from him, from our own thoughts and preferences, or from Satan, who is good at using our thoughts and preferences to deflect us from our actual vocation. In Saint Ignatius' case, he was severely injured in combat and sent to his brother's house for his convalescence. He used to love to read books of chivalry and asked for some. But they had only two books in the house: *Lives of the Saints* and the *Life of Jesus* taken from the Gospels. So out of boredom he read them. He found to his surprise that he experienced a similar excitement in reading the lives of the saints as when reading about chivalry and worldly exploits. In both cases he felt attracted to doing great or important deeds, but there was a key difference. His worldly excitement left him empty, and the deeds of the saints left him with a deep peace that came from above.[10]

I had experienced something similar in thinking about being Protestant or Catholic. The motives favoring the Protestant option

---

[10] See St. Ignatius of Loyola, *Autobiography*, chap. 1.5–8, in *Ignatius of Loyola: Spiritual Exercises and Selected Works*, ed. George E. Ganss (Mahwah, N.J.: Paulist Press, 1991), 70–71.

were human reasons, whereas the motives favoring the Catholic faith involved an inner experience of peace and joy that I did not fully understand, or give enough importance to.

But despite all those experiences and my misgivings, we were still baptized together with our three-month-old baby in the Anglican church in Florence. It was a very beautiful and reverent high-Anglican liturgy, but I do not remember being touched interiorly at all, as we had been previously in the Catholic Mass. We were confirmed there a few months later (again, with no interior emotion) and made plans to return to the United States. I actually wrote to the Episcopalian bishop of New York inquiring about eventually studying for the priesthood.

Saint John Henry Newman

Just after that, shortly before leaving Italy, we were browsing in the British Library in Florence, and I "accidentally" picked up a book entitled *The Newman Reader*, a selection of works by Saint John Henry Newman, a great nineteenth-century convert from Anglicanism to Catholicism who was canonized in October 2019. It immediately spoke to my heart.

The first thing that most struck me was what Newman called the "dogmatic principle", which is simply faith that God's revelation comes from above. It is his word, not our words that we project onto him. Like most in our society, I had very negative associations with the notion of "dogma" and "dogmatic". We equate it with intolerance. For an atheist deeply interested in religion, as I used to be, religious beliefs are understood to be human aspirations that are projected onto God. This projection might be more or less noble or profound, and there is beauty in our groping attempts, but no possibility of dogmas. The dogmatic principle means that there is a Word to follow that liberates us as we follow it, a Word that speaks in conscience, a Word that is the source of our being, and is Love.

Newman contrasted the dogmatic principle with the principle of liberalism in religion, which he understood as a principle of private judgment with regard to the faith by which "we may safely trust ourselves in matters of Faith, and need no other guide,—this is the principle of philosophies and heresies, which is very weakness."[11] This was my default world, but the tragedy is that it does not sufficiently take one out of oneself or offer a sure basis for hope. As an atheist coming to faith, this kind of position was all too familiar to my former way of thinking.

The dogmatic principle, on the other hand, has the strength of faith rather than religious opinion, as Newman explains: "That there is a truth then; that there is one truth; that religious error is in itself of an immoral nature; that its maintainers, unless involuntarily such, are guilty in maintaining it; that it is to be dreaded;...—this is the dogmatical principle, which has strength."[12] Religious conversion involves an "obedience of faith",[13] letting go of self as the ultimate criterion. This presupposes that God has revealed himself and that there is a Church who is God's oracle, declaring his Word today and resolving disputes.

Faith presupposes the fact of revelation and, ultimately, the existence of a Church who makes the claim to speak infallibly when necessary to preserve and transmit the deposit. What seems to the world as an argument against the Catholic Church—her claim to an infallible Magisterium—is part of what makes it believable that she can speak with the authority of her Founder. This intrinsic connection between revelation, the infallible teaching office of the Church, and the obedience of faith is what I first found so moving in Saint Newman.[14] Faith is about adhering to God's revelation and being in communion with him, and the Church is where we find the fullness of that revelation and communion. At the same time, it expands communion to the whole world.

I had been thinking about the question of the Church too much from the perspective of personal advantage, career choices, and cultural preferences or prejudices, and Newman's conversion was a

[11] Newman, *An Essay on the Development of Christian Doctrine*, 6th ed. (Notre Dame: University of Notre Dame Press, 1989), 357–58.
[12] See ibid., 357.
[13] See Vatican II, Dogmatic Constitution on Divine Revelation *Dei Verbum*, no. 5: "'The obedience of faith' (Rom 16:26; see 1:5; 2 Cor 10:5–6) 'is to be given to God who reveals, an obedience by which man commits his whole self freely to God, offering the full submission of intellect and will to God who reveals' and freely assenting to the truth revealed by him."
[14] See Newman, *Essay on the Development of Christian Doctrine*, 88–90; Newman, *Apologia pro Vita Sua* (Mineola, N.Y.: Dover, 2005), 158–63.

reproach to me, for he had so much more to lose. The question was simple: What was God's will for his one Church?

This prepared me for the second great insight that I drew from Newman, which concerned the beauty of the Church in her catholicity. Christ wanted his Church to go out from Jerusalem to all creation while still remaining one, built on the apostolic foundation. The Church was to be one, holy, catholic, and apostolic. How was she to remain one and apostolic while being universal in time and place and being alive with intellectual and moral vigor and growth? Newman's *Essay on the Development of Christian Doctrine* helped me to see the beauty of the Church as a supernatural organism whose life, ever new, permeates and transforms culture as she grows organically through the centuries while remaining both one and catholic in space and time. The Church is like a tree that starts as a seed—the mustard seed spoken of by Jesus—that slowly and organically grows into a tree. In the process, she changes and develops and is expressed in different ways in different cultures and times, but still retains her inner unity of faith, sacraments, and government.

One of the great things about studying the history of Christian art is that one sees the Church express her faith in very different and complementary ways, each of which shows a different face of the faith. Here, too, beauty—the beauty of the *catholicity* of the Church (the "beauty of her varied face")[15]—played a decisive role in our coming to see the truth. I wanted to be in the Church that embraced the whole world and all of history since Christ and the apostles and that, like the Church of Pentecost, still speaks all languages and is present in all cultures, transcending them but taking root and flesh in all. If the Church is the Bride of Christ, the beauty of the Bride cannot be restricted to one tongue, time, or place.

In art history I had seen that no one artistic style or school could be the queen, for every style, while gaining expression in one aspect, lost it in another. The cultures of the world were complementary, as

---

[15] John Paul II, apostolic letter *Novo Millennio Ineunte*, no. 40: "Christianity, while remaining completely true to itself, with unswerving fidelity to the proclamation of the Gospel and the tradition of the Church, will also reflect the different faces of the cultures and peoples in which it is received and takes root. In this Jubilee Year, we have rejoiced in a special way in the beauty of the Church's varied face." This expression is quoted by Francis in his apostolic exhortation *Evangelii Gaudium*, no. 116.

family members are. No culture, artistic style, or philosophical style, method of prayer or spirituality, could overcome this limitation of our condition.

The Catholic Church is seen by many as one of those complementary "cultures", and I suppose I had been looking at her that way when I was trying to choose between Catholic and Protestant. But the Church of Pentecost made a typological claim, which she has long realized, to speak through the language of every culture and tribe and, thus, to be exempt from this law of particularity by bringing forth all her varied children from her one womb. This is expressed in Psalm 87:5–6: "And of Zion it shall be said, 'This one and that one were born in her'; for the Most High himself will establish her. The LORD records as he registers the peoples, 'This one was born there.'" That all cultures are to bring their cultural treasures to the service of the Church is indicated in the prophecy of Daniel 7:14: "All peoples, nations, and languages should serve him." Or in the words of Psalm 72:10, "May the kings of Tarshish and of the isles render him tribute, may the kings of Sheba and Seba bring gifts!"

Saint Augustine has a beautiful commentary on the significance of the miracle of tongues at Pentecost:

> At the beginning the Church was not yet spread throughout the entire world, making it possible for Christ's members to speak among all nations, and therefore the miracle happened in each person as a presage of what would later be true of all. Today the whole body of Christ does speak in the languages of all peoples, or, rather, if there are any tongues in which it does not yet speak, it will. The Church will grow until it claims all languages as its own. . . . I dare to say to you, "I speak in the tongues of all men and women. I am in Christ's body, I am in Christ's Church. If Christ's body today speaks in the languages of all, I too speak in all languages. Greek is mine, Syriac is mine, Hebrew is mine. Mine is the tongue of every nation, because I am within the unity that embraces all nations."[16]

An implication of this is that there is a beauty and wisdom proper to our own time and culture that is still to be more fully incorporated

---

[16] Augustine, *Exposition of Psalm 147*, no. 19, in *The Works of Saint Augustine, Expositions of the Psalms 121–150*, trans. Maria Boulding (Hyde Park, N.Y.: New City Press, 2004), 20:464.

into the Bride of Christ. The beauty of the Bride is open to the whole of human experience. If the Bridegroom is the Logos made flesh, the Bride of the Logos must be catholic and be in continuous mission to be ever more so.

During this time, I sought out a Catholic catechism and happened to come upon Father Hardon's *Catholic Catechism*. (This was a few years before the publication of the *Catechism of the Catholic Church*.) This, together with the works of Newman, made me resolve to enter the Catholic Church.

Throughout this process, Marsha had not been doing research regarding Christianity but relied on me to do the reading and to explain it to her. She was not afraid to ask questions and raise objections! However, she trusted me as a guide, and I could usually explain things in a way that allowed her to take the next step forward with me. I remember telling her that I thought we should enter the Catholic Church. She had known that it was an issue and, though surprised that it was actually going to happen, did not hesitate to see that it was the right thing to do, even though it meant losing the attractive prospect of being the wife of an Episcopal priest. I contacted our local Catholic pastor on Long Island on December 8, 1988, feast of the Immaculate Conception, about three months after being baptized. Like many RCIA programs, the instruction was not very good. We were not taught about either the Real Presence or confession.

We entered the Church on March 25, 1989. This time God gave me consolation. I remember experiencing a peaceful and profound joy that day that has remained. I can make the words of Saint Newman my own. Newman writes:

> From the time that I became a Catholic, of course I have no further history of my religious opinions to narrate. In saying this, I do not mean to say that my mind has been idle, or that I have given up thinking on theological subjects; but that I have had no variations to record, and have had no anxiety of heart whatever. I have been in perfect peace and contentment. I never have had one doubt.... It was like coming into port after a rough sea; and my happiness on that score remains to this day without interruption.[17]

---

[17]John Henry Newman, *Apologia pro Vita Sua* (Mineola, N.Y.: Dover, 2005), 155.

As I mentioned, I felt called to leave aside sculpture and study theology. I decided to take some courses as a lay student at the local Catholic seminary in my hometown in 1989–1990. As a new convert, I was surprised to find that they were getting rid of their extra copies of Aquinas and were focusing on contemporary theologians like Karl Rahner, Josef Fuchs, and Raymond Brown. The seminarians were frustrated. What struck me as relatively absent was the dogmatic principle of Newman, the organic development of doctrine (through addition, not subtraction) and what Pope Benedict XVI would later call the hermeneutics of continuity,[18] which means that the Church develops and is reformed in continuity through the centuries, and not through rupture or revolution.

It is interesting how God uses things from our personal history to further our vocation and growth. My conversion as an artist, stimulated by Prof. Smith, consisted in returning to the classics like Michelangelo and rediscovering the beauty of tradition. It also meant looking at the moderns in the light of the classics, comparing their ethos, and resisting the hermeneutics of rupture. So it was natural on entering the Church and theology to start with the classics, which for me meant Saint Augustine and Saint Thomas Aquinas, with whom I fell in love. Similarly, it was natural to seek to engage in a living Thomism, open to all the riches of the Church's patrimony and to the breadth of reason, while remaining rooted in the Fathers and Doctors and, in a particular way, in her common Doctor.

This turned out to be a vocational experience. I felt called to get the best theological formation so as to teach seminarians later. Since we already knew Italian, we decided to go to Rome, where I studied for nine years at the Pontifical University of the Holy Cross. It has been an answer to prayers to be able to participate in the formation of seminarians at Kenrick-Glennon Seminary, where I have been very blessed to teach full-time since 2012.

[18] See Benedict XVI, Christmas Discourse to the Roman Curia (December 22, 2005), in *Origins* 35, no. 32 (2006): 536. See also Benedict XVI, Address of February 14, 2013, in *Origins* 42, no. 38 (2013): 607–8.

Chapter 4

THE LOVE OF TRUTH
AND THE TRUTH OF LOVE

by

Scott Hahn

Right round the turn of the century a book came roaring into America's households, including mine, and occupying young and old with its innovative taxonomy. It was *The Five Love Languages* by Gary Chapman. First published in 1992, it proposed that each of us tends to express love in a particular way: either by acts of service, or by gift-giving, or by physical touch, or by quality time, or by words of affirmation. We may, moreover, prefer to receive love *from* others in a way that is different from the "language" we prefer for showing our love *to* others.

My wife instantly took to the book, and the older children soon followed. In short order, we easily pegged each other as to our languages—both *from* and *to* others—except for me. The first part was easy enough, the family agreed: I prefer "words of affirmation" to express my love *to* others. But the second part, how I best receive love *from* others—this remained an uncracked code for many years.

More recently, my daughter Hannah, now a mother of four, looked on as her daughter, Tessa, then barely two, was crawling around the floor—carrying a book. "She does that all day", she said. "Her love language is books!" All family members present, in that moment, recognized that that was true for me as well. Everyone immediately agreed. The code was cracked.

I do love books, and books are indeed the "language" in which I show and receive love. If you've ever spoken with me for longer than a few minutes, you know this. Once I've figured out your interest or passion, I'll bring up the books I've read about it. If you tell me your problems, I'll prescribe books as the solution. If I find we share a common fascination, I may send you away with a book or two in hand. One of my longtime friends jokes about the time, years ago, when I sent him home with four boxes of books in his trunk.

Books represent the kind of affection that has always come most naturally to me—since long before I took up the academic life. Books are the common words in my love language.

But, like words in every language, they stand for something. They have meaning that is complex. For me they stand not only for love, but also for truth. They convey truth. They reveal truth. They represent truth.

It would be easy for me to compose this brief memoir—this intellectual itinerary of my conversion—as a bibliographical essay. In my mind, I remember the road to Rome as a cobbled street paved with books. But, for reasons that will eventually become clear (I hope), I am resisting that temptation. First of all, because it can be misleading. Depending on the day and the immediate triggers for my revery, I can recall my conversion as a different sequence of books. In fact, in several of my own productions I have explored my past in this way: as a catena of Marian titles, Eucharistic titles, sacramental titles, or ecclesiological titles. Each telling is true. Yet each telling is incomplete, as all tellings must be—and as this one will be.

So this telling will be about books, but not exclusively about books. It will be about teachers, conversations, and friendships, too, though even these, for me, are often based on books. I should say from the outset that this love of books was always about a much higher love; for me, it was always a consuming, passionate love of truth.

᷍ ᷍ ᷍

"Of making many books there is no end", said Qoheleth (Eccles 12:12). Well, the same can be said of the consumption of books. That endless supply needs to go somewhere, so why not to me? My home library currently houses more than fifty thousand books, and there is no end in sight.

But even the beginning of my consumption is indistinct. I was an early reader. I know I read the usual run of Weekly Reader and

Scholastic titles. In seventh grade, however, my reading shifted into high gear. I took an interest in World War II, which was then only twenty-five years in the past. My parents encouraged what they saw as a healthy curiosity about history, and they subsidized my purchase of around eighty books on the subject.

My World War obsession led to a fascination with aircraft. My knowledge grew more specific, detailed, and concrete; and what I discovered in books I wanted to bring into being. So I soon filled my bedroom with a hundred model military planes. Let the reader understand: when something catches my attention, I go at it with intensity and intentionality. That was true in seventh grade, and it has been true ever since.

With adolescence came other interests, and I let each in turn consume me. Music was one. I took up the guitar, and I hardly ever put it down. I read somewhere that Eric Clapton got good by locking himself up for a month with his guitar. My parents would not have let me go that far, but since they were paying for my lessons, they were happy to see me practice—a lot.

Not all my interests, however, could pass for healthy. Like many teens, I found myself enthralled with rebellion—and not just with the *idea*, but with acts of rebellion. Like Augustine pilfering pears, I chased the adrenaline rush of petty crime and mischief: lighting fields on fire, shoplifting record albums, experimenting with drugs. I liked the declaration of independence that each act represented. It was an upending of all authority: I alone was the boss of me, and I would do whatever I wanted. The same intensity and intentionality I had once applied to model airplanes I now lavished on subversion.

I rarely acted alone. I had friends who were similarly disposed, and we fed off each other's encouragement and provocations. It was inevitable that we should get caught, and we did—stealing record albums at a shopping mall. My friend got away, only to be brought into custody later. I was taken away in the police cruiser, ashamed and fearful. We seemed to have met our doom. But then a strange thing happened. I somehow managed not only to lie my *own* way out of the trouble, but to get my friend exonerated as well. I should have taken my lesson then and there and cleaned up my act. But the escape just left me feeling invincible—emboldened and energized for more trouble.

The next time, though, was for real. We got caught. We got tried, and we got sentenced. I faced a year in juvenile detention, which the judge mercifully commuted to six months' probation. This time I heard the message. Faced with the very real prospect of time in a lockup, I knew I had to turn my life around. I had to find a way to reject my worst impulses and make it through probation.

My parents were not particularly religious, and we attended a mainline church whose pastor confessed—from the pulpit—his own doubts about the Resurrection. So I did not have strong spiritual resources to fall back on. I was, moreover, just about to face a new challenge, entering high school, where new temptations were certainly waiting. Freshman year was a lonely struggle.

It was my singular grace my sophomore year to meet Jack Fitzmier, who showed me an entirely different way of living life. In his way, he was no less passionate and curious than I was; but his way was essentially different from mine. An undergraduate at the University of Pittsburgh, he was majoring in mathematics; but he volunteered all his spare time for Young Life, an Evangelical parachurch ministry that tried to reach kids like me, who were unchurched and spiritually feral. He did not match my stereotype of religious people. He was not a goody-goody. He was brainy, witty, and even cool. He liked to shoot hoops. He had a friend, Walt, another Young Life leader, who played guitar even better than I did and listened to all the right music.

I did not realize it at the time, but Jack was modeling a kind of maturity for me. He was living an intellectual life that excited him the way rebellion had thrilled me. He could talk about salvation—and important historical figures like Paul and Martin Luther—while we shot our free throws. He used plain language, but he could go deep. There was nothing uncool about him. I could see myself living such a life. In time, Jack would get his doctorate from Harvard and become a church historian and university administrator of great repute—and eventually executive director of the American Academy of Religion (AAR). I was just fourteen years old, and I was the beneficiary of his generosity and private tutelage.

From Jack I learned that the Bible was a Christian's sole authority; but I, like the young Augustine, found the Bible unreadable. It was rough and rude, and it did not stimulate my mind the way our philosophical conversations did. In principle I revered Scripture; but in practice I usually fell asleep within minutes of opening the Good Book. I felt the same way about prayer. I wanted to pray, but when I tried it, nothing "happened". I felt bored and restless.

I was ashamed of this, and I prayed to God to take away whatever impediment I (evidently) had to Bible study and prayer. Not long afterward I was sitting alone in my bedroom, praying, when something strange came over me. I began to pray in a way I had never prayed before. I was uttering syllables, but they were not recognizable as words. They just flowed out from me. I had heard of the phenomenon of "speaking in tongues", but I did not expect to experience it. My Christian companions and heroes were Calvinist and tended to be wary of Pentecostalism. I felt uneasy about the matter, so I decided that was enough prayer for the night. I reached over and switched on my radio and turned the dial. I remember the moment vividly, because it was Sunday and the first station I hit seemed to be broadcasting a religious service—but it was not in English. Nor was it in Spanish, French, German, or any of the other languages taught at my high school. It was just passionate preaching in a tongue that was utterly foreign to me. It sounded, in fact, a lot like the prayers I had offered a few minutes before!

I am not exaggerating when I say that, the next time I opened my Bible, the words on the page excited me. I flipped around in the big volume, and everywhere my eyes landed the Scriptures seemed to dance with delight. I wanted to keep the book open forever and never stop studying with it, praying with it, worshipping with it. It was as if the Holy Spirit had flipped a switch and turned a light on. Suddenly I had the gift of appreciating Scripture—desiring it— something I had utterly lacked before that evening. And I had the gift of prayer, which now seemed more like sailing than rowing, at least sometimes.

From that moment forward, the Bible became my consuming interest. It kept me up late at night. It got me out of bed early in the morning. I began a project of reading the Bible all the way through in one year. After I finished, I started all over again.

ᶾᴥ ᶾᴥ ᶾᴥ

I wanted to do the kinds of things that Jack did, and I soon found opportunities. My English teacher, Miss Dengler, was introducing us to the rigors of academic writing, and her lessons resonated with me. Some students grew excited by the technical requirements of the sonnet. I was intrigued by the precision of the forms prescribed for footnotes and bibliography. At last the time came for us to write a full-length term paper.

Jack often talked about the great figures of the Reformation, so I decided I would write about Martin Luther. My high-school and town libraries yielded little on the subject, so I made a raid on nearby Mount Lebanon Presbyterian Church, which was known for its library. I signed out about twenty books, and I devoured them. Writing that paper, I felt something like the confidence I felt playing the guitar. Of course, I did not have the mastery yet, but it seemed like something I could do well if I tried. I still remember the A+ Miss Dengler wrote on my title page, and I think I can quote her comment verbatim from memory: "You certainly have a mature writing style; but I must ask, how much are *you* writing, and how much are you manipulating quotes?" Advice taken. She saw that I was showing off—piling on sources to impress her with the depth and breadth of my research. Now in hindsight, which is 2020 (literally), I had all the makings of an uppity Ph.D. candidate.

Young Life began to absorb more of my young life. It was a place I could play guitar with other musicians. It was a place I could meet girls. It was, strangely enough, a place where I could speak more freely than in other places. As Jack graduated and moved on, a man named Art Lindsley took his place in my life, and Art was a worthy successor: a graduate student at Pittsburgh Theological Seminary with wide-ranging interests and profound mastery. He introduced me to the field of apologetics, focusing especially on its philosophical, theological, and historical dimensions.

With Jack and Art, it was OK to be smart and intense. It was OK to ask hard questions—though I had to be ready to *answer* hard questions in turn.

While still in high school I began to accompany my older friends, mostly theology grad students, to evening and weekend programs at the Ligonier Valley Study Center, about an hour away from my home. This proved to be another breakthrough for me.

The Study Center, as we called it, had only recently been founded, in 1971, near Ligonier (Pennsylvania) by a young, rising star in the Reformed world, R. C. Sproul. He had mighty and noble ambitions. His aim, he said, was to fill the gap "between Sunday school and seminary". He wanted nothing less than a widespread renewal of Protestant theology, and not only in academic settings, but in Christian churches and homes, among ordinary believers. He wanted to communicate and share an *intelligent* faith with as many people as were willing to listen and engage. In time, he would launch a radio show, *Renewing Your Mind*, and publish a magazine, *Table Talk*. In the course of his life he would publish almost a hundred books.

At the Study Center, Sproul lectured constantly, in a systematic mode, examining Scripture and doctrine over the course of weeks and months. Soon after one series stopped, he began another. The lectures were recorded and distributed as cassette tapes. They were reshaped into articles and books. R. C. wasted nothing, and he made the most of every effort, because it was all—and only—for God's glory. I wanted to be just like him, deep yet clear, profound yet passionate, orthodox yet dynamic.

I sat awestruck at his talks. They did not feel like lectures. We were not sitting in a classroom. It was more like a gigantic living room with comfortable furniture and lots of folding chairs, right there in his home! R. C. paced in front us while he was speaking, and he had a natural, engaging, entertaining delivery. He could be very funny. He could be very dramatic. He told stories, but he was delivering difficult points of philosophy, theology, and Scripture. In good weather, the events drew forty to fifty people.

I must have looked comical, a scrawny teen who looked even younger than my years. I went once or twice a week through my high school years, and I rarely saw other high-school kids there. But everybody treated me with a dignity and seriousness that I wanted to grow into.

I recall in particular R. C.'s lectures that would years later find canonical form in his 1985 book *The Holiness of God*—a bestseller and perhaps his masterpiece. At the podium, he referred to the work of Rudolf Otto, a German Lutheran theologian of the early twentieth century, who was best known for his book *The Idea of the Holy*. Otto's category of the "numinous" resonated with me. I had experienced God's power in strange and inexplicable ways. I could sense this power bringing order and discipline to the chaos that had been my life. I felt that I could only bow before the Almighty who had condescended to save me.

Otto spoke of God's *holy* presence as the *mysterium tremendum et fascinans*—a mystery that makes us tremble—yet also fascinates us. It attracts us and repels us. Peter could honestly say, "Lord, I am ready to go with you to prison and to death" (Lk 22:33), and yet, "Depart from me, for I am a sinful man, O Lord" (Lk 5:8).

This made sense of much that I was feeling and experiencing at the time. It left me with a deep desire for God, but also a keen sense of my own weaknesses and propensity to sin. This was a salutary thing for a teenaged boy.

The Ligonier programs were also strikingly different from what I was hearing everywhere else. In school and in the mainline churches we were still suffering a hippie hangover. The Summer of Love was past, but it was still all we talked about. The world and even the churches kept telling us: *luv, luv, luv.* But R.C. echoed the Scriptures, which told us: *Holy, Holy, Holy* (Is 6:3, Rev 4:8).

I could see why Jack and Art were so enthusiastic about the activities at Ligonier. And it was not a one-man show. R.C. invited others to speak, including his own teacher and mentor, the legendary theologian and church historian Dr. John Gerstner from Pittsburgh Theological Seminary. We felt as if we were in on the ground floor of a great moment and movement in Christian history. I sensed that God was calling me to be part of it.

ℰ ℰ ℰ

For my particular vocation—and my particular inclinations—I seemed to be living in the ideal location. By the end of my senior year in high school, my mind was fairly well formed and informed. Like my mentors, I was Evangelical in style, Calvinist in substance. Western Pennsylvania was home not only to the Ligonier Valley Study Center, but also to an excellent college that fit my profile.

I applied to Grove City College, and I was never disappointed by my choice. My teachers varied in style and theological approaches, but they all insisted on rigorous thought. And most of them were Reformed, like me. Near the start of my first semester a number of my classmates took an interest in a local Pentecostal fellowship where

the preaching was exceptional, and the services were replete with
"signs and wonders", words of prophecy, and instances of apparent
healing. The pastor was a firm believer in "believer's baptism". He
encouraged those who had been baptized as infants, which was most
of us, to do it again—this time for real—by full immersion.

While that was normal in Baptist and Pentecostal churches, it did
not square with the positions of John Calvin or Martin Luther. Nonetheless, my friends were moved by the excitement of the preaching,
and they made plans to get themselves rebaptized. And in less than
subtle ways, they coaxed me to join them. I mentioned this casually
to one of my professors, Dr. Robert Vande Kappelle. He raised an
eyebrow and said, "Rebaptized? Why?"

I told him about the cool new church, and I added, "I was baptized as a baby, and it didn't mean anything to me?"

"So?" he responded.

"Besides," I said, "where is it in the New Testament?"

He never changed his even tone, but asked, "Have you looked
into it?... Maybe you should." He encouraged me to make infant
baptism the topic for my term paper in his class, Biblical Ideas: Old
and New Testaments.

I did; and I decided to defer my decision about baptism until I
had researched the matter. I dug into the literature, ancient and
modern, and learned that Calvin had good reasons for retaining the
long-customary practice of baptizing babies. Jesus himself had said:
"Let the children come to me, and do not hinder them; for to such
belongs the kingdom of heaven" (Mt 19:14). The Lord made clear
that the kingdom belongs to those children, and baptism is somehow the sign of the kingdom's coming (see Mt 28:18–19). When
Peter preached the Gospel for the first time on the first Pentecost,
he put the matter in the same terms: "Repent, and be baptized
every one of you in the name of Jesus Christ for the forgiveness
of your sins; and you shall receive the gift of the Holy Spirit. For
the promise is to you *and to your children*" (Acts 2:38–39, emphasis
added). These and other New Testament passages made the case for
infant baptism plausible to me, if not quite as explicit as I would
have preferred. But Calvin's authority was important, and he was
backed up by a respectable number of thinkers from the early centuries of Christianity.

The classic Reformers seemed to be arguing from biblical doctrine, both the Old and New Testament, whereas the Pentecostals claimed to base their beliefs almost entirely on New Testament practice. I came to appreciate the words of Jesus, "Do not think that I have come to abolish the law and the prophets; I have come not to abolish them but to fulfil them" (Mt 5:17).

The incident taught me to keep a certain reserve in religious matters and not act impulsively. I learned rather quickly that there was usually more to religious tradition than meets the eye. By asking simple leading questions like "Why?" and "So?" Dr. Vande Kappelle taught me to raise those queries in my mind if I found myself suddenly in the thrall of some novelty.

He also taught me not to be afraid of modern biblical scholarship. For my project, he had me engage with historical critics, as well as the early Church Fathers, and he taught me to test their claims and sift them.

The experience awakened me to the question of the relationship of the Old Testament and the New. It was obviously important to the early Reformers. What should it mean to us today? More importantly, my research made me intensely aware of the biblical covenants and the "signs" of those covenants. It also led me, for the first time, to encounter the writings and customs of ancient Christianity.

It was pure joy to be in such an atmosphere with such teachers. I threw myself into my studies and made the decision to *triple*-major in theology, philosophy, and economics. For me, though, it was one major. I wanted to build an all-encompassing biblical worldview.

In economics I leaned Libertarian, influenced by the Austrian School. (My first published article, "The Outcome of Income Tax", written while I was at Grove City, appeared in *The Freeman*.) In theology I was Calvinist, of course. In philosophy I considered myself a Thomist. This surprises my Catholic friends when I tell them today. But Aquinas was the favorite philosopher of R. C. Sproul and Dr. Gerstner. They had a keen appreciation for the Angelic Doctor's demonstrations of the existence of God, his Five Ways. I recall R. C. once saying that if Presbyterians could canonize saints, he would nominate Thomas Aquinas without hesitation.

Studies were important, but not the only thing in my life. In my second semester I applied to enter leadership for Young Life. I was told that it was unusual for a freshman to do that, but I persisted. I felt that Young Life had saved my life, and now I wanted to pay it forward. I made it clear that I would not take no for an answer, so they let me in.

I started by helping to lead the programs for high-school kids, and I targeted those who were in a halfway house affiliated with the nearby juvenile-detention center. They could live there because they had earned the privilege through their good behavior. So they seemed ripe for conversion. Three days a week I would go over for a couple hours with the guys.

In Young Life we called this "contact work", "incarnational ministry", and "winning the right to be heard". I did the things Jack had done for me. I talked. I listened. I learned to play their favorite songs on the guitar. They enjoyed the company, but they never seemed interested in the next step. They could not seem to muster interest in Jesus.

I found it frustrating, because I loved them and they seemed to have real affection for me. I wanted what was best for them. But I came to see that their obstacles to faith were rather large. In my younger years, I had at least an intact family and a lifelong experience of love. Many of the kids at the halfway house had never known a stable, intact family. I had committed my crimes out of a desire for rebellion. But some of these kids had never known any life but crime and neglect.

I saw slightly more progress among the more typical students at Grove City High School. But even among them I saw that a bad family environment was often the impediment to growth.

My frustration led me reflect on the nature of family—and, of course, it led me to do more research. I began to see that, in Scripture, family was inseparable from the idea of covenant, and covenant was the dominant theme in both the Old Testament and New Testament. In fact, the very word "testament" in those titles is a rendering of the Hebrew *berith* and the Greek *diatheke*, both of which are ordinarily translated as "covenant". In ancient Israel the marital covenant made the family not just the basic unit of society, but a sacred organism, a divine institution.

It was a providential convergence of circumstance and syllabus, of curricular and extracurricular concern. My work with Young Life had me thinking much about family. I ended my senior year with an independent study in theology, directed by Dr. Andrew Hoffecker. It culminated in a fifty-page paper: "A Covenant Theology of Family for the Ministry of Young Life in Grove City". Dr. Hoffecker loved it. I was becoming a *relational* dogmatist.

My studies at an Evangelical Calvinist college kept the idea of covenant always before me. Covenant theology arose in the seventeenth century among the Scottish Presbyterians. The idea was so central to them that they were known as "the Covenanters". Covenant theology came to New England with the Puritans and continued to thrive in the United States for centuries, especially at the major Presbyterian seminaries: nineteenth-century Princeton and twentieth-century Westminster. Practically every paper I wrote in college, quite intentionally, centered on some aspect of covenant.

To my professors, a covenant was a form of sacred *contract* that created a binding relationship between two parties. It established legal obligations and rights for both parties. In the ancient world, treaties between nations were enacted with covenants. A covenant was sealed by a solemn ritual oath that invoked God (or the gods) as witness.

But I began to notice a consistent pattern in the relationships created by the ancient covenants (in ancient Israel as well as its neighboring societies). Covenantal relationships were *family* relationships—sacred kinship bonds. Even if a conquering king was imposing a treaty upon a conquered people, he still spoke of himself as a father and the conquered people as his sons and daughters (2 Kings 16:7). This was certainly true of the divine covenants found in Scripture—with Adam, Noah, Abraham, Moses, David, and Jesus. In each, God was raising up a family for himself. In the divine oracles, the earthly partners are addressed as God's spouse, brother, or child (2 Sam 7:14; Ps 2:7; 89:26–27; 1 Kings 20:32; Deut 21:13; Hos 2:2, 16, 23; Gen 2:23). From such covenants, cultures arose, and from them, societies, nations, and religions. But they all arose as families.

The issue would become more personal for me when I met Kimberly Kirk, a fellow student with whom I was immediately smitten when I first spoke with her. We got to know one another, and she eventually volunteered to join my Young Life team. She came to share my passion to reach the kids *and their families*. She also came to appreciate my emerging insights on the notion of covenant.

Kimberly was not only brilliant and beautiful, she was royalty in my world. Her father, Jerry Kirk, was a renowned pastor and evangelist—and a friend and colleague of R. C. Sproul. Dr. Kirk pastored a church in New Wilmington, Pennsylvania, right across the street from Westminster College, during the years R .C. taught as a professor there. Dr. Kirk later invited R. C. to serve as a theologian-in-residence at his next parish, College Hill Presbyterian Church in Cincinnati. From there R. C. went on to found a study center in Ligonier, Pennsylvania.

My future plans dovetailed nicely with Kimberly's. We both planned to go on to advanced studies in religion. I intended to prepare for eventual ordination as a Presbyterian pastor. I chose Gordon-Conwell Seminary, an Evangelical powerhouse that had been launched by Billy Graham and others in 1969. Not coincidentally, Gordon-Conwell was home to some of the world's greatest Evangelical biblical scholars and theologians, several of whom specialized in biblical and covenant theology. Nicknamed the "Harvard of the Evangelical seminaries", Gordon-Conwell had the reputation for academic rigor as well as solid pastoral formation.

Kimberly and I got engaged, and we planned for our wedding to fall between our graduation from Grove City and my matriculation at seminary.

In my waning days at Grove City I completed yet another independent study, this one in philosophy. With Dr. Richard Trammell, I slowly worked through Michael Polanyi's *Personal Knowledge*, his Gifford Lectures from 1951 to 1952. Polanyi stretched my Thomism in unexpected and exciting ways. He challenged thinkers like me to confront the personal commitments, tacit dimensions, and fiduciary aspects inherent in the pursuit of all knowledge, whether it is from reason and science or from revelation and faith.

Between my last two semesters, I was able to spend the month-long Christmas break living at Ligonier and studying closely with R. C. Sproul. I spent many hours with him and shared dinner at his house with his family. It was the capstone of my educational experience thus far; and afterward I felt I was going forward with the blessing of one of my heroes.

⁂ ⁂ ⁂

How do I begin to measure the influence of someone with whom I shared the whole of my mind—and whose mind I came to know as well as my own? Kimberly and I shared the same creedal commitment and the same theological orientation. We had attended the same college, taken many of the same courses, and read many of the same books. When our theological interests diverged, they were complementary. Her spiritual formation ran deeper than mine, as hers had begun in a pastor's home. She often knew by instinct what I had yet to master by study. We tested each other's thoughts; we tried each other's thoughts; we completed each other's thoughts.

We had great expectations for Gordon-Conwell, and the place did not disappoint. We arrived at our apartment complex in Ipswich on a Saturday night and spent the night in the U-Haul truck. In the morning, we went to the Presbyterian church down the road in South Hamilton.

We had no sooner pulled into the church parking lot than I felt like a starstruck fanboy. I nudged Kimberly and tried to point as discreetly as possible. "Do you see that man?" I whispered. "That's M. G. Kline!"

Meredith G. Kline was an Old Testament scholar and one of the world's most respected experts on covenants in Scripture and the ancient Near East. He had already written two groundbreaking historical studies, *Treaty of the Great King: The Covenant Structure of Deuteronomy* and *By Oath Consigned: A Reinterpretation of the Covenant Signs of Circumcision and Baptism*—and he was still in his prime. Both books had exercised a profound influence on me. And when I arrived, I discovered that he was finishing up two other books, *Images of the Spirit* and *Kingdom Prologue: Genesis Foundations for a Covenantal Worldview*. When I found out that he was sharing with students the article versions and drafts of these books in the making, I was excited beyond words. It felt like being an extra on a Hollywood movie set.

We later attended the church pastored by Gordon Hugenberger. He was then very young and known as Dr. Kline's protégé. He was pastoring full-time at a local church and had turned down a full scholarship for doctoral studies at Harvard. In his classes, he was already working out the ideas he would later set down magisterially in his doctoral dissertation and his 1994 book *Marriage as a Covenant*. His academic interests and mine coincided rather closely. I attended his church and had him for a year of intensive Hebrew and a course on 1–2 Samuel.

In our second year in Massachusetts, Kimberly started taking courses. We were on different "tracks" with different requirements. Mine was designed for those who planned to enter ordained ministry. Kimberly had become convinced that Scripture did not allow for the ordination of women. At home at the end of the day, we shared everything we had heard and learned in the classroom or the library.

Early on, she took a course on Christian ethics. I had taken it the year before, so I knew how it went. The professor divided the class into small groups and had each group examine a particular topic of contemporary interest. Kimberly's group chose contraception—a subject that no one had bothered to pick the year before when I had taken the course.

The topic seemed strange to me—a non-issue. What was controversial about birth control? We were practicing it at the time, because we wanted to devote ourselves entirely to our studies. It was practiced almost universally in the Christian world as we knew it. Only the Roman Catholic Church opposed it, and I did not consider "Romanism" to be a legitimate expression of Christianity.

But Kimberly approached her research as she always did (and does): with thoroughness and an open mind. She read everything she could lay hands on, including books by Roman Catholics. She even read *Humanae Vitae*, the controversial 1968 encyclical of Pope Paul VI. At the dinner table one night she informed me that until 1930 *all* Christian churches had opposed contraception, without exception, including our Presbyterian denomination. I explained this away as residual Catholicism, which had taken centuries to wither away. But Kimberly helped me to see that the old Protestant arguments against birth control were deeply biblical—and the newer arguments in favor were *not*. She was trying to be fair.

She asked if I would read one book on the subject: *Birth Control and the Marriage Covenant*. The last word leapt off the page at me. I considered myself a rising master of all things "covenant". How had I not heard about this book? I looked at the author's name, John Kippley, which I did not recognize. Then I saw the imprint on the spine was Liturgical Press. Ah, Catholic. But it could not hurt to read it, and so I did.

It did hurt, because by the end of the book I was convicted. Here was a cogent moral argument—expressed in covenantal terms—refuting a practice I had blithely accepted without hesitation or thought. Why had I never heard this before? Why had it been scrubbed from the moral memory of even the most serious Protestant thinkers? I had to conclude that the Catholic Church stayed right on this subject when all the rest of the world went wrong.

It was unsettling—though it did not tempt me to become Catholic. I remember saying to Kimberly what my mother and grandmother had often said to me: "Even a blind hog finds an acorn now and then."

In the past I've described myself as "anti-Catholic" at this point in my life. I've decided that is not entirely accurate. As a convinced Calvinist, I did not consider myself anti-anything. I opposed Catholicism, but I also opposed Methodism. But was I anti-Catholic? Was I anti-Methodist? Neither label would have made much sense to me at the time. "Evangelical" I could accept, because I was all about the *evangel*, the Gospel. From high school onward I delighted in arguing against anyone I considered to have strayed from the biblical way. When I lived in Western Pennsylvania, however, I met far more Catholics than Arminian Wesleyans, and I never met a single Catholic willing to argue for his faith on biblical terms.

This case against contraception was the first compelling argument I had heard for a distinctively Catholic doctrine. It compelled Kimberly and me to change our marital practice, and that led, very soon, to significant changes in her anatomy.

Everything in life seemed to be moving at warp speed. All my life to that point I had been a student. That is the box I would have checked on any form. Now I had become a husband and then a father. And I was about to become a pastor.

My studies, too, were taking me into unexpected places. Gordon Hugenberger focused not merely on the legal aspects of covenant, which had fascinated me, but also on their ritual expression— the *covenant oath* forms that sealed the deal. I reflected on how in ancient Israel baby boys at eight days were incorporated into the Old Covenant by circumcision, and how Paul's epistles compared Christian baptism to Jewish circumcision (Rom 4–6; Col 2:11–12). Kline explained how the early Church came to celebrate—and refer to—these as "sacraments" (*sacramentum*, Latin for covenant oath). My teachers also led me to understand the ancient Passover as a ceremony for covenant renewal—and I came to understand the Lord's Supper in the same way. I began to see an overarching pattern and plan in the unfolding of history: a law that governed God's household, a divine economy.

This marked my discovery of *biblical theology*—which was something more than exegesis but less than systematics. My initiation came through the writings that Dr. Kline assigned, notably the works of Geerhardus Vos, an early-twentieth-century biblical scholar at Princeton. His *Biblical Theology: Old and New Testaments* was a lodestar that showed me how to read Scripture as a canonical unity, in terms of what he called redemptive history. He also taught me how to compare and contrast the Old Testament and the New Covenants, to trace the profound continuity and to recognize the discontinuity.

Also around this time I won a coveted position as teaching assistant for Dr. Roger Nicole, a world-class expert on the New Testament's use of the Old Testament. The field was on fire back then with the question of whether it was safe for modern Christians to read the Old Testament as the New Testament authors did—that is, typologically, as a foreshadowing of redemption in Christ. I tended to think we could, but in those days that was a minority view in the Protestant world.

Knowing my interest in the family dimension of covenant, Dr. Kline directed my attention to a recent and important work on the subject. It was *Treaty and Covenant* by Dennis McCarthy. McCarthy's book led me in turn to another book: *Declaration and Covenant: A Comprehensive Review of Covenant Formulae from the Old Testament and the Ancient Near East*, by Paul Kalluveettil. I consumed both. They seemed to confirm—from history, archaeology, and biblical exegesis—everything I had intuited about the biblical covenants.

Both books, I learned, were written by Roman Catholics.

Perhaps the contraception issue had softened me enough that I could let my guard down. Though I was not yet attracted to Catholicism, I could no longer dismiss its adherents out of hand. I had to admit that at least a few "papists" were producing biblical scholarship of the highest quality. This was an awkward and painful thing for me to accept.

On visits to bookstores (my favorite recreational activity) I began
to notice titles—about covenant, about Jewish and Christian ritual,
about the relationship between the Old Testament and the New—
that were by Catholic academics. I developed an appreciation for
Jean Daniélou, Henri de Lubac, Yves Congar, F. X. Durrwell, Louis
Bouyer, M. J. Scheeben, V. Soloviev, and finally a German named
Joseph Ratzinger.

These men led me, in turn, to their sources from antiquity: the
Fathers of the Church and the literature of Second Temple Judaism,
the Dead Sea Scrolls, and the Targums. I plunged into the study of
covenant ritual, the sacrifices and annual festivals in the Temple(s)
of ancient Israel. This led me, in turn, to the liturgical texts and other
writings of the primitive Church. I had encountered these before, of
course, but only in cherry-picked quotes. Now I was reading them
in full and in their proper context.

I was surprised by the ways the earliest authors differed from the
practice of modern Christianity as I knew it. Clement of Rome (second half of the first century) lived in a Church that was liturgical
and hierarchical. Ignatius of Antioch (died A.D. 107) assumed that the
clergy in every city were ordered uniformly: bishop, priest, and deacon. The *Didache* (first century) described a Church that was centered
on the Lord's Supper to a degree I had never seen in the Evangelical
world. And yet everything these men wrote seemed to stand in clear
continuity with the Church I encountered in the pages of the New
Testament. It did not look the same in every detail. It was bigger now,
more widespread. The Church was encountering new cultures and
situations, and as she did, she proved the universality of the Gospel.

Nevertheless, I was troubled by that list of practices and beliefs
that seemed universal in the first, second, third, and fourth centuries.
Why should the basics back then differ from the basics in Christian
life today? Perhaps I could help to close that gap between the first
century and 1982.

೨ಀ ೨ಀ ೨ಀ

Ordination came, and morning followed, a new day. I left Gordon-
Conwell with a master's degree, *summa cum laude*, and I walked into
the dream job. I was hired as an assistant pastor at Trinity Presbyterian

Church in Fairfax, Virginia. Trinity was, like R. C. Sproul's Ligonier Ministries, one of the hot spots of the Reformed world of Calvinism in the eastern United States. It was a small congregation with
an outsized reputation, known internationally as the home of the
theonomy movement—also known as Christian Reconstruction.
Theonomists sought ways to apply biblical law to civil law in our
modern context. Trinity hosted regular classes and conferences with
the leaders of the movement: R. J. Rushdoony, Gary North, Greg
Bahnsen, and James B. Jordan.

The church had been thriving for decades and had established its
own school, Fairfax Christian (K–12), which was well regarded for
its academics. Senators, representatives, and prominent conservative activists sent their children there. The year before I arrived, the
school had been featured in *People* magazine.

With Ronald Reagan in the White House, American Evangelicalism was riding a new wave of confidence; and there Trinity was, just
outside the Beltway and enjoying a fair measure of influence.

I had my pulpit for preaching on Sunday mornings and weekly Bible
studies on Sunday nights, and I was assigned to teach four daily classes
in theology, philosophy, the Bible, and economics at the high school.

Like any newly ordained clergyman, I was eager to put to use all
that I had learned at seminary. In my case, that meant helping people
to understand the meaning of covenant, of baptism as the sign of the
covenant, and of the Lord's Supper as a covenant renewal. These
were consistent themes in my teaching and preaching. I even began,
gradually, to tinker with our church's order of service, to emphasize
the covenantal signs. Eventually, we went from a quarterly observance of the Lord's Supper to weekly. We also adopted the regular
profession of the Nicene Creed. I saw all of this as consistent with our
biblical roots as Presbyterian Calvinists.

One or two members of the congregation, however, were ex-
Catholics and saw my actions in a different light. Some remarked
that my services reminded them of what they had left behind. They
warned me against my "Romish" tendencies. I assured them that
there was nothing "Catholic" about what we were doing. I still truly
believed that our services represented the *antidote* to Catholicism.

Not that I knew much at all about Catholicism. My impressions came mostly from lunchroom discussions with badly informed

Catholics in high school and college. In apologetics manuals I had read critiques of Catholic doctrine and practice; and most of the Catholics I met seemed unable to refute or deny what I found in those hostile sources.

I was, in fact, more ignorant than the Catholics with whom I sparred. They at least had attended Catholic worship on occasion. I had never done so, and in fact I had an aversion to the idea.

Yet the remarks continued to dog me. In fact, my students at the high school—at least one of whom knew more about actual Catholicism than I did—began to call me out with some regularity.

At first I was irritated. But soon I was rattled. What if they were right? What if I had failed to filter out the Catholic elements in those books by Daniélou and de Lubac?

And I began to have an even more frightening thought: What if the Catholic Church is right?

These were not thoughts I wanted to entertain. I was a young husband and father whose job depended on his fidelity to Calvinist principles. I was, moreover, a devoted disciple of Sproul, Gerstner, Kline, Nicole, and Hugenberger.

I examined my conscience and soon arrived at a most unwelcome conclusion: I could not continue doing what I was doing. I had been presenting myself as a preacher and teacher of Calvinist doctrine, as taught by historic traditional Presbyterianism, and I was the last person to realize that I was none of the above.

I needed time to think. But I also needed a job that could support my family. We stepped out in faith and moved back to Pennsylvania. Several days after our arrival, I ran into the president of Grove City College while I was filling out a job application at the local supermarket. He mentioned that he was looking to hire an assistant. My prayers were answered.

ʒ❦ ʒ❦ ʒ❦

The job in Grove City was perfect for my purposes. It was hard work, mostly nine to five, but it was not difficult work most days. I was invited to teach courses in Scripture and theology, while I worked alongside of my former professors, some of whom were experts in my various fields of interest. I already knew the profs, and they knew me well. My nights I could spend with Kimberly and the kids—and with books culled from the library.

During my second year, I enrolled in the Ph.D. program in theology at Duquesne University in Pittsburgh, about an hour down the interstate, and took three doctoral seminars on Thursdays. I even visited with an Opus Dei priest to seek his counsel. (He was better informed than the guys in my high-school lunchroom had been.)

It was a full year. My graduate courses forced me to think systematically about my current preoccupations. I wrote a paper on "Marriage as a Covenant" and then reworked it the following semester to emphasize the differences between covenant and contract. (Much of my subsequent work as a Catholic has been a further reworking of the seminal ideas in those papers.)

I was actually more congenial to Catholic doctrine than some of my classmates who were Catholic. They thought my support of traditional Catholic teaching against contraception was odd or quaint. I called as my witness the current pope, John Paul II, who was then delivering the Wednesday addresses that would come to be known as the "theology of the body". On my long drives home late at night, I asked myself: *Why am I doing this? Why am I defending a church that's not mine?*

I kept asking. I did not know where I belonged. I could not go back to the world I had loved—the world of my heroes. It already seemed alien to me, because I believed it was alien to the life and intentions of Jesus Christ and the apostles. But I could not go forward toward the Catholic Church. In fact, it was hard for me even to think about such a course of action.

Kimberly was patient and kind. She showed all the qualities of holy love you'll find catalogued in 1 Corinthians 13. But I knew that our situation pained her. She was a Presbyterian pastor's daughter, and she had signed on to be a Presbyterian pastor's wife. She was the one who had catalyzed my first "Catholic thoughts" with her study of the morality of contraception. But Rome seemed to elicit no further interest from her. She knew me, and she knew my struggle. But she found it increasingly hard to sympathize, and I knew that she felt abandoned and desolate. This was devastating to me, and yet there was nothing I could do to fix it.

I found myself in orbit, at a certain distance from both my Protestant past and any possibility of a Catholic future.

My colleague John Bergsma often jokes that the natural impulse of a young man in a crisis of faith is to enter a doctoral program. It is funny because it is true, not only in John's case, but also in mine.

2& 2& 2&

In all my life, that two-year period was probably the single most exciting and productive time in the development of my thought. I read close to two hundred books on Catholic theology, including the documents of Vatican II, Vatican I, Trent, and other councils. I discovered the writings of John Henry Newman, of course, and devoured his *Essay on the Development of Doctrine* and the *Apologia pro Vita Sua.* I read countless scholarly articles, including a number of luminous studies of the Eucharist in Hebrews by James Swetnam, S.J. I also led a number of Bible studies for young people (college and high school); one of the regular attendees was R. C. Sproul, Jr.! Many of these young men and women eventually became converts and lifelong friends.

But I could not stay. I applied to the prestigious doctoral program at Marquette University in Milwaukee and was awarded a full scholarship, so I could afford to study full-time. I would press forward in my studies of the biblical theology of the covenants.

It seems foolhardy now. I had no realistic job prospects. A few years before, I had seemed to be at the beginning of a great career. Now that door was closed and locked. Yet I had no expectations of employment in Catholic academe. I had no patience with the doctrinal dissent that was fashionable in those days. And I felt I wore my Protestant past like a scarlet letter.

I was biding my time and working out my thoughts in a safe space. I had no reasonable expectations of employability at the end of the program. But still I pressed on.

Early in my time at Marquette I made the decision to attend a Mass. I had read enough about it, and I figured I was ready. I had good academic reasons, too. Though I had read the texts of the ancient liturgies, I had never seen one in real life. So one day I set off, trying to look casual as I sneaked downstairs to a basement chapel for the regular weekday Mass at noon.

I thought I was prepared, but I was not. The experience was overwhelming. The prayers and the readings delivered more Scripture, in sheer quantity, than I had ever experienced at an Evangelical worship service. But that was not what got me.

What got me was the undeniable Presence of Our Lord Jesus Christ from the moment of the Consecration onward. He was there, and I knew it. I found myself salivating, so much did I want to receive him.

At that moment I knew what I had to do. Once home, I began to prepare Kimberly and discuss my path forward. I wanted to make it as easy on her as I could.

I continued to attend Sunday services with her at her Evangelical church, but the preaching did not hold my interest. I found myself using the time to plan my future. Assuming I would be unemployable as a theologian, I jotted down other career paths. Perhaps I would follow after my father, a respected jeweler, and make rings for a living. One week, I wrote a list of my long-term goals. Chief among them was my fond wish to teach Scripture for a parish adult-education class someday.

I received instruction in the Catholic faith from Msgr. Fabian Bruskewitz—a brilliant theologian and former professor (and the future bishop of Lincoln, Nebraska). At the following Easter Vigil (March 29, 1986), I was received into full communion.

I went on to write more papers for my doctoral seminars at Marquette. One in particular, "*Familia Dei*: A Covenant Theology of the Family, Church and Trinity", was over a hundred pages. But Father Donald J. Keefe, S.J., my esteemed mentor, read it anyway, making extensive comments, mostly positive and encouraging. It would resonate throughout my later books. My wife, to my great surprise, did follow me into full communion, though several years later (April 14, 1990). And I did eventually finish up my doctorate (1995). It took forever, but I finally got around to revising my dissertation (cutting it down to a mere 589 pages, from 775), for Yale University Press to publish it in the Anchor Bible Reference Library; it is entitled *Kinship by Covenant: A Canonical Approach to the Fulfillment of God's Saving Promises* (2009). To be sure, it is not easy breezy like most of my other titles, but I still stand by it and recommend it, especially for insomnia. In the end, I also managed somehow to find a teaching job.

ᕫ᠍ ᕫ᠍ ᕫ᠍

When I was younger, I looked back on my conversion and it seemed a relatively simple and straightforward matter. I told the story as if it were an argument won by the Catholic Church, because the Catholic faith is true. And I had a passionate love for the truth.

Over the years, I came to realize that every time I told the story I told it somewhat differently—not in a contradictory way, but rather in a way that revealed multiple dimensions of the event: intellectual, spiritual, interpersonal, theological, and moral.

In my memoir *Rome, Sweet Home* (coauthored with my wife), I focused mostly on the apologetic arguments. In a trilogy of books (*The Lamb's Supper, Consuming the Word,* and *The Fourth Cup*), I retraced the covenantal research that led me to Eucharistic faith. In *Swear to God,* I examined my gradual development in sacramental theology. In *First Comes Love,* I detailed my coming to terms with Catholic ecclesiology. In *Letter and Spirit* (my favorite book currently), I expounded a *liturgical hermeneutic* for "reading Scripture in the tradition", that is, from the heart of the Church. In *The Kingdom of God as Liturgical Empire,* I showed how this approach can make even stale and forgotten books like 1–2 Chronicles come alive. And so on. I love to tell the story because each time I relive the mercy.

My story began with an attachment to books and the love of truth—and it ends with the truth of love—and I do not mean the diagnosis of my love language. God is indeed awesome and holy, as I learned from R. C. Sproul and Rudolf Otto; but holiness is not reducible to God's ability to strike fear in us. It is not measured simply by his unapproachability.

In the Mass I saw that holiness is the perfection of love. It is complete in the Holy Spirit, the third Person of the Trinity, whose second name is Love. And holiness envelops us like a glory cloud in the Mass. "The glory of God", said Saint Irenaeus in the third century, "is man fully alive ... beholding God." And we are never so alive as when we receive Holy Communion. Before that moment I had experienced many graces and mercies in life, including the covenantal consummation of a loving marriage, but none was near what I saw at the altar. No one deserves this; yet God gives it freely. I understand why the early Fathers described the Eucharist as "the dread sacrifice". But I also know why they quoted the Song of Songs as they compared the sacrament to spousal union.

It is the grace of this communion that makes us saints. Holiness is nothing we have by nature; but we receive it superabundantly from the altar.

In spite of all these changes, I see more continuity than rupture in the story of my life and thought. My conversion began with my last arrest and court hearing at age fourteen—and is not over yet. I owe so much to my mentors of those early years—Jack Fitzmier, Art Lindsley, R. C. Sproul, John Gerstner, M. G. Kline, Roger Nicole, Gordon Hugenberger—and it is a joy to remember them with gratitude.

R. C. in particular is a man whose work I have imitated, consciously and unconsciously, in many ways, small and large. He strove to communicate rigorous thought to as large an audience as possible, by whatever means necessary. He strove to fill the gap between Sunday school and seminary, and he succeeded. If I too have succeeded to some degree, it is because I had the privilege of his mentorship.

I really am the proverbial midget who got to stand on the shoulders of giants.

I am so much older now than I was then, but I am still the boy who thrills at theological discoveries and gets excited about books. I am still the man who hungers daily to know the covenant more deeply and live it more faithfully. And I am still the sinner who longs to grow up—as a son of God our Father—to become a saint, and nothing less, by the power of the Holy Spirit and for the glory of God.

Chapter 5

ONE CANNOT HAVE CHRIST
WITHOUT THE CHURCH

by

Paige E. Davidson Hochschild

1. University of King's College (Halifax, Nova Scotia)

At one time, I was a very good Protestant. During my first few months of university, I fell very hard for Jesus Christ. My college chapel (at the University of King's College in Halifax, Nova Scotia) announced times for prayer with bells rung at annoying hours. When I eventually sought after the reason for these daily interruptions, I found myself drawn into a life of regular prayer according to the Anglican Book of Common Prayer. Matins and Vespers were prayed, utilizing a rich and ancient lectionary that managed to lead a congregation through the entire Psalter every month and the better part of the Bible every year (including the Gospels and Acts twice per year). It was the opportunity to sing in a choir, however, that first got me in the door, and we sang Holy Communion on Sundays and High Mass on Thursdays, with the glorious praises of Tallis, Lassus, Palestrina, Victoria, and so on. I was confirmed by the Anglican bishop of Nova Scotia in the Easter season of my first year.

No doubt related to the awakening of faith in me, I committed myself to the study of classics, which was housed in an unusual department at Dalhousie University, where King's students normally completed their undergraduate studies after their first-year great books boot camp. We studied Latin and Greek, of course, but the

remainder of my coursework privileged ancient and medieval philosophy, along with the Church Fathers. I participated in an eclec-
tic range of seminars on figures such as Origen, Pseudo-Dionysius,
Eriugena, Dante, and Siger of Brabant. An intellectual culture of
Hegelianism might explain the unusual prominence of pagan Neo-
platonism in the curriculum and a tendency to historicize Aristotle as
slightly dualist. These years were a time of liberty, shaped by a wholly
new intellectual discipline, and deep joy.

My family was distressed at my new and dual strangeness, since I
seemed to have abandoned the path of professional success expected
of me. Perhaps because I am a parent now, I am more sympathetic
than I was then; even when one acknowledges that it is typical of the
young to define oneself "against" expectations, I have no doubt that
I caused harm with annoying flourishes of piety and a lack of practical
concern about the years that would follow college. The foundation of
this strangeness, however, was clear to me and nonnegotiable: I had
a whole new center for my personhood—Jesus Christ. While I surely
failed in observing the filial piety minimally expected of the faithful,
I rejoiced in the daily expansion of a new and radical freedom. I
knew that I had received a gift, in the form of an ideal experience of
higher education. The freedom that I had been granted was inevitably imperfect, but this can be accounted for by my own youthful
choices; despite my own sin, I enjoyed the veritable freedom of the
Cross, having received the life-defining gift of faith. From this place
of faith, arising from love for Jesus Christ, the indwelling Word, I
chose to devote my life to the study of the true and the good.

In those undergraduate years, I immersed myself in the glories
of liturgy and spent my evenings in the library with the Protestant/
Anglican version of Migne—the blood-red volumes of the Parker
Society.[1] The preoccupation with liturgy, combined with a general
lack of spiritual (or just adult) oversight, created some unhealthy pat-
terns of fellowship. The classroom became the most important locus
of intellectual and spiritual formation, especially under the tutelage of
a beloved mentor, Robert Darwin Crouse, a celibate Anglican priest

---

[1] The Parker Society (named after Matthew Parker, Anglican archbishop of Canterbury,
1555–1575) was formed in 1841 to publish writings by the early Anglican reformers; fifty-four
volumes were published until 1853. See Peter Toon, "The Parker Society", *Historical Magazine of the Protestant Episcopal Church* 46, no. 8 (September 1977): 323–32.

(and, incidentally, the first non-Catholic scholar invited to join the faculty of the Augustinianum in Rome). Eventually, a move away from the culture of college became important, providing an occasion for new friendships and the growth that can perhaps only be gained from parish life. An undergraduate, university setting is, of necessity, a bit unreal; the danger therein is the possibility of not really growing up and, in my case, of not actually seeing and living the faith "in action", with all of the good and the bad. The rector of a remarkable parish in Halifax, a young family man and scholar, Gary Thorne, became a spiritual father and a good friend. He was a fellow melancholic soul who preached the Gospel with the burning heart of Christ; he felt duty-bound to unsettle the bourgeois culture of his maritime parish. I still remember one day when he caused particular discomfort in the congregation: pointing out the beautiful Georgian windows of the historic church, in the direction of the north side, the adjacent poorer neighborhood of Halifax, he cried from the pulpit: "If Jesus returned to us today, do you think he would be *in here*? No! He would be seeking the poor, the broken, and the lost, *out there*." I later observed to him, probably with some insolence, "The ones who sense themselves 'in' the church ... aren't they *also* the poor, the broken, and the lost?" I do not recall his response, but I think he was pleased. He longed desperately for the holiness of those under his care.

Through both of these men, pastors, teachers, and friends, the Lord unfolded the theological and spiritual traditions of the church, which gave me a doctrinal foundation that allowed for the integration of the riches of grace received through the liturgy together with a lived faith. Such integration put to the side a twofold danger not uncommon with the young: liturgy as merely aesthetic play (as opposed to grace-effected *theosis*), and the reduction of faith to prideful intellectual Gnosticism. Though I only gathered a few crumbs of the Christ-wisdom that fell from their tables, these crumbs were the sustenance that the Lord judged needful at the time—and his providence can never fail, despite our best attempts to frustrate it.

2. University of Notre Dame (South Bend, Indiana)

I went to graduate school, at the University of Notre Dame, for an unlikely reason: for love. Study was the one place in which praying and living seemed to come together. I wanted nothing else except to "meditate on [the Lord's] precepts" day and night, in a posture of loving adoration (Ps 119:15). I had investigated two religious communities in Nova Scotia before committing to graduate school, one Anglican and one Catholic, and they terrified me. I did not have the ecclesial tools to make sense of, or locate, religious life within any existing conception of the church at that time. I began a course of study at the Medieval Institute, which allowed me to keep the disciplinary conversation between philosophy and theology open, even as my commitment to higher theological study became more concrete. In many ways, I was unhappy in graduate school: my institution's desire to be truly great, to compete ambitiously with the wealthy mainstream of American academia, tended to infect all of its elements, cultivating an atmosphere of competitiveness, anxiety, and vanity that had little to do with the mission of the church or my own motives for ongoing study. I admit that I was naïve. I had no inclination to intellectual competitiveness. I wanted a life of contemplation; I was seeking a form and *via* for such a life, but I did not find it at that time. I had little thought of marriage and family life. I realize that the privilege of graduate school is really that of the gift of time and the luxury of study—which I enjoyed, once again, at the feet of some truly good and wise people, such as John Cavadini, Father David Burrell, Father Brian Daley, Mark Jordan, Christian Moevs, Duncan Stroik, and more, including many wonderful graduate students.

I found myself singing in a small choir at the Basilica on campus, and while this gave me a first opportunity to experience Catholic liturgical prayer regularly, I fell into a posture of mild critique of everything that seemed inadequate to me. I beheld the generosity of Catholic devotionalism. I was inclined to investigate Catholic doctrine, and my courses no doubt contributed to this inquiry; nevertheless, I had no sense of urgency or anxiety about my ecclesial home. I recall a significant moment when I had lunch with a student of medieval philosophy, a brilliant man and Catholic philosopher who now teaches at Notre Dame; I asked him to explain a theological idea that seemed to recur in Catholic theological writing, the nature of "dignity". He pondered for a moment, then shrugged and said, "I don't really know." On the whole, I felt that as an Anglican, moderately well-versed in the theological tradition, I had the best of both worlds:

the riches of these same spiritual traditions, without the unnecessary baggage of Catholic practices and hard-to-articulate traditions, as well as the apparent confusion between things that seemed to be primary (such as faith in Jesus Christ) and things secondary (such as the saints, devotional practices, and so on). Over time, however, my attempt to perpetuate a lived form of the rich Anglicanism that had shaped me, while now living in the midwestern United States, would lead me from one place of worship to another, ultimately baffled by the unhealthy diversity within global Anglicanism and the overall state of Protestantism in the United States, tending as it did to Evangelical moralism, on the one hand, and perpetual schism, on the other. This Protestantism was very different from the beauty of the liturgy, from the transformation of self into the likeness of Christ through the Christian Year, and from the Eucharist-centered worship that won me to Jesus Christ in my years in Halifax.

3. Wheaton, Illinois

I was married after my first two years attending graduate school at Notre Dame—as often happens, to another graduate student. In retrospect, the spiritual gift of marriage is simply the Cross, or the privilege of the opportunity to be conformed to Christ through privileging the good of the other over one's own. I think I would have been a very selfish celibate—albeit, in all fairness, I did have a very individualist conception of religious or vowed life. Initially, I put to the side the completion of my Ph.D. for the sake of supporting my spouse's academic prospects.[2] This was a difficult thing to ask and to expect of me, but as suggested by my initial motives for graduate school, I was not primarily "career-driven"; moreover, the evolving of family life when one spouse is in a graduate program requires a disciplined commitment and habitual frugality from all members. Before my spouse earned his first teaching position at Wheaton College in

---

[2] I left the Ph.D. program at Notre Dame after the successful completion of the oral and written candidacy exams; about two years later, just before the birth of my first child, I was accepted at Durham for the completion of the Ph.D. Due to coursework and exams done at ND, I was admitted directly to the stage of writing the dissertation.

Illinois, I was moved by a sensed providential-vocational urging to finish my Ph.D.—but I knew I would have to do this in a way that privileged family life. I did my research with a much-valued mentor, Carol Harrison, at the University of Durham in the U.K. Carol is now the Lady Margaret Professor of Divinity at Christ Church, Oxford, but at that time, Durham simply had the largest and best department for the study of historical theology in either Canada or the U.K. I did my research and dissertation on the place of memory in the anthropology of Saint Augustine. This was a challenging time, and a test of both love and discipline; those years of near-total lack of sleep permit rare glimmers of memory. I was far away from my family in Canada; my primary job pertained to making a home and setting out on "adult" family life with almost no money. I taught dance lessons to children in our parish, hugely pregnant with a second child, in exchange for babysitting hours so that I could work at the local library for a few hours each week. The people at and around Wheaton College were remarkable: this is one of the finest "Evangelical" colleges in the country, with smart and driven students whose love for the Lord was evidenced by the large number of those who did missionary or service work after graduation. During these four years, two very important elements of my spiritual journey into the full faith of the Church came to the forefront of my consideration.

First, my confusion about the state of Protestant America that I had begun to experience while living in South Bend only deepened further. The specific parameters of my confusion, however, became clearer: Evangelicalism seemed to be the only remaining life-blood in the major Protestant churches. The reader should consider that these were the years of the ascendancy of the mega-church, the legacy of the great Billy Graham, Jr. and of a supposed political "conservative consensus" on moral issues. My family attended a wonderful Episcopal church in Glen Ellyn, Illinois. After two or three years, a casual conversation revealed that no one in that parish, least of all the pastors, actually believed in sacramental grace. Not long after, the Episcopal Church in America fractured endlessly, missionary dioceses were somehow established, and good friends had to make hard decisions about where to worship and whom to join. Less denominationally inclined Evangelicals had an easier time: they might attend a particular church one Sunday, and if they objected to the sermon of the week, they would simply go to a different church the next Sunday. In a "worst-case scenario" they might have recourse to a "home church". This way of dealing with a baffling diversity of doctrine and practice had a certain logic to it; but it also seemed deeply sad to me, and clearly influenced by a distinctly American consumerist culture. There was a perfection, or at least a correctness, being sought after. This was laudable in one way; but, in another way, it was a brittle foundation for actual ecclesial membership. I knew from my historical studies that the church had never been an entity of manifest perfection, and that those who stepped away from a particular or local church to find such perfection usually found themselves *outside* of the church.

Wheaton College undergraduate students are very smart, and they seemed to be vulnerable to a different set of issues, perhaps because of the dimension of self-definition appropriate to "young adult" maturation. I would sum these up as pertaining to history and liturgy. Many of these students were raised in denominations marked by only one common theological element—"ABC", or "anything but Catholic". On more than one occasion, I came across apologetic pamphlets similar to those published in the years of Martin Luther's most fiery preaching. In these, I beheld the papacy represented as the whore of Babylon and Catholics depicted as the enslaved victims of theurgic magical rituals, paying cash to "get into heaven". It was actually an amusing display of propaganda and willful ignorance. With intellectually curious young people, gross misinformation cannot abide for long, and it seemed to take little more than a few sermons by Augustine or an article from the *Summa Theologiae* to bring about an intellectual crisis. History is the primary locus of revelation, and the historical study of philosophy and theology compelled these young people to realize that they were beneficiaries of a living tradition that had not simply vanished between the fourth and the nineteenth centuries. This in turn tended to lead to a discovery of, and a hunger for, liturgical worship: any realistic sense of the richness of the spiritual tradition fueled an even greater desire to enact the faith in light of this tradition. The principle of ABC, however, was a deeply ingrained cultural prejudice, and so many undergraduates ended up at Episcopal or Orthodox churches. This membership rarely lasted for long, nor did it have the depth and character of being at home, or

permanently planted. To their credit, Evangelicals make the "plant-
ing" of churches primary to their mission; but seedlings are easily
uprooted. The greatest cultural solidity, and oddly enough, the most
consistent theological certitude in Evangelicalism, pertained to marriage and family life and cultural symbols of community life. However, Evangelical undergraduates seemed to struggle with the tension
between the internalism of their faith and the sensed need to observe
the virtues of religion through appropriate outward and communal
acts of praise, sacrifice, and worship.[3] I suppose the key reflection for
me, in the context of the unhappy state of the Episcopal Church, was
as follows: you kids are looking desperately for the church. Good
luck with that.

Between lack of sleep, life at home with young children, and supporting my spouse's busy schedule, these reflections were only points
of distant curiosity for me. Another and much more important seed
was planted—albeit one clearly related to my ongoing reflections
on Evangelical Protestantism at Wheaton College. One evening, I
attended an event at the college, at which a famous biblical scholar,
J. I. Packer, spoke alongside Richard Neuhaus, a Catholic priest, former Lutheran, and the founder of the magazine First Things. This
event was related to an initiative known as Evangelicals and Catholics Together—something in which I would participate, briefly, a
long way down the road. The discussions centered upon a document about the unity of the church, and Professor Mark Noll's words
seemed to sum up the initial mood in the room: "the Reformation is
over!" The closing exchange between Packer and Neuhaus created a
deep, complex, and exciting disquiet within me.[4] Neuhaus spoke in
earnest terms of the first mark of the Church, unity, as it is confirmed
by the ancient and universal Creeds. He discussed the high priestly
prayer from John 17, the Lord's prayer "that they may be one"; he

---

[3] I would later see these reflections summed up with clarity by my theological master,
Joseph Cardinal Ratzinger, in his book The Spirit of the Liturgy, trans. John Saward (San Francisco: Ignatius Press, 2000).

[4] Since that time, a number of Evangelical publications have observed that the Catholic
Church has not really changed and, given the ambiguity of her theological language, may actu-
ally have intended subterfuge at this particular event. See, for example, James G. McCarthy,
Talking with Catholic Friends and Family (Eugene, Ore.: Harvest House, 2005), 195–96; alluding
directly to the event held at Wheaton College, he argues that false teachers who "claim to be
Christian" (presumably Neuhaus?) are the greatest threat to the true faith.

argued that Christian unity is a serious and demanding task, but, in light of the words of Scripture themselves, a nonnegotiable one. Packer responded with great caution. He spoke carefully about the problem of the pope, or of papal primacy as an issue of governance and theological authority. Then, to a surprising degree for a self-described man of the Scriptures, he demurred on the importance of Christian unity as presented by Neuhaus. Packer returned to the safer territory of the unique authority of the Scriptures *in general*, rather than engaging Neuhaus on the texts from the Gospels and Saint Paul that exhorted Christians to the difficult task of unity as a corporate reflection of the *unity* of Christ's person, and of the *uniqueness* of the "way" of salvation. The form of the impasse seemed to propose a serious problem; I sensed some incipient intellectual theophany on the horizon.

I knew full well that the authority of the Sacred Scriptures, in general, was not that much of a matter of theological divergence between Catholics and Protestants. The larger question of revelation was indeed an issue, including necessary reflection about the nature and role of the Church, tradition, and theological reflection, for interpreting the Scriptures. But these questions were matters of ongoing discussion and disagreement even within particular ecclesial communities; moreover, an individualist-rationalist understanding of truth as something attained by *sola scriptura* seemed to be on the way out. Packer did indeed appeal to the principle of *sola scriptura*, but this was done to present the Bible as an alternative to the Church, or any authoritative tradition or person of theological authority; it seemed like a total evasion of much more difficult questions. Whatever was going on between these two men was not about the Bible. It was about the Church. As a matter of rhetoric and ecumenical charity, Neuhaus was willing to admit that the papacy was a problem for Protestants; but he also gave many reasons for why this was still a conversation worth having. The theology and governing role of the papacy was demonstrably subject to development over time. The pope no longer has rule over the Papal States, nor does he ride through the streets of Florence in shining armor. Neuhaus observed multiple ways in which Pope John Paul II had proposed forms of compromise as part of his desire to reach out to separated Orthodox churches, even in matters of governance, discipline, and basic dogma—see, for example, the remarkable paragraph that relativizes the *filioque* in the *Catechism*.[5] The overall message from Neuhaus was this: there are a number of things to talk about, but there are some good reasons for thinking we can move forward, together; if lived, theological unity is a pressing desire from the Lord himself; please, at least come and talk. Packer's response to Neuhaus, even supposing the possibility that he entertained feelings of conflict between his cultural formation and his theological intelligence, was stark: *no thank you*.

It was not clear to me at the time what was actually going on or how to explain Packer's surprising and contrasting lack of concern about Christian unity. Was it about the practicality of governance? Most Protestants lack effective structures of governance—never mind anything like a Code of Canon Law; some Protestants are explicitly against such structures; in some cases, governance coalesces around fundamental doctrine. Was it about authority and teaching? Perhaps at heart it might be this. But in the context of the discussion, in a place like Wheaton College, Packer's "no" seemed to be little more than a return to ABC as the sole foundation of Evangelical ecclesial identity. By the end of the evening, there was a new specter of fearfulness in the room, as though rejecting the foundational character of ABC might in turn reveal a host of other "nos" to be weak, illusory, or tertiary. Insofar as Neuhaus was hardly offering compromise—something he could not have the authority to do—but instead offered reasons for why this was a discussion worth having, the implication of the asymmetry between these two men was disturbing. Behind Packer's "no" there might have been motives and concerns, theological or professional in nature, entirely foreign to me; maybe there was academic exhaustion or a lack of goodwill; far worse, however, was the possibility of a total failure of charity.

I remember being stunned, sitting in that room with my mind in turmoil. I recalled that I had delivered a response to an academic

[5] See *Catechism of the Catholic Church*, no. 248; after observing in no. 247 that the formulation of the *filioque*—the procession of the Holy Spirit from the Father "and the Son"—is patristic in origin, but only admitted into liturgical prayer between the eighth and eleventh centuries, the next paragraph goes to some effort to explain how the Eastern and Western "traditions" have distinct but complementary ways of expressing, or impressing (*imprimis*), the same orthodox truth about God the Trinity.

paper at a small conference long before, when I was finishing my undergraduate studies in classics at King's/Dalhousie. In my response, I presented Augustine as someone who holds the Church to be "a living hermeneutic of Scripture", according to the later books of *Confessions*. I do not think this reading is incorrect. However, the Packer-Neuhaus exchange made me realize that my analysis was overly abstract and, therefore, inadequate. Such an approach, while failing to honor what those books are actually about (the Church), could never generate a sense of what the Church actually, visibly, happens to be; nor did it make the thorny questions of the *interpretation* of Scripture, in light of the Church and her living tradition, go away. I further recalled being part of a reading group with Gary Thorne, looking at the Edwardian *Book of Homilies*. At first published as a corrective to barely literate parish homiletics during the early years of the English Reformation, these homilies were clearly also a program to implement a new theological perspective. The first and foundational homily is on the sufficiency and fruitfulness of reading Scripture—even in a time of, as yet, low to moderate literacy.[6] Depending to some extent on Saint John Chrysostom, the benefit and veracity of reading Scripture is attributed to the direct intervention of the Holy Spirit. I recall my friend and mentor musing: "Here, you see the grave cost of the opening of the Scriptures. The danger is that you might end up with as many 'churches' as you have readers of Scripture. But this danger is surely worth the cost, for the sake of opening up God's Word." To this day, his words seem both correct, while also deeply problematic. The Calvinist-Augustinian in me was quite certain that *I* could not possibly *be* the Church; I would have to hang it all on the Scriptures themselves, in some way as Packer attempted. Such a task seemed to involve a host of preexisting intellectual commitments that could not defensibly be the fruit of actual biblical or theological inquiry; they just had to be "there" and basically closed to theological examination.

I was experiencing in my life of faith and prayer in Wheaton the fragility of a faith that is, or pretends that it can be, divorced from the life of the visible Church—precisely because it only finds its substantive visibility, at best, in a community of the doctrinally like-minded. This kind of approach was more congenial to my spouse as an academic philosopher.[7] I needed to reconcile the visible and lived faith with the theological and invisible reality of the Lord of history. Practically speaking, I could not imagine a cruciform life in which the veracity of the Church somehow depended upon my own theological judgment. The principle of unity under discussion at the event at Wheaton College: this is the first mark of the Church and the first wound of the Church, addressed early in the Acts of the Apostles in reference to Jewish practices expected from adult converts to faith in Christ. Of this I was certain: the principle of unity, the actual glue that binds together the Body of Christ, can only be God himself, the Holy Spirit. I had many, many questions, but all of my questions now gravitated around the central question of the nature and purpose of the Church. As a result, something seemed to me to be very wrong in the lived structure of my personal faith. The issue of criteria of veracity of interpretation was an evasion. A much more pressing question was reframed for me as follows: Does the God of Abraham, Isaac, and Jacob actually *work* in history in a way that is effective? In a more Thomistic form, the new question was about the interaction between primary and secondary causality, grounded in the goodness of creation as a manifestation of the divine life, however real the problem of sin and evil. In a more concrete form, this question was simple: Is the Church, as our Lord clearly intended it (from scriptural and historical evidence), even possible?

---

[7] During this time, my husband was confirmed in the Roman Catholic Church—a long but somewhat inevitable journey for him—and, consequently, he was not allowed to teach at Wheaton any longer. I championed his intellectual battle, but the chief talking point in the final stage was about "who gets to say what the Scriptures mean". Put another way, his dispute was about the question of authority. Having studied *Dei Verbum* in class with Catholic students, and having worked with inerrancy and inspiration as a very difficult locus for articulating the Church-Scripture relationship, I would say that the matter is clearly much more complicated. These issues may not in fact be about authority, or even about the relationship of tradition to Scripture—the question that initially framed discussions at Vatican II about revelation—but first about ecclesiology *in se*. Ratzinger's summary points about *Dei Verbum* are a poignant reminder that even this groundbreaking document opens up more questions than it can possibly hope to resolve, revealing many "traces of its difficult history" (in committee), as the "result of many compromises", while remaining "a synthesis of great importance". See Joseph Cardinal Ratzinger's essay on the origin and background of the Dogmatic Constitution on Divine Revelation in Herbert Vorgrimler, ed., *Commentary on the Documents of Vatican II*, vol. 3 (New York: Herder and Herder, 1969), 164.

4. Mount Saint Mary's University (Emmitsburg, Maryland)

Life with young children is a daily experience of human dependency—not only that of children but that of the family as a whole, situated as it is within the various individualisms of contemporary Western culture. Saint Thomas Aquinas observes that the family is an "imperfect form of community", which simply means that it is inadequate to secure the goods necessary for human flourishing. We relocated for the sixth time in ten years of marriage when my husband was compelled to leave his position at Wheaton College and take a new position at Mount Saint Mary's University. This move involved many challenges, with a third child recently arrived and a fair bit of personal illness. Finding anything like a communally rich place to live in rural or small-town Maryland was difficult, and an overall feeling of being on my own was only deepened by acceding to the experiment of homeschooling. With something like dogged desperation, I finished my dissertation on Saint Augustine and defended it with success and strong recommendations to publish. Knowing full well that religious division within a family tends to breed an impoverished culture of faith formation, I agreed to raise our children as Roman Catholic, and I started attending daily Mass with them.[8] This experience afforded me fodder for critique: unbiblical preaching, bizarre liturgical moves, and so on. I recall walking up to the Grotto at Mount Saint Mary's and studying a plaque that promised a plenary indulgence to pilgrims who made a good confession, prayed for the pope's intentions, etc. These seemed to me to be rank Pelagianism. On Sundays, I attended an Episcopal church in Blue Ridge Summit, Pennsylvania, while also attending our local parish, across the road from the house in which we eventually settled; this parish, full of wonderful local families and many faculty families, would not have a pastor for many years, which resulted in a confusing progression of religious and lay administrators. My spouse was necessarily very busy with a new teaching position at a new institution, and the individual

---

[8] This was a fact that seemed intuitively true, but about which I was able to reflect later, both in "counseling" student-advisees and also in writing; cf. my review of Naomi Schaefer Riley's book 'Til Faith Do Us Part (Oxford: Oxford University Press, 2013), published in Commonweal, December 2014, https://www.commonwealmagazine.org/til-faith-do-us-part.

character of his own spiritual journey into the fullness of the Church
seemed to provide yet another basis for my own personal resistance,
since I was never going to enter the Church just for the sake of unity,
especially when I had principled objections.

Still, given my agreement to raise the children in the Roman Catholic faith, I decided to take the RCIA[9] course on campus offered
through Campus Ministry—*strictly* as an inquirer. I had read the
Catechism of the Catholic Church when I was in college, but when I
arrived at the first session with my heavily annotated copy, I was told
that this was not going to be used, nor would it normally be used as
a teaching tool for the laity. This was a disappointment. There were a
handful of undergraduates in the group, along with three seminarians
(two from the Archdiocese of Atlanta, one from Worcester, Massachusetts), loosely involved with Campus Ministry for their pastoral
field experience. Sitting there, with my copy of the *Catechism* in hand
and ready to have at it, I soon realized that I made the seminarians
nervous. I decided to have fun with RCIA. Interestingly, the most
important aspect of this experience turned out to be the relationships
that I developed with the seminarians in the room, who welcomed
me into a theological fraternity of sorts, and continued conversations
outside of the sessions.

Looking back at RCIA, the content and approach were not nearly
as important for me as the overall shift that I needed to make in my
attitude, which I would compare—perhaps presumptuously—with
that of Saint Augustine. Around the time that he discerned a real
desire to enter the Church, Augustine had overcome many of the
problems raised by his studies and bizarre cultic choices; moreover,
thanks to the fatherly guidance of Saint Ambrose, he had come to
embrace the Scriptures and their study in and through the ministry of
the Church; but the most important thing remaining for Augustine
was that he had to *submit*.[10]

---

[9] RCIA stands for the Rite of Christian Initiation for Adults and is a catechetical course
that culminates, for those who desire it, in reception into the Church.

[10] When book 7 of *Confessions* is studied, attention is usually given to Augustine's use of
the "books of the Platonists" in correcting his errors about the nature of God, providence,
and evil. Far more important for the narrative path of the argument, however, is the problem
with these "Platonists"—intellectual pride: their philosophical acumen excludes, in their own
minds, the necessity of mediation, even as they themselves become an obstacle to mediation,

I used to frame my understanding of my own submission, or conversion—from combative inquiry to an earnest desire to be grafted into the fullness of the Church—through the dual herme-neutic of *intellective* and *affective*. On the one hand, I had theological problems that I needed to work through, with the help of appropriate texts and guides; on the other hand, I clearly had a certain arrogance, resistance, or absence of desire. I no longer think this is the best way to understand the situation, because these shifts are about the whole of life and, therefore, must arise from, or reach to, a more anthro-pologically central faculty—perhaps what Saint Augustine and Saint Paul mean when they speak of the heart (*cor*) as the center of a person. When one is moved fundamentally by love, all the other issues and elements take secondary place; they are not unimportant, but they must find their place in an ordered relation to that same love. Love, of course, is not primarily a feeling or even an act of the will. It is about a will-act in relation to a particular object or end.

Certain theological issues remained. The papacy was not much of a problem anymore: in light of comments made above, realistic histori-cal sensibility (as both historical context and development of doctrine) was clarifying and liberating. Moreover, years of reciting the Creeds as an Anglican had generated a clear sense that the four marks of the Church—as "one, holy, catholic, and apostolic"—somehow rested historically, and thus theologically, on the foundation of the claim to apostolicity. If the Church is first established upon "the Twelve" in some way, the living link to the apostles, including (and perhaps especially) Peter, must be reliable. Biblically speaking, this argues for continuity with the fidelity of God promised to Abraham, which extends throughout the covenant theology of the Old Testament and finds its final form in the reliable presence of the Holy Spirit given to

---

because the boundary between the creature and the Creator cannot be spanned by human effort. At 7.9.13–14, Augustine observes that "[you, Lord] wanted to show me how you 'resist the proud and give grace to the humble' ... and with what mercy you have shown humanity the way of humility in that your 'Word was made flesh and dwelt among' men." Good clas-sical philosophy discerns that any *logos* must be equal with God, because if it is the wisdom of God, it must also be divine; nevertheless, these philosophical books did not, and could not, have taught Augustine that the *logos* who is the Son of God, "took on himself the form of a servant and emptied himself, [being] made in the likeness of men ... humbled himself [and was] made obedient to death, even the death of the Cross" (translated by Henry Chadwick; Oxford University Press, 1991).

the Church at Pentecost. For an Anglican, or for any Protestant who hopes to lay claim to continuity with the early Church—and thus be "catholic" in the minimal sense of the word—any sudden historical break in continuity becomes arbitrary, implying that human sinful-ness or infidelity ultimately defeats the Lord's promise of faithful love. Even more dangerous, the exercise of identifying such moments of disjunction runs the risk of unreasonably privileging the criterion of a modern scholarly or faith-based "God's-eye view" on sacred history. I found a form of this crisis in the writings of Newman on patristic history, especially his study of Arianism.[11]

A greater theological (and therefore devotional) problem con-cerned Mariology. Many people do not understand the difference between worship (due in justice to God alone) and veneration (or honor, or piety; due in justice to parents or saints, for example, in appropriate degrees). For an Anglican, high feast days included All Saints, Saint Michael the Archangel, and more; the lectionary in the Book of Common Prayer provided for the "falling asleep of the Blessed Virgin Mary" on August 15, which sounds closer to the Orthodox theological tradition. Nevertheless, the observance of this day was optional, and diminished as a not-in-bold item in the calen-dar. The Mariological problem therefore had two distinct aspects for me: on the one hand, the two dogmas (the Immaculate Conception and the Assumption of the Blessed Virgin Mary) that the Church required Catholics to hold as principles of the faith, with full assent of heart and mind; on the other hand, a radically new view of the Church as the Mystical Body of Christ, which includes the living and the dead, especially the saints in glory, in a unity that is marked by effective intercessory prayer. The flexibility of allowing the theologi-cal tradition to have its due authority, as opposed to dogmatic formal-ism commanding assent of mind and heart, was attractive to my own traditionalism; nevertheless, this flexibility allowed for a breadth of practices within Anglicanism that inevitably extended to significant differences in core beliefs. This has been, and perhaps remains, the weakness of an otherwise rich and hopeful *via media*, a best attempt

---

[11] See "Tract 19", https://newmanreader.org/works/times/tract19.html (on the impor-tance of apostolic succession for Anglicans); *Lectures on Certain Difficulties Felt by Anglicans in Catholic Teaching Considered* (London, 1850), lecture 12, no. 2; *An Essay on the Development of Christian Doctrine* (London, 1845), intro., no. 17.

at consensus for a relatively young and diverse national church, since the early years of the Reformation. Unity with diversity requires the deep, stable soil of culture. In its absence, fundamental doctrinal diversity becomes a problem and an inevitable matrix for crisis—in my case, taking the form of the two aspects of Mariology, one about authority (and dogma vs. doctrine), and the other about the nature of the Church.

The first aspect was and is complex as a theological matter. It is an easy matter to discover that, from the earliest decades of the Church, when the reality of martyrdom fueled a deep veneration for heroic saintliness, the Mother of our Lord was an object of singular honor. Still, I resented, in perhaps Newman-esque ways, the Church's move to concretize centuries of devotion as mandatory dogma in the modern era. Moreover, while patristic and medieval texts approached theological reflection on Mary through the biblical lenses of Mary as "the new Eve", or as the icon, mother, and first member of the Church, Catholic dogma—but perhaps even more, the witness that I had of Marian devotions—seemed not only to set Mary apart from the economy of saintly intercession, but more dangerously to honor and pray to her in a way that supplanted the primacy and clear uniqueness of Christ's salvific power. She was and is not divine, and only God has the power to raise the dead. Even when Mary's unique holiness was explained as a fruit of the saving work of her Son, the Catholic tendency to subvert the order of historical time—e.g., to bring about a retroactive or preparatory sanctification—seemed to conflict with the theological importance of the historicity of revelation. Why could she not be sanctified precisely in and through the act of Jesus' conception? It did not help that some apologetic works that I read, for example by nineteenth-century English theologians, leaned heavily on a more moral-physicalist (instead of cultic) sense of purity; the implication was that everything about the conception and birth of Christ simply *must* evade the corruptibility and "yuckiness" of sex, pain, and, frankly, the female body in its reproductive capacities. This seemed to approach the early heresy of Docetism, whereby Christ's full humanity is minimized or rendered illusory out of a desire to preserve and uphold his full divinity. There is much that I could say about the process of working through some of these questions, but I will simply share with the reader that Joseph Cardinal

Ratzinger—who was and remains my theological mentor, both in ongoing academic work and in my journey into the Church—wrote a little book, *Daughter Zion*, that made all the difference for me.[12] Instead of beginning with strong theological claims, followed by high praise and veneration for the Blessed Mother, he works with Scripture and a brilliant sense of the trajectory and unity of salvation history. Right away, he puts his cards on the table: one cannot open the Bible and "get" Catholic Mariology out of it. One must approach Scripture as revelation and with intelligence, allowing it to have life and meaning within the theological *tradition*. This was nothing short of liberating for me, because, while this book offered ideas, arguments, and meditations beyond proclaiming "this is what the Church teaches" and then moving into a posture of devotion, it more importantly directed me to the necessity and centrality of the Church in all matters theological.

This leads to the second aspect of my problem with Mariology. I mentioned the importance for Anglicans of certain feast days, to which I would add the observance of All Souls; of course, most Protestants do not observe these days, and so any conversation about the saints and their intercessory power is a non-starter. However, "high" Anglicans share with the "low", and perhaps with Evangelical Protestants more widely, a basic paradigm of the Church that may be the root problem. It is more profoundly an issue of the theology of grace and secondary causality. From a big-picture perspective, for a Protestant not raised in a culture of local or universal saintly veneration, turning in prayer to the saints, even Mary, feels like dealing with middle management; why not go straight to the "big guy", especially

---

[12] *Daughter Zion: Meditations on the Church's Marian Belief*, trans. John M. McDermott, S.J. (San Francisco: Ignatius Press, 1983); see also Hans Urs von Balthasar and Joseph Cardinal Ratzinger, *Mary: The Church at the Source*, trans. Adrian Walker (San Francisco: Ignatius Press, 1997). Useful and important, in addition, at that time: Raniero Cantalamessa, *Mary: Mirror of the Church* (Collegeville, Minn.: Liturgical Press, 1992); Luigi Gambero's two historical books on Marian devotion and theology, both from Ignatius Press: *Mary and the Fathers of the Church* (1999) and *Mary in the Middle Ages* (2005). After my confirmation, two other authors became more significant: John Henry Newman's Mariological writings, which are scattered throughout his oeuvre and collected in a volume entitled *Mary: The Virgin Mary in the Life and Writings of John Henry Newman*, ed. Philip Boyce (Grand Rapids, Mich.: Eerdmans, 2001); and Caryll Houselander's *The Reed of God* (Notre Dame, Ind.: Ave Maria Press, 1985).

when the heroic virtue of the saints is consistently attributed to Christ's salvific grace? In the order of causality, the saints look to many Protestants like "extras", figures who stand *between* the faithful and the Lord. This perspective had to be reevaluated. Moreover, I needed to consider the use and value of prayer as an effective secondary cause in the order of grace: that is, rather than think of prayer, or religion in general, mainly as constituted by various acts of increasing intimacy with God through submission of will to his own, I needed to incorporate what is true (in this view of religion) into some sense of the objective reality of the Church. Why do we pray? Clearly, it is about conformity to the will of God; but what is the visible effect of the action so consistently enjoined by our Lord? And why is it necessary both to pray for one another and to pray in a petitionary posture? God "already" knows what I want or, better, what I need. It therefore seems that we pray chiefly to habituate ourselves to total dependency upon God. But our Lord asks much more than this. Perhaps we pray for one another not simply to increase individual intimacy with God or a sense of solidarity in the Church; perhaps we are commanded to pray precisely because the Holy Spirit is *in* the Church, and the Church is the effective means of salvation, established to complete the work of Christ in history. Perhaps God acts in the Church, in the world, through the effective means (or secondary causality) of prayer, just as he does in an analogous way through the sacraments.

"Solving" the problems of Mariology—this was not exactly what I needed to do; all questions directed me to the Church over and over. The Mariological questions could remain on the table; however, they needed the right perspective, or paradigm, for ongoing study and meditation. The real issue continued to be that of the Church. And here we come to the true *locus* of conversion as *metanoia*—a total shift of the whole person, beginning and ending in the center, with the heart.

At some point during that year of RCIA classes and uninspiring daily Masses, I began to take advantage of our proximity to campus, and after the children were settled for the night, I walked and walked, turning over in my mind questions and frustrations. I discovered that Eucharistic Adoration was held regularly in Saint Bernard's chapel on

campus, in the seminary: this was so strange to me, even as an Anglican convicted of the Real Presence of the Lord in the sacrament.
Why kneel before a Consecrated Host? The heart of the Anglican
objection to Adoration is that the sacraments are for *use*.[13] An even
more important space for me was the chapel up at the Grotto—this is
not an architectural masterpiece, but a glass-walled chapel is ideal not
only when one must find time for solitude and prayer "off-hours",
but also when one requires a visual frame for the tabernacle that bal-
ances a dialectic of presence and distance, fullness and poverty. The
glass walls permitted total visibility while also emphasizing my own
feeling of being "outside". Our Lord meets us first and last in the faces
of his children; but the "still, small voice of calm" is heard by living
ears above all else when we are *quiet*.[14] Any narrative account of my
own conversion from resistance to submission fails at this point. I can
only attain recollection in pieces, making reference to fragments of
the verses that I poured out, crouched on the concrete wall, alone
in the dark, outside that chapel. They mean little when abstracted
from that context, but these words arose from overwhelming feelings
of desperation and desire. The theophanic presence of the Lord in the
tabernacle provoked me; the tension between alienation and longing
opened up some space within, suggesting an identity between the
tabernacle and the sepulcher of my own wasted heart. I was so very
tired. From within that physical and spiritual exhaustion, I came to
see that I had

---

[13] In historical context, there is no justification for interpreting the term "use" in a way
that is typically modern and functionalizing, implying technique rather than a process and
the eventual discarding of elements—this is an important critique that Pope Francis has
taken up (for example, in *Laudato Si'*) from previous magisterial teachings. Any sixteenth- or
seventeenth-century Anglican would affirm that to behold something in loving adoration is a
"useful" action; the critique at that time arose from the practice of infrequent reception of the
Eucharist by the people (as opposed to the priest) and the popular sense that processions and
other devotions were "for the people"; a more Calvinist-inflected critique concerned popular
confusion between worship and veneration.

[14] Cf. "Dear Lord and Father of Mankind", a beautiful hymn adapted by the American
Congregationalist Garrett Horder in 1844 from a poem by John Greenleaf Whittier and normally sung to the tune "Repton". The two final stanzas are as follows: "Drop Thy still dews of
quietness / Till all our strivings cease; / Take from our souls the strain and stress, / And let our
ordered lives confess / The beauty of Thy peace. Breathe through the heats of our desire / Thy
coolness and Thy balm; / Let sense be dumb, let flesh retire; / Speak through the earthquake,
wind, and fire, / O still, small voice of calm."

eyes that cannot see,

I saw that

I was sick, of love,

and I saw that

> between rest and act, what is;
> Will holds to the fixed point,
> humility opens the heart,
> the purity of the round window, gathers in.

I was confirmed in Immaculate Conception Chapel on the campus of Mount Saint Mary's on Divine Mercy Sunday by the auxiliary bishop of Baltimore. I took the name of Benedict as the moniker of my Christian adulthood, since the Holy Father was then, as now, my patron (albeit alive and well). The best account that I can offer of what cannot be represented by theological narrative is as follows:

a. if this is Jesus, wholly present in the Eucharist, then
b. this is the Church—or, the Church simply has to be what she says she is, and therefore
c. the doctrinal stuff I should and would continue to study; but this could only be done with integrity *within the Church*.

5. Mount Saint Mary's Seminary (Emmitsburg, Md.)

About a week or two after my confirmation, I received a call from the academic dean of the seminary, who said that they needed someone to teach the two philosophy courses housed in the seminary and that would serve as bridge courses to theological study. He hoped to find a woman—"it's good for them"—and of course she would have to be fine with little in the way of remuneration. This is the norm with adjunct university-level instruction, and it mattered very little to me. The intellectual fruit of years of enjoying the privilege of higher study would be put to the service of the Church. My ongoing formation as a Catholic and a theologian would be deeply shaped by my experience teaching in the seminary. My friendship with several individuals working in the Theology Department at the Mount, along with the eventual experience of teaching undergraduate core theology courses, would be more formative of my sense of the ecclesial vocation of a theologian, and of the specific issues that recur in the pedagogical universe of Catholic theology. Still, beginning at the seminary, in service to priestly formation, had a certain logic to it. Going back to my college years, the role of intellectual mentors who were also spiritual fathers, as well as the centrality of mediation as enacted by liturgical worship and sacramental generosity, testified to the importance of the priesthood in my journey. In the years immediately preceding my confirmation, and as suggested above, the stable foundation of apostolic succession was the obvious historical basis for the reliability of the Holy Spirit's presence in the Church. My toughest moments of spiritual agony always directed me back to the embrace of the Lord under the specificity of the divine name of "Father". At times, attending daily Mass before confirmation, I felt something akin to rage as I considered the fearfulness of the Real Presence and the apparent lightness with which sacred things were handled by hands unsacred. A once-baffling image hanging in the Grotto chapel now made more sense to me: Mary was depicted holding the infant Jesus, who had his hand raised in a priestly gesture; in front of both, at about the level of her womb, was the Blessed Sacrament, a Host hovering over a chalice. Mary is not divine; she is a fragile vessel, a tested mother; but just as fire has passed through her, so also, in an analogous way, grace must pass through the priest so that it can pass into me. If God is the Lord of all history, then the sacred and the unsacred must find a home in which to dwell, together. This is the Church.

My first class of seminarians was a fantastic group. Two-thirds of the men in the class were several years older than I was at the time, and I worried about my ability to establish something like appropriate authority. I experienced the fruits of being welcomed into their fraternity, and I was warmed by their humor, their kindness, and their total commitment to Christ and the Church. The courses that I developed returned me under a new rubric to the texts of Saint Thomas. At that time, *Fides et Ratio* was the dominant teaching moving most thinking about pre-theological intellectual formation.[15] I had to confront

---

[15] *Fides et Ratio* (1998) is a papal encyclical written by Pope John Paul II that deals with the relationship of faith and reason.

a danger that can arise with the very idea of natural theology—the first course I was asked to develop—namely, the distinctively modern polarity of rationalism-fideism. Natural theology is often described as an area of study concerned with "things knowable about God without recourse to revelation", and Saint Thomas helped seminarians to see that anything like a strict "two-column" summary of truths (revealed tenets of faith on one side, rationally demonstrable truths on the other) would generate a desiccated sense both of the scope of reason and of the glorious intelligibility of the faith. JPII's emphasis on anthropology—going all the way back to the Christological recentering of *Gaudium et Spes* attempted in his first encyclical, *Redemptor Hominis* (1979)—which is further developed in Ratzinger's writings on the nature of theology and the place of reason within human experience, suggested that a false vision of the human person might lurk behind every modern intellectual and ecclesial crisis.[16] This might include questions about the nature of conscience, the sensed opposition between experience and authority, the transformative possibilities of the teaching office of the Church, or the various moral issues that are primary cultural *topoi* for many American Catholics. And so, in the second course that I was asked to develop, I tried to put the anthropological question in the forefront, while (over time) discerning the importance of softening any "Church-world" opposition. To be more specific, both intellectual and pastoral necessity dictated the importance of not simply critiquing the modes of modernity, but instead encouraging intelligent and sympathetic reflection on the complexity of human experience, including goods such as culture, tradition, healthy work (and leisure), and failing or revitalized modes of human community.

My time in the seminary was deeply formative in other ways. I experienced a moderate "outsider" status as adjunct, as lay, and as female; nevertheless, I was called upon to serve in a multitude of ways, becoming more involved in formation than was ultimately fruitful for me. The seminary gave me a view of some of the dysfunctionalities of the visible Church. The wounds of Christ are present in his Body at all levels; at the same time, however, I saw the priestly face of Christ

---

[16] On the "perspective of redemption" as a basically "humanistic" one, see *Redemptor Hominis*, 8–10; see also Ratzinger, *Principles of Catholic Theology*, trans. Sister Mary Frances McCarthy, S.N.D. (San Francisco: Ignatius Press, 1987), 333–64.

embodied daily in both students and colleagues, and his grace powerfully at work. I was being formed in a way that allowed my love of God the Father, and my sense of honor for the priesthood as a mediation of divine fatherhood, to remain primary. The most important and fundamental aspect of my work in the seminary pertains in the end to the relationship between intellectual and spiritual formation—or, to put it in the words of a wonderful man and priest who would become my first department chair: the goal of intellectual formation is to know Jesus Christ more, and thereby to love him more. Seminary formation can be inflected with American pragmatism, fueled by an urgent and laudable desire to give people the pastors they desperately need.[17] The sacramental essence of the Church—and the veracity of transformative grace—demands that every act of true studiousness be a service to the Lord who is truth and life. Nevertheless, the wellspring of every effective Christian witness is simply this: to choose the "better part" first and last, by sitting at the feet of our Lord in patient adoration, in the deepest intimacy of friendship.

6. Mount Saint Mary's University: Conclusion

Scholarly invitations compelled me to expand my primary focus on Latin Patristics into new areas. These opportunities served to ground me more deeply in the life of the Church. Study of the Modernist Controversy made clear the profound implications of a theology of revelation—as seen, for example, in the poor integration of reflection on the development of doctrine and critical biblical studies in the early twentieth century. Papers given on *Gaudium et Spes*, and particularly focused on marriage, opened up the integral relationship between canon law, moral theology, and contemporary culture. Mary, the Mother of God, invited me to deepen our intercessory relationship through study, and I was able to spend time with Our Lady, Seat of Wisdom, by delivering essays integrating Newman, Ratzinger, early modern intellectual history, rhetorical attention to

---

[17] Even though the following is about seminaries in Germany, there are interesting analogues with North American formation; cf. Ratzinger, *The Nature and Mission of Theology*, trans. Adrian Walker (San Francisco: Ignatius Press, 1995), 121–28.

modes of theological argumentation, and ecclesiology. One particular project, a book chapter on the Vatican II document on education, *Gravissimum Educationis*, entailed a kind of professional summary of my journey into the Church, linked to my primary vocation as a parent and ordered to my incipient roles as a teacher and theologian. I applied for and earned a full-time, tenure track position in the Theology Department on the undergraduate "side" of Mount Saint Mary's. While I continued to teach at the seminary, I had found an intellectual and professional home. The classroom experience with undergraduates is, in some ways, very different from that of teaching seminarians; in other ways, not so much. The kinds of intellectual projects that moved me from working on Augustine to working more deeply in twentieth-century Catholicism, with *Ressourcement* theologians such as Jean Daniélou, and more, afforded an opportunity to reflect on the cultural-spiritual crises that afflict modern persons—seminarians, priests, laypeople, and undergraduates alike. The clearest shape of my vocational service as an academic within the Church would somehow be about the nature and rationale of Catholic education as *formation*, whether at home or in the parish, in a university or in a seminary. It would be about anthropology, or about the nature of the human person as a rational being and a child of God, called to be transformed daily "according to the mind of Christ Jesus". But it would be about the Church, insofar as the prophetic gift of teaching makes Catholic higher education to be an essentially ecclesial work, and, more importantly, because the Church is the Lord's providential means for establishing and building up the city of God.

A dear mentor, about a generation older than I, sometimes quips that converts "make no sense". In truth, he is articulating a critique that speaks to much of my own journey, addressing the dominant voluntarism of contemporary culture. By "voluntarism" I mean something like: "I am a radically free being, and my choices determine my identity, or my truth." For this mentor, growing up in a Catholic slice of American culture defined by the presence of religious and a close and organic relationship between home, parish, and school, the idea of "choosing" your faith or your church simply made no sense. In a way, he simply struggled to live within the sad reality of the demise of any recognizably "American Catholic culture". There is no causality involved in this demise that can be accounted for in a useful way by academics, or counteracted by cultural criticism. He was presciently correct in seeing that a new voluntarism, which tended to reduce any sense of faith not grasped by the active hand of individual will, would be brittle and easily politicized; it would inevitably privilege the individual over and against the communal nature of the Church as the Body of Christ. This convert-faith would be shot through with anxiety, involving a perpetual search for tropes of political-cultural identity—and then, it would abandon these when their usefulness had been exhausted, or when lived faith became impossible in the face of actual life. Even more theologically dangerous: lurking behind this cultural individualism lay the specter of the refusal of the fundamental primacy of divine grace as the glue that binds together the Church as well as the whole of the spiritual life. I suspect this is why Ratzinger diagnosed modernity as fraught with a tendency to Pelagianism.

Cradle Catholics draw encouragement from hearing "convert stories"; this essay may fit the bill, since my story has a coherence and, thus, a compelling character for me and, therefore, perhaps for others. What is "story" unless it is "thinking as memory"? The important part of any story, which is also the more difficult part, is everything that one brings to a narrative, as well as all that remains unspoken because it comes after. It is the sum of everyday, embodied human living.[18] All it takes is a son or daughter falling into faithlessness; or a fellow seminarian, more priest-like than any other, leaving formation months before ordination; or a spouse or beloved relative more desperate to prevail on the false cross of self than upon the Cross of Christ, to realize the fragility of any narrative coherence discerned at a particular moment of one's life. The Lord is good and gracious, providentially at work in times of great personal drama; perhaps he is at work even more powerfully in the everyday and banal, speaking from the hiddenness of that "still, small voice of calm". He showers us with blessings far beyond what we could ever deserve. But

---

[18] For this reason, for Tolkien, the essential part of his *Lord of the Rings* trilogy is the final part that is set in the Shire: everything that has transpired as a matter of high drama has been a preparation for returning home and setting things "to rights". Gandalf refuses to return with the Hobbits because they are now "grown up" and must heal the wounds of their community by using their gifts, on their own. *Return of the King* (New York: Ballantine Books, 1965), bk. 6, chap. 7; see also *The Letters of J. R. R Tolkien* (New York: HarperCollins, 2014), letters 105, 160, 183.

the faith puts before our eyes the Cross, as the center and source of all possible meaning. As a remarkable and neglected spiritual master tells it: "The conditions of today, of the whole world's pain, of the poverty and sweating and grief in my city, and my personal grief: the Cross was there before. He did not give us the Cross, but He gave us Himself on the Cross.... Receiving His Cross, we receive Him."[19]

I will conclude with a cue borrowed from Augustine's *Confessions*, perhaps provoking the reader: Even if I know why I am writing these words, why are *you* reading them? Augustine poses a simple question, distilling all wisdom to its essence: "What do I love when I love my God?" In light of the centrality of the Cross, it would appear that the faith is simply not about *me*. It is not about an identity crafted from the bits of my experiences and my judgments: What liturgy do I think most authentic? What hymns do I judge to be non-heretical? What gestures and life choices do I consider truly pious? How am I taking theological control of my own destiny? If the Church is the Lord crucified, lived out in time, she must be more than a group of people sharing (or ideally sharing) a set of theological agreements. The Church is nothing apart from radical unity with Christ as her head, and in a democratic age, and in a culture that celebrates autonomous freedom above all else, those who have indeed been born "[not] of the will of the flesh nor of the will of man, but of God" (Jn 1:13) must find a way to live in the simple, mystical truth of the Church as a mediation of all that the Cross means. The self-gift of the Lord: this must include the cultivation of less popular virtues, such as docility, obedience, studiousness, and sacrifice; moreover, such a life will look like the daily privileging of the good of others over one's own. History, as revelation, is the ongoing exercise of allowing God to work in and through each of us, individually and collectively—but these two are not alternatives, or really distinct, because individual holiness arises from and presupposes the primacy of the common good. For this reason, salvation is located "within" the Church. The logic of the Cross demands nothing less. The completion of the Church's mission in history depends upon the realization of this simple truth.

So "what do I love, when I love my God?" We are not asked to love the Church, but only the face of Jesus Christ on the Cross—he who is Love himself. It is not easy, because the cost of such love is so

---

[19] Caryll Houselander, *This War Is the Passion* (London: Sheed and Ward, 1941), 69.

very great. This same Christ commanded Augustine to return to the Church—in effect, to "the world". Even in a time of political unrest and theological struggle, Augustine discerned that the peace of the divine life would have to be found, somehow, within the Church. This is not an easy matter, nor can it ever pretend to have any completeness in this life; but it is for this peace that we are made, and according to which we are called, and by which we are sanctified, by grace. This is the purpose and the gift of the Church. And so I ask the reader to pray for me, a sinner; and let us pray for one another without ceasing.

Chapter 6

POST TENEBRAS LUX: DISCOVERING THE FULLNESS OF TRUTH IN THE CATHOLIC FAITH

by

Joshua H. Lim

Months before I was received into the Catholic Church, I was asked how it was that I became convinced of the truth of the Catholic faith. In what must have been a grueling twenty minutes for those at the dinner table, I detailed my journey (listing the various authors of the different books that I had read, detailing how such-and-such an author led me to this-or-that idea, which further allowed me to see the solution to this-or-that theological difficulty, etc., etc.). Sister Dominic Mary (then Audree) Heath, who had unsuspectingly provoked this deluge of excited though disorganized jumble, politely nodded along. When I at last concluded, Father Thomas Joseph White, who had been sitting beside me, turned and graciously recommended that, going forward, I simply tell inquirers that I "read my way into the Church". Though my story will not be so brief, nevertheless, in what follows, I hope to provide a less circuitous account of my path to the Catholic Church.

My journey to Rome is divided into two parts. The first has little to do with the Roman Catholic Church and consists primarily in the development of my religious ideas within Protestantism, which developments would eventually place me on the path to Rome. I began each of the various phases of my Protestant journey with an attitude of docility rather than suspicion; it was only when I experienced an absolute incongruity among the various principles within a given Protestant tradition that I would ultimately be forced to find a new way. Thus, through my Evangelical pastors, I became convinced of the doctrine of *sola scriptura* and, later, through the Reformed tradition, the doctrine of justification *sola fide*. I abandoned Evangelicalism when I recognized the incoherence of denying any and all human traditions in understanding Scripture; I left the Reformed church when I realized that there was no internally coherent way of defending the most fundamental tenets of Christian dogma on the grounds of the Protestant rejection of Sacred Tradition and natural reason. With each step, I was moving closer and closer to the Catholic Church even as I thought myself to be moving farther and farther away from her. In terms of chronology, this first part spans my baptism in the Presbyterian church up to my final year at Westminster Seminary. In the second part, I recount the more or less rapid movement from a practical loss of faith to a recognition of the truth of the Catholic faith.

1. Baptism to Seminary

My mother and father were the first in their respective families to convert to Christianity, my mother from Buddhism to Protestantism, my father from a nonreligious background to Catholicism. My father eventually converted to Protestantism on the advice of his priest, who told him it would be better for a happy marriage. By the time my older sister and I came along, my parents had immigrated to the United States from South Korea and were members of a Presbyterian church, in which I was baptized. My upbringing, to the degree that it was informed by Korean cultural standards, broadly reflected Confucian norms, which, above all, emphasized the importance of moral duty and deference to elders and tradition. From childhood, therefore, I was inculcated with a fundamentally conservative outlook that saw the path to wisdom as always beginning with submission and trust.

In my youth, it was my sister who had the greatest spiritual influence upon me. She was precociously religious—one time she surprised my parents by dressing up like Billy Graham for her grade-school career day. Following her lead, I took to reading the Bible regularly, often looking to Saint John's Apocalypse in an attempt discern how and when the world would end. In middle school, after reading the account of the life and martyrdom of Jim Elliot, a missionary to Ecuador, I decided that I wanted to devote my life to missionary work. Such aspirations quickly faded, however, once I reached high school. Again, through my sister's influence, I discovered the punk rock scene. For about a week, I thought myself an anarchist and then, after reading Marx and Engels, a communist. Within a year, I grew tired of punk rock and, in a bout of adolescent despair, stumbled upon C. S. Lewis' *Mere Christianity*. It was reading Lewis' thoughtful and lucid appraisal of God's existence, of universal moral norms, and of the goodness of religion that re-enlivened my interest in Christianity, which would continue throughout high school all the way up to seminary.

Fortuitously, my freshman year of high school coincided with the hiring of a new youth pastor who had an indelible impact on my spiritual formation. He emphasized the importance of holiness and introduced me to the serious study of Scripture. His sermons and Bible studies confronted us, mere high-school students, with the costly call to discipleship. Recognizing my interest in Scripture, he took me under his wing and even helped me begin studying Greek. I enthusiastically took up the study of Scripture, spending hours of my time in and out of school systematically working through various books of the Bible. In my senior year, after controversy surrounding the Presbyterian church leadership's decision to hire a more liberal college pastor, my pastor decided to leave for a more biblically oriented church. I followed him, joining a small Baptist church aptly named after the Bereans in the Book of Acts.

At Berean, I learned the importance of biblical interpretation. Much like the original Bereans, we saw it as our duty to search the Scriptures diligently and confirm for ourselves the knowledge of saving truth. Berean conscientiously adopted a method of interpreting Scripture called the grammatico-historical approach. Rooted in nineteenth-century Dispensationalism, this method of biblical interpretation eschewed all forms of allegorizing or spiritualizing the biblical text in favor of a strictly literal approach. Such an approach was thought to be a necessary extension of the Reformation doctrine of *sola scriptura* and was held in sharp contrast to the practice of patristic and medieval exegesis. Scriptural texts were thought to possess only a single, literal meaning that could be clearly discerned through careful attention to grammar and historical context. By emphasizing the perspicacity of the text, we thought it possible to avoid turning the Bible into a wax nose, devoid of any intrinsic meaning. Only thus could one avoid dependence on human traditions. Thus, it was at Berean that I first encountered explicitly the Protestant approach to Scripture under the Reformation banner of *sola scriptura*. Both intellectually and spiritually, I found this approach to Christianity exhilarating. Scripture, the very Word of God, became to me the sole wellspring of the knowledge of Truth.

Yet, if knowledge of Scripture was prized, intellectual truth was not considered an end in itself. In fact, the pursuit of knowledge for its own sake was seen as a deviation from that saving knowledge of God. Knowledge had an end that was above all practical; it was ordered to the love of God and neighbor, in sum, to lived obedience. One positive aspect of this approach was Berean's commitment to the Great Commission. True religion did not consist merely in a personal relationship with God but naturally flowed outward to evangelization. For my part, I took to evangelizing on my college campus and through regular conversations with atheists, Muslims, Catholics, and people from all backgrounds, I was confronted with a host of difficult questions that quickly became my own.

Though I initially turned to popular Christian apologetical works (here I first discovered the presuppositionalism of the Dutch Reformed theologian Cornelius van Til), I eventually discovered the deeper waters of traditional Protestant theology. From the more contemporary works of Evangelical theology, I gradually worked back through the topical works of the Puritan tradition (Bunyan, Owens, Baxter, Edwards, et al.), to the formidable luminaries of the Presbyterian and Reformed tradition (Charles Hodge, Herman Bavinck, Louis Berkhof, B. B. Warfield, et al.). My excitement in discovering this world of theological inquiry was readily apparent to those around me; for it was not long before I was mildly rebuked for spending too much time in the writings of men rather than in the Word of God.

Concerns that I was being led astray by human writings were not without warrant. Through my reading, I came to question the grammatico-historical hermeneutic, which appeared to be contradicted by the apostles' own methods of interpreting the Old Testament. Furthermore, I became convinced of the ancient practice of infant baptism. (By this point, I had been baptized three times, once as an infant, again at a middle-school retreat, and, thirdly, at Berean.) Unbeknownst to me, by accepting infant baptism, I was taking an initial step toward recognizing the untenability of *sola scriptura*. While Scripture nowhere explicitly enjoined the practice of infant baptism, neither did it condemn it. It seemed incredible to me that a practice that had been uniformly adopted by the earliest Christians, by the disciples of Christ's own apostles, should be rejected purely on the basis of Scripture's relative silence on the matter. It seemed more reasonable to view the silence of Scripture as a sign of the practice's unanimous acceptance rather than the ground for its rejection. In this case, it was not a matter of choosing between the Bible, on the one hand, and human tradition, on the other, but about choosing between two traditions, the one relatively recent and the other traced back to the apostles. I did not, however, see my admission of infant baptism as a concession to a Catholic notion of tradition. Rather, it was a simple recognition of the unavoidable fact that any approach to Scripture would be informed by some kind of tradition. So long as the tradition in question admitted the possibility of reform through Scripture, its adoption did not compromise the absolute authority belonging to Scripture alone.

This relatively positive assessment of tradition resolved certain tensions I experienced in my attempts to understand theological and biblical truth. It was clear that I did not arrive at my understanding of Scripture on my own. I relied on pastors, biblical commentaries, and theological works to arrive at the clear meaning of the text. With this more optimistic appraisal of tradition, I turned to that tradition most proximate to me, namely, that of the Reformed and Presbyterian churches. I studied the Westminster Confession of Faith as well as the parallel Three Forms of Unity of the continental Reformed churches (i.e., the *Canons of Dort*, the *Heidelberg Catechism*, and the *Belgic Confession*), seeing in these works something akin to a rule of faith. Beyond the confessions, I delved into the writings of Calvin and subsequent Protestant Scholastics, where I discovered a more sophisticated theology whose historical and traditional identity was clearly defined in opposition to Rome. Specifically, it was Luther, the father

of the Reformation, whose writings had the greatest impact on me.
Luther's *On the Freedom of a Christian* and his *Heidelberg Disputation*
cemented in my mind the central article of the Christian faith, *articulus stantis et cadentis ecclesiae*, the doctrine of justification *sola fide*.

Through reading Luther, I eventually became convinced that
Berean, along with the bulk of Evangelicalism, had, in fact, abandoned the Gospel. That Luther's heirs would practically abandon
the central tenet of the Christian faith was consistent with my Calvinist assumptions regarding the insidious nature of sin and pride. It
was precisely for this reason that Luther deemed it necessary to view
the Reformation as a constant and ongoing struggle, *reformata semper reformanda*. Still, the accusation was a surprise to my pastors, who
saw themselves as faithful inheritors of Luther's teaching. Nevertheless, I saw in Berean's emphasis on the necessity of human works
for the assurance of salvation what amounted to a practical form of
works righteousness. For they regarded the assurance of salvation as
grounded most proximately in the visible fruits of sanctification in the
believer's life. Given the possibility of self-deception, believers, particularly the spiritually lax, were exhorted to test regularly the verity
of their faith through an examination of such fruits. This seemed to
me a roundabout way of pointing the believer away from Christ's
righteousness, freely received through faith, back to human works.[1]
Against this backdrop of introspective scrupulosity, Luther's gospel of
imputed righteousness brought about a sense of freedom. The human
act of faith, which grounded the justification of the sinner, was not at
all a human work, a "doing", but the mere receiving of an alien righteousness. Taking my stand on conscience and Scripture, I left Berean.

Along with a very small group of friends from Berean (who would
eventually enter the Catholic Church), I joined a denomination that

---

[1] This approach is present in Edwards' response to the Great Awakening. See Jonathan
Edwards, *A Treatise concerning Religious Affections* (New York: Leavitt, Trow, 1845), p. 53:
"But this doctrine [Christians living by faith, not by sight], as it is understood by many, is,
that Christians ought firmly to believe and trust in Christ, without spiritual sight or light, and
although they are in a dark dead frame and, for the present, have no spiritual experiences or
discoveries. And it is truly the duty of those who are thus in darkness, to come out of darkness
into light and believe. *But that they should confidently believe and trust, while they yet remain without spiritual light or sight, is an anti-scriptural and absurd doctrine*" (emphasis added). Nevertheless,
such a tension is apparent already in Calvin. See John Calvin, *The Institutes of the Christian
Religion*, III.ii.11–12. I am grateful to Barrett Turner for this reference.

held more closely to the Lutheran doctrine of justification and, more broadly, to the Reformed tradition. This step represented a further deepening in my intellectual journey. Joining a traditional Reformed church definitively freed me to explore the Protestant tradition. I saw this no longer as a turn away from God to men but, rather, as a turn away from my own ability to understand Scripture toward a dependence on the wisdom of teachers who went before me. "How can I understand, unless someone guides me?" It was precisely through others, through tradition, that I recognized the path to the attainment of a true understanding of Scripture. Most of all, I inherited that important doctrine which fundamentally differentiated Protestantism from Rome, the doctrine of justification *sola fide*.

It was not long before intellectual curiosity led me beyond the confines of traditional Reformed theology, expanding to the world of contemporary biblical scholarship. In particular, through questions about the historicity of the Old Testament, I was introduced to the Yale school of theology in Hans Frei and Brevard Childs; and it was through the latter that I was finally disposed to that twentieth-century Swiss Reformed theologian who would be most consequential in the latter part of my Protestant journey, Karl Barth.

In my senior year of college, I decided to read through the entirety of Barth's *Church Dogmatics*. Barth had on me the same effect that Hume had on Kant, awaking me from my dogmatic slumber. Though an inheritor of the Reformed tradition, Barth was nevertheless regarded with suspicion by those in conservative Reformed circles. Not without reason, he was viewed as nothing more than a liberal Protestant in disguise. Yet, I found myself drawn to him precisely because of his vehement insistence, against liberal Protestantism, on the relentless priority of divine action. In Barth, I discovered a theology that sought to confront all of liberal Protestantism through critical engagement with modern theology and philosophy. (Barth's commentary on the Letter to the Romans, *Der Römerbrief*, has aptly been described as a hand grenade lobbed into the playground of liberal Protestantism.) Through Barth, my horizons were opened to the "strange new world" of modern theology. Unlike much of the conservative Reformed tradition, whose engagement with modern thought tended to consist in an all-too-easy hearkening back to the pre-critical era of the Magisterial Reformers, Barth grappled with the problems of modernity with utmost seriousness. It was through Barth that I first grasped the challenge that modernity posed to any serious theological project. I became acutely aware of the danger of attempting to talk about God by speaking about man in a loud voice.

When I entered Westminster Seminary, I still found myself reeling from the aftershocks caused by the earthquake of the *Church Dogmatics*. Although I discovered a more thoughtful engagement with modern thought, I nevertheless could not bring myself to follow in Barth's footsteps. Barth's emphasis on the event-character of revelation—a pox on any human attempt to reify God's act of self-revelation—not only seemed to call into question much of classical Christian theology, it also appeared to undermine Barth's own project. Reading certain followers of Barth, such as Jürgen Moltmann and Eberhard Jüngel, only confirmed my suspicions. Their revisions of the doctrines of divine immutability, simplicity, and impassibility ran contrary to the core of the Christian doctrine I had received.

Nevertheless, I was troubled in seeking an adequate response to their claims. I saw how their views were, in many ways, logical extensions of Luther's own approach to theology, the *theologia crucis*.[2] These thinkers viewed God's historical revelation of himself *pro nobis* not only as constituting the basis of any human knowledge of God but, more radically, as the basis of God's very being. I attempted to reject such teachings on the grounds that they introduced extrabiblical philosophical assumptions into theology, an implicit breach of the principle of *sola scriptura*. In this vein, such modern developments appeared as speculative attempts (*à la* Luther's *theologia gloriae*) to get behind the God revealed in Christ to a glimpse of God in himself, the *Deus nudus*. Implicit in my rejection, however, was the naïve idea that traditional Reformed theology already possessed a fully "Christian ontology", which purportedly had its foundation, not in human speculation, but in divine revelation alone. But how was I to know whether it was not I who was, in fact, limiting the fullness

---

[2] See especially theses 19 and 20 of Martin Luther, *The Heidelberg Disputation* (1518): "(19) That person does not deserve to be called a theologian who looks upon the invisible things of God as though they were clearly perceptible in those things which have actually happened [Rom. 1.20]. (20) He deserves to be called a theologian, however, who comprehends the visible and manifest things of God seen through suffering and the cross." *Luther's Works*, trans. Martin H. Bertram, ed. Jaroslav Pelikan and Helmut Lehmann (St. Louis: Concordia Publishing House, 1955-86).

of God's self-revelation in Christ? For according to Moltmann and Jüngel, the classical doctrines of immutability and impassibility were not founded upon Scripture at all, but upon Hellenistic philosophy. If the specter of Hegel loomed behind modern theological projects of divine passibility, it was Plato, not Saint Paul, who was alleged to be hiding behind the classical doctrines of God. I was becoming aware that appeal to Scripture alone was insufficient to resolve what was, in fact, a philosophical dispute.

Yet, in seeking a philosophy that corresponded with traditional Christian belief, I found myself in a bind. In my seminary classes, despite the best intentions of my professors, I learned what was a fundamentally competitive view of the relationship between faith and reason. To be sure, faith was not held in absolute contrast to natural reason considered in itself (i.e., in abstraction from the economy of sin). Yet, since every concrete instance of this natural, speculative knowledge of God could not but be stained by the deleterious effects of sin, it would only ever pose an obstacle to a true and saving knowledge of God. This was an application of Luther's Law-Gospel distinction to the epistemological realm. For only through the corruption of man's natural ability to know God could Luther maintain an absolute contrast between revealed faith and human works. As such, the philosophical speculations of the ancient Greeks, the Church Fathers (insofar as their thought betrayed the influence of Greek philosophy), and, most of all, the medieval schoolmen could only be regarded as sinful attempts to circumvent the true revelation of God in Christ, a manifestation of the much-abhorred *theologia gloriae*.

Such a scathing assessment of natural human reason formed the basis for a sweeping theological narrative that viewed Plato as the primary foil to biblical Christianity. The Platonic priority of the unchanging and eternal over and above the material and historical was seen as necessitating a quasi-Gnostic rejection of the latter. Against what was deemed to be an undue intrusion of Platonic and Neoplatonic philosophy into early and medieval Christian theology, my professors contraposed the strictly historical character of revelation through the biblical covenants. This emphasis on the historical over and above the eternal was most clearly seen in the Protestant rejection of the Catholic view of salvation as consisting in a knowledge of the divine essence, the *visio Dei*. In contrast to the Catholic teaching, the salvation brought about by Christ was thought to consist not in the supernatural elevation of the natural powers of the soul to behold God in himself, but in a resolute affirmation of the material and historical order of reality, in what could only ultimately be a purely temporal "age to come".[3] Thus, any mystical and speculative endeavors consisting in a "flight from this world", beyond the contingent and historical, were viewed as evidence of the corrupting influence of Greek philosophy. If the philosophy of Plato suggested a natural human desire for eternal and absolute truth, this was only accidentally a reflection of man's innate desire for God; essentially, it was evidence of the cancerous effects of sin, which infected all of fallen man's attempts to reach the divine. All such endeavors to ascend to God through human reason were but echoes of that human pride most clearly displayed in the construction of the tower of Babel.

Yet, by continuing the Magisterial Reformers' repudiation of the "vain speculation" of the medieval schoolmen, we unwittingly rejected the metaphysical foundations of the most central dogmas of Christianity. For in the place of a realist metaphysics, the Reformers posited *sola scriptura*. If any of the philosophical assumptions of Catholic Christianity were true, these could ultimately and only be deduced from Scripture alone. By denying the fundamental integrity of man's intellectual desire for God in the fallen state, however, the Reformed tradition had inadvertently barred access to any extrabiblical knowledge of that human reality which is ontologically *prior* to revelation—that is, the knowledge of natural reality that forms the concrete foundation for the human intelligibility of divine revelation. Instead of beginning from what was better known to us through the human experience of reality, we took as our fundamental starting point the revealed will of God—not only according to the order of discovery (in which case one might work backward, aided by revealed truth, to discover principles proper to nature) but also according to

---

[3] See, for instance, Michael Horton, *The Christian Faith: A Systematic Theology for Pilgrims on the Way* (Grand Rapids, Mich.: Zondervan Academic, 2011), 75: "However, at this point at least it was a Platonized form of religion that [Nietzsche] was rejecting rather than the Bible's world-affirming narrative of creation, incarnation, redemption, resurrection, and the consummation of created reality. Not in a flight into a 'beyond,' away from the supposedly lower world, but in the arrival of the age to come; not in a renunciation of life here and now, but in the embrace of life as the anticipation of feasting with God and each other in joy, does Christian hope prove itself the only true rival of Platonism."

the order of reality. Thus, I saw that the epistemological claim of justification *sola fide* (i.e., that God cannot be known through human effort) was part and parcel with the ontological claim implied in the doctrine of *sola scriptura*. In order to ground saving truth solely in the divinely revealed will, Luther thought it necessary to deny access to such truth through natural human ascent.

In this regard, human philosophies were, at best, neutral instruments. Once purified by a thoroughly biblical "Christian ontology", they could be used to aid in the explication of what was known through revelation alone. This entailed the naïve assumption that Scripture could be approached without being substantially influenced, indeed distorted, by the reader's own human assumptions about reality (whether colored by the regnant philosophies of the time or based on a more conscientiously assumed philosophical outlook). While meticulously exposing the nonbiblical assumptions of all other theologies, we remained blind to the possibility that we ourselves might have been beholden to unbiblical philosophical assumptions. As a result, we failed to subject our own theology consistently to the scrutiny of God's Word.

This approach colored our assessment of modern thinkers. Rather than argue on the basis of philosophical principles as to why Kant or Nietzsche was wrong, my professors argued from accidents of history. It was thought sufficient to give purely historical accounts as to why certain modern views missed the mark. For, at base, we presupposed that our particular version of Christianity successfully evaded all serious critique. Thus, since Kant's critical philosophy had as its proximate religious background German Pietism, his works could be seen as providing a salient critique of various forms of Christian pietism, but not of Reformed Christianity. Similarly, since Nietzsche's critique of Christianity was based on a "Platonized" form of Christianity, it was applicable to those Catholic and Evangelical versions of Christianity that were influenced by Platonic thought and not to our own. We even dared to adopt these critiques as our own. For we rightly saw Kant and Nietzsche as following Luther in his reaction to what were deemed the speculative excesses of any philosophical claim to divine truth.

When forced to deal more directly with the substantial elements of the Kantian critique, however, fissures in the Reformed foundation became all too apparent. Here, again, it was history, not metaphysics, that grounded our response. Against Kant's prohibition of any direct metaphysical knowledge of God, we thought it sufficient to point to the historical event of the Incarnation. Since the Word became Flesh (i.e., the noumenal entering into the phenomenal, historical realm), Kant's claims about the noumenal had to be false. It was a *reductio* that began from the presumed truth of the metaphysical claims of Christianity (which lay concealed under purely historical claims). While compelling as a matter of rhetoric, such responses did not go much beyond that. For it was clear to me that Kant's critical philosophy posed a challenge to the very foundation of any theological science. If Kant were correct, there would, in fact, be no way to know that what we claimed to know about God, even if only through history, was true. For the historical evidence did not provide a proportionate warrant for belief in what were fundamentally metaphysical claims. Yet, in the face of Lessing's "ugly ditch" between the particular events of history and the universal truths of reason, the solution was not an affirmation of the human soul's natural capacity for spiritual truth but a reduction of the divine to the purely historical plane. The Reformed response to Kant amounted to a *petitio principii*. It was an assertion based on subjective interpretations of purely historical events. For it is one thing to recognize that religion must be objectively grounded, which we certainly did, and another thing altogether to have an objectively grounded religion, which we did not. Having rejected any claim to the possibility of metaphysical objectivity on the grounds of sinful human experience, we had no way to give a rational defense for the possibility of revelation.

By superficially inuring our theology to modern philosophical criticism, we did not see that we were, in fact, undermining the very grounds of the intelligibility of Christian revelation. By dismissing the allegedly "Platonic" aspects of the traditional Christianity of the East and West, which appeared too much concerned with the ontological transformation of human nature, we were left with a view of humanity whose end could only consist in purely material and sensible manifestations of God in history. Indeed, the very *ratio* of the Incarnation no longer made sense. For what need was there for God to become man except to elevate man and, in Saint Peter's words, make us partakers in the divine nature? I saw that many of the Reformed "defenses of the faith" were mere capitulations of basic metaphysical premises entailed in the most central Christian dogmas of the Trinity and the Incarnation. Yet, deprived of the ground of truth, it seemed that even our boldest attempt at objective theology could only ever amount to a poorly disguised attempt to speak about man in a loud voice.

2. The Turn to Rome

All of this came to a head when I attended a conference on Karl Barth and Thomas Aquinas. The conference, billed as an "unofficial Protestant-Catholic dialogue", consisted mostly of Barthian Protestants and Thomist Catholics. I attended the conference in the spirit of an outsider. The Barthian project held little appeal to me, and the Catholic Church was, to my mind, still the Church of the Antichrist. In fact, I was beginning to regard the entire project of Christian theology as tendentious. As a traditional Reformed Protestant, I found myself much more sympathetic to the Thomists than to the Barthians. Yet, I was beginning to see that those aspects of traditional Christianity that I had received through the Reformed tradition could only exist and thrive when rooted in their original source, the Catholic Church.

More than anything else, it was through a providential encounter with one Dominican theologian that I recall the definitive beginnings of a turn, a *conversio*. I was curious to hear how exactly a Catholic theologian would respond to the various and sundry objections against Rome that I had been taught. Thus, I approached Father Thomas Joseph White and unloaded all the major objections that, I thought, should have prevented any reasonable person from being a Roman Catholic. Beyond the substance of his responses, which were compelling enough, I was able to attain a glimpse of my own tradition from the outside, more precisely, from the perspective of Rome. While I had hitherto approached opposing views from within, I had resolutely refused to do this with Catholicism. Yet, for the first time, I was struck by the possibility that it was I, as a Protestant, who was in error. In continued contact with Father Thomas Joseph White, I began to search the Catholic tradition from within.

As I studied Catholic theology, I began to see that the seemingly intractable problems I encountered in and through modern philosophy and theology were, in fact, rooted in the Reformation itself. My quarrel was not with Christianity as a whole, and certainly not with Rome, but with Protestantism alone. It was at this time that I began to consider more seriously a point of one of my church history professors, namely, that the *via moderna* or "nominalism" of late medieval Scholasticism formed the necessary condition for Luther's doctrine of justification.[4] In making such a claim, my professor merely intended to provide a historical basis for the Reformed tradition's catholicity; yet, in it, I found something more disquieting. Was it not possible to see in Luther's own reforms, in Protestantism as a whole, an approach to Scripture that was, in fact, based not on Scripture alone, but on purely human assumptions about reality? In other words, was not Luther's own Herculean attempt at "Scripture alone" curtailed at the outset by his own philosophical assumptions?

A closer look at the immediate medieval background of the Reformation showed this to be incontrovertibly true. While Luther, a self-professed Occamite, was reacting most of all to Pelagian strands in the *via moderna* of late medieval Scholasticism, his own "Augustinianism" (most proximately tied to other members of the *via moderna*, Gabriel Biel and Gregory of Rimini) was emphatically shaped by this same intellectual background. While the Erasmian renaissance brought about a renewed appreciation for the Greek and Hebrew texts of Scripture, it was, in fact, Luther's philosophical assumptions that formed the most proximate backdrop to his reactionary interpretation of Saint Paul.

Specifically, it was only through the philosophical assumptions of the *via moderna* that Luther could take the Greek term for justification (*dikaiosyne*) a step farther by restricting the word's meaning to what was only conceivable within the context of a particular

---

[4] By "nominalism" was meant that broad movement of late medieval thought that rejected the realist epistemology of the High Middle Ages, made use of the dialectic between the two powers of God (the *potentia absoluta* and the *potentia ordinata*), and emphasized the notion of extrinsic denomination with respect to justification based on the voluntarist notion of the *acceptatio divina*. On the influence of the late medieval movement on the Reformation, see Alister McGrath, *The Intellectual Origins of the European Reformation*, 2nd ed. (Oxford: Wiley-Blackwell, 2003); Heiko A. Oberman, *Forerunners of the Reformation: The Shape of Late Medieval Thought* (Minneapolis: Fortress Press, 1981); *The Dawn of the Reformation: Essays in Late Medieval and Early Reformation Thought* (London: Bloomsbury, T&T Clark, 1986); *The Harvest of Medieval Theology: Gabriel Biel and Late Medieval Nominalism* (Grand Rapids, Mich.: Baker Academic, 2001).

human philosophy. Rather than implying an ontological transformation occurring in the sinner (in the parlance of the high medievals, the notion of grace as a created habit perfecting the soul), Luther approached the Pauline text with the nominalist assumption that divine righteousness did not have to conform at all to created, human notions of righteousness. Most radically, "to be righteous" in the Pauline sense did not entail an intrinsic quality in the human soul. A sinner could be declared righteous without being made righteous (i.e., without the internal transformation of grace), through a purely extrinsic imputation by divine fiat, *simul iustus et peccator*. The advent of sin was thus the occasion for God to act in ways apparently contradictory to his wisdom in creation. If such a view went against notions of justice founded upon human reality, this was because the latter was, in fact, the corrupted "wisdom of this age". In contrast, Luther's *theologia crucis* did not take its cues from human wisdom but from the revealed text alone. Teachings that the earlier Christian tradition would have rejected as incoherent and absurd found their ground of possibility in the milieu of late medieval philosophy.

Yet, what enabled Luther's key doctrine of justification by faith alone was precisely what cordoned off access to rational human discourse about God. The basis of Reformed theology's "Christian ontology" lay, not in Scripture, but in the all-too-human intellectual background of nominalism. Indeed, the very call to Scripture alone betrayed the philosophical vision of a reality that was really only knowable by recourse to revelation, in which one could discover God's *potentia ordinata*. At the root of both modern critical philosophy as well as the distinctively Reformed doctrines of the human capacity to know God was the rending of natural reality from divine revelation. Whether later Protestants accepted nominalism as such, to the degree that they accepted Luther's doctrine of justification and *sola scriptura*, they unwittingly adopted these philosophical assumptions. I saw that a consistent rejection of Luther's philosophical assumptions required a rejection of his doctrine as well. Once I had recognized that my theological quandary was rooted in a philosophical problem, I increasingly began to see in the Catholic tradition, and in Saint Thomas Aquinas in particular, a more reliable guide. I no longer had to deny that which had to be assumed in order for Christianity to be rationally defensible; for human reason was not so corrupted as not to be able to know meaningful truths about reality. I read through the entirety of the *Summa Theologiae* and saw, beyond the superficial similarities between Thomas and the post-Reformation Protestant Scholastics, a vastly different approach to God and reality.

Yet, two lingering issues prevented me from immediately becoming Catholic. The first had to do with the doctrine of justification. It was not at first clear to me how I could accept the Roman Catholic doctrine of justification, which I regarded as semi-Pelagian. Though I had doubts about the Reformed explication of the doctrine, as a whole, my entire understanding of the history of redemption through the framework of Reformed covenant theology hinged on Luther's understanding of justification.[5] Second, I could not bring myself to

[5] My eventual acceptance of the Catholic understanding of justification was made possible by the study of Scripture. As a part of the Reformed covenantal understanding of redemptive history, I was schooled in a particular version of covenant theology that is much controverted within Reformed circles. Labeled by opponents as the "Escondido theology", this particular version of covenant theology saw in the covenant that God made with the First Man in the Garden of Eden one devoid of any grace. Grace, specifically understood as *de*-merited favor, was only thought to exist in the context of sin. The stipulations of God's first covenant with man, the covenant of works, required perfect and perpetual obedience on the part of Adam; on the condition of his obedience, he would be admitted to eschatological glory. On account of Adam's failure to guard the garden from the Serpent, however, humanity was cut off from covenantal relationship with God. Because he was the federal head, Adam's Fall plunged all of humanity into the morass of guilt, sin, and death: humanity was henceforth separated from God, barred from a return to the garden and, more significantly, barred from the possibility of eschatological beatitude. Through his earthly active and passive obedience, Christ did what Adam had failed to do. As foretold in the protoevangelion, Christ crushed the head of the Serpent, thereby fulfilling the stipulations of the original covenant of works. As a result of Christ's perfect, perpetual, and personal obedience, which would be imputed to those who had faith, humanity was able to enter once again into covenant with God—unlike the original covenant of works, however, membership in this covenant was by faith and not by works.

This understanding of the biblical narrative would be challenged through my study of the New Perspective on Paul. The basic thesis of the New Perspective was that Luther had fundamentally misinterpreted the "works of the law". Luther had not so much unearthed Saint Paul's true meaning against alleged corruptions of the biblical text by the Catholic Church as much as he had read his own sixteenth-century introspective crisis into the Pauline text. According to the New Perspective, the "works of the Law" against which Saint Paul inveighed were not to be understood as Luther's generic "principle of works" but, rather, as the particular works associated with the Mosaic covenant. Consequently, in pointing to the need for faith and baptism, Saint Paul was not excluding all human work, but only excluding those purely external human works that were associated with the Old Covenant.

So much effort was exerted in Reformed attempts to rescue Luther's interpretation from the challenges posed by the New Perspective. Yet, these arguments were only secondarily arguments from Scripture; primarily, they were theological in nature, already assuming the truth of Luther's Law-Gospel distinction. One of the arguments, hailed as a victory for the traditional Protestant view, argued for a variegation in Second Temple Judaism, among which one might conceivably find the sort of proto-Roman Catholic view against which Saint

submit to a Church that required a subjection of intellect and will that was due to God alone. As I thought through these two issues, however, I gradually began to see how these two doctrines were entailed in the very logic of the Christian faith.

With respect to justification, my development as a Protestant consisted in an increasing recognition of the centrality of the Law-Gospel distinction. Even if the doctrine's implications were not consistently worked out, I had nevertheless been taught from my youth that Christianity was to be distinguished from every other form of religion (especially Catholicism) on the grounds that it was a religion of faith, of believing, as opposed to one of human works, of doing. While all other religions provided various ways for man to ascend to God through human effort, Christianity alone was thought to provide "good news" based on faith alone. "Say not in thy heart, who shall ascend to heaven?" It seemed that becoming Catholic would require assent to a doctrine of salvation through human effort rather than through grace—which appeared to me to be a thorough repudiation of the Augustinian doctrine of grace. Yet, I soon discovered that this was not the case.

Unbeknownst to me, the grounds for accepting the Roman Catholic doctrine of justification had already been laid in seminary. One of my seminary professors, attempting to show that Calvinism was not a fatalistic determinism, had adopted a view of divine and human freedom that was, in reality, borrowed from the Thomist tradition. Rather than positing divine freedom as mutually exclusive with human freedom, this view argued that the former was, in fact, the very ground of the latter.[6] As I studied the Catholic teaching of justification and merit in Saint Thomas, I found a far more thorough explication of the teaching. Far from being semi-Pelagian, the

---

Paul could have been writing (the positive evidence for this was to be found in Paul's letters themselves, which, of course, presupposed the Lutheran interpretation). As with the traditional doctrines of Christianity, the traditional Reformed position was ultimately defended by recourse to a system of doctrine that was already assumed to be true, received from the Reformed and Lutheran tradition on faith.

[6] Cf. Horton, Christian Faith, pp. 261–62: "Tyrants stalk the earth devouring the freedom of their subjects. The flame of their power can burn only to the extent that it consumes the liberty of others. However, God 'gives ... life and breath and everything' to us (Ac 17:25). God is a producer, not a consumer, of our creaturely freedom, and his presence fills our creaturely room with the air of liberty. Precisely because God alone is sovereign, qualitatively distinct in his freedom as Lord, creaturely freedom has its inexhaustible source in abundance rather than lack, generosity rather than a rationing or negotiation of wills."

Catholic doctrine saw all human action, both natural and supernatural, as grounded in the metaphysically prevenient divine action. In the first three canons of the Council of Trent, often conveniently passed over in silence, I found an unequivocal condemnation of the view that the first grace could be merited (against the semi-Pelagian interpretation of the Scholastic dictum, *facientibus quod in se est Deus non denegat gratiam*, "to those who do what is in them God will not deny grace").[7] Furthermore, contrary to what I had been taught, the Catholic doctrine did not merely posit habitual grace at the beginning of conversion, leaving the believer to complete on his own the work that God had begun. Far from it, as Saint Thomas taught, the divine help, *auxilium*, was necessary for every human movement toward God. Far from detracting from God's glory, human merit contributed to it. To my surprise, this teaching was grounded in Saint Augustine himself. "God who created you without you does not justify you without you."[8] In denying the possibility of human merit on the ground that it diminished the glory due to God alone, the Protestant understanding of justification betrayed a fundamentally competitive view of divine and human agency, which, if followed through consistently, could only lead to the denial of the latter, even in the act of faith.

With respect to the Church's claim to infallibility, I simply needed to work consistently through the views I held as a Protestant. Any claim to a correct scriptural interpretation (i.e., any scriptural interpretation of the Gospel that required the assent of theological faith) entailed the corollary claim to infallibility. Claims to present the "true" Gospel implied that the interpretation presented was, in fact, true and certain; for it was ultimately divine in origin. If someone had openly contradicted this Gospel by his own "human" interpretation, he was rightly regarded as worthy of excommunication, not only from the local church but from all true Christianity. In practice, we acted as though the sure and indubitable message of the Gospel could be infallibly handed down through fallible human mediators.

Notwithstanding the nominal distinction between ministerial and magisterial authority, the same was true in the Reformed tradition.

[7] See Saint Thomas Aquinas, *Summa Theologiae* I-II, q. 109, a. 6, and *The Council of Trent*, sixth session, canons 1–3.

[8] Cf. Saint Augustine, *Sermo* 169, 11, 13 (*PL* 38:923), where Saint Augustine describes at length how God does not justify us, does not make us righteous without our own volition.

When I became Reformed, I looked to the Reformed symbols, not as opposed to Scripture, but as helpful and necessary guides to understanding the truth revealed in Scripture. While we freely admitted the confessional documents to be fallible in principle, nevertheless, they were and could only be infallible in practice. The logic of the Gospel's demands required that its human proclamation be regarded as infallible. Even if secondary matters might be subject to alteration, we considered the core of the confessions to be based on a true and reliable interpretation of the Gospel message. When Evangelicals dismissed the Reformed confessions as a paper pope, we simply pointed to their own tacit acceptance of human traditions. We recognized that an explicit confession of faith, a human tradition, was necessary to guard fallible humans from error.

Finally, the philosophical difficulties arising from my engagement with modern theology revealed the need for affirming a true account of reality that was not explicit in Scripture but necessary for its proper understanding. For the very possibility and coherence of the Christian *kerygma* depend on an accurate and true understanding of human reality, about the nature of created truth, goodness, and justice. Not finding an explicit account of this in Scripture alone, I saw that it was the Church's task to maintain, through Sacred Tradition, aspects of a perennial philosophy that would prevent the corruption of the Gospel message by those who unwittingly brought their own erroneous philosophical assumptions to their reading of Scripture.

Far from an overreaching human grasp at divine authority, I therefore saw in the Catholic Church's claim to infallibility a necessary corollary flowing from the very logic of the Gospel itself. This was a demand to a submission of intellect and will, not to an arbitrary human authority, but to a visible authority guaranteed by Christ himself. Just as God worked through human authors in Sacred Scripture, I saw that God worked through visible human institutions (in the Book of Acts as in the Old Testament) to fulfill his saving plan. If the Church was to have any realistic claim to saving truth, it could only be through a claim to infallibility.

If I did not submit to the apostolic tradition found in the Catholic Church, I saw that I would inevitably be submitting to another human tradition (whether of my own devising or another's). Since Christ transmitted the Gospel of the kingdom of God through fallible humans, it was necessary that Christ also grant to the Church an outward form that would guarantee the stability and truth of this Gospel message—not merely through the invisible working of the Holy Spirit in individuals, but through the working of a visible human institution guarded by the Holy Spirit. For Christ did not form a disparate group of individuals, but his Body, the Church. I saw that the visibility and infallibility of the Church was but an extension of the logic of the Incarnation itself: God accommodated himself to the level of human realities of space and time so that, through Christ, he might lead humanity back to God.

Conclusion

In 2012, I began to meet with a Norbertine priest of Saint Michael's Abbey, Father Sebastian Walshe, for private instruction. One remark by Father Sebastian in particular struck me and is reflected throughout my journey: as long as one seeks the truth above all things, one will be saved. I was received into the Catholic Church on the feast day of Saint Anselm of Canterbury, only a few months before I graduated from Westminster Seminary. It is fitting that I was received into the Catholic Church on the feast day of a saint who had such an influence on the Western intellectual tradition. For it was chiefly through Saint Anselm's Scholastic heirs of the high medieval period, in whom the project of faith seeking understanding reached its zenith, that I was finally led to the Catholic Church.

While I regarded my various movements within Protestantism as forms of abandonment, forsaking erroneous traditions and philosophies in the pursuit of the truth, I regard my conversion to Catholicism most of all as the cumulation and purification of those partial truths that I had received as a Protestant. It was only through my baptism, through the biblical instruction I received from my pastors, and from the Catholic elements that I received from the Reformed tradition that I was able, with the divine help, to come to the fullness of the Catholic faith.[9]

[9] I am grateful to Micah D. Throop for his constructive feedback on particular points pertaining to the Reformed tradition and to Julieanne Mitchell (Dolan), Fr. Bruno Shah, O.P., and Sr. Dominic Mary Heath, O.P., for their valuable comments and suggestions.

Chapter 7

THE RELUCTANT CONVERSION OF A SKEPTIC

by

Jeffrey L. Morrow

It was the Easter Vigil of 1999, and I was a young college sophomore, only twenty years old and doing something I would never have imagined or expected just a few years prior. Having not been raised Catholic—or even Christian—this was my first time ever attending an Easter Vigil Mass. And I was there, not as an interested outsider or even a curious observer (as I had been at other Masses), but rather as someone celebrating Christ's Resurrection in a special way, with my own baptism, First Communion, and confirmation.

That I would want to be received into the Church was no doubt unexpected to many that had known me during my childhood. To some in my family, it seemed not just unexpected, but disappointing, as a forsaking of my nominally Jewish upbringing. Others, familiar with my skeptical, agnostic high school years and emphasis on science as the only avenue to truth, would no doubt be confused at this abrupt change. Perhaps a few suspected it was just another phase, driven by extra free time and the passion of youth in those college years.

Yet more than twenty years have passed since that Easter Vigil when I was received into the Church, and with each passing year, the grace of my conversion becomes more evident. The youthful decision—seemingly rash to many—has never wavered. Instead, it appears in retrospect as the beginning of a new life that I would never have imagined when I began college as a Jewish agnostic. Even my wife would say that the story is so unlikely that she probably would not believe it if she did not know it to be true. In the years since that Easter Vigil, God has led me to earn an M.A. and Ph.D. in Catholic theology, to become a professor at a Catholic seminary, and, in my most humbling role, to live as a Catholic husband and father to seven children. While the story of my conversion may seem unusual, or even unlikely, its veracity is a testament to God's grace and mercy.

Mixed Religious Confusion

Looking back on my childhood, I can see in hindsight the ways in which our Lord reached out to me, ways of which I remained oblivious at the time. My parents came from quite different religious upbringings. My father came from a Jewish home and at the time of his bar mitzvah had considered studying to become a rabbi, but instead he sought a path in the medical profession. Although most Jews coming from Europe would have fit in with what we call Orthodox Judaism, American pressures to work on the Sabbath, amidst a host of other factors, led many to practice Judaism within either Reform or Conservative Judaism; most of my family wound up in the latter. My father's paternal grandfather, however, was an ardent Zionist and even hosted Golda Meir, who would become Israel's first (and thus far only) female prime minister, at his house in Cleveland, Ohio.

My mother's home was not particularly religious. Her mother had come from a long line of Scottish Presbyterians but never took to religion. In her youth, my grandmother had abandoned a quiet, rural Midwest life to become a Hollywood flight attendant. My maternal grandfather's father was a lapsed Mormon, and his mother had left Lutheranism to become a Christian Scientist. Although there are hints of some traumatic experience connected with religion, my grandfather's encounter with a host of intellectual ideas coming from logical positivism (especially in the work of Alfred Korzybski) and also the thought of Charles Darwin were his answer to religious faith. In the course of his military service, first with the Marines in World War II and Korea, and then in the Coast Guard, he went to graduate school for semantics, where he studied with S. I. Hayakawa, in the tradition of Korzybski.

My mother and father married but did not raise my brother and me in a particularly religious environment. The only prayers we had were the Hebrew prayers my non-Jewish mother taught us, e.g., for Hanukkah, but I did not know anything about God, or even that prayers were directed at God. Even though I attended a public school, I did not learn that Christmas had anything to do with Jesus until about the third grade, and it would take until my first semester at college to learn that Easter was a celebration of Jesus' Resurrection. For a few years my parents took us to a Unitarian Universalist church, where we children learned about classical Greek mythology . . . I never found out what the adults learned. My parents separated when I finished third grade, and both my brother and I initially lived with our mother, who married my stepfather soon after the divorce. This stepfather was a professor of psychology, formerly at Princeton, who, as a graduate student, had been intimately involved in the now-famous Stanford Prison Experiment. He had very similar intellectual preferences to those of my maternal grandfather; they shared Darwin as a towering influence, but instead of the logical positivists and semanticists, behaviorists like B. F. Skinner were more prominent for my stepfather.

School Violence and Rationalist Proselytism

We moved to a very rough school for my fifth- through seventh-grade years. During this time I took up the practice of martial arts for self-defense. Getting bullied and beaten up in fifth and sixth grade made me determined to learn to defend myself. My grandfather taught me the basics of how to punch—he had been a golden gloves boxer—and he taught me some very useful wrestling moves from his days as a wrestling champion—as well as some of the hand-to-hand combat he learned in the Marines (most of which was too lethal for me realistically to use on the playground).

God played no explicit role in my life at this point. I do not remember the term "God", or "Jesus", ever being used in my home growing up. When friends at school explained to me in the most childish and simplistic terms possible about God, I took the question to the most intellectual sage I knew at the time, my skeptical maternal grandfather. Our conversation went something like this:

"Grandpa, does God exist?"

"Well, Jeffrey ... Can you see God?"

"No."

"Can you hear God?

"No."

"Can you feel God?"

"No."

"Can you smell God?"

"No."

"Can you taste God?"

"No."

"Well, I think you found your answer."

I thought this was the most brilliant response I had ever heard. It made perfect sense to me. I was about nine years old. I did not yet have the intellectual tools to challenge this empiricist idea, which assumed that only that which is directly verifiable by one or more of the five senses is real—a notion that is self-refuting since such an idea (indeed, any idea) is itself not directly detectable by any of the five senses.

I would enjoy sitting at my grandfather's feet listening to his rationalist sermons. He would sit in his comfortable chair and pull down books from his shelf, replete with yellow highlighting, ink underlining, and marginal notes that would make any medieval scribe blush. These were his go-to books that he had read and studied over and over again; he was one of the only men I knew who kept virtually all of his college textbooks. He even used a trigonometry textbook to help in his building projects, which included building his own boats; he had been an avid sailor since his childhood growing up in California. The books he brought off his shelf, and eventually new copies of which he provided me for my own "childhood" library, included Darwin's *Origin of Species*,[1] Korzybski's *Science and Sanity*,[2] and Hayakawa's *Language in Thought and Action*.[3] I became captivated

---

[1] Charles Darwin, *On the Origin of Species by Means of Natural Selection or the Preservation of Favoured Races in the Struggle for Life* (London: John Murray, 1859).

[2] Alfred Korzybski, *Science and Sanity: An Introduction to Non-Aristotelian Systems and General Semantics*, 3rd ed. (New York: Institute of General Semantics, 1948).

[3] S.I. Hayakawa, *Language in Thought and Action* (1941; New York: Houghton Mifflin, 1972).

by Darwin, and by the fifth grade was reading his *Voyage of the Beagle*[4] along with the works of Harvard evolutionist Stephen Jay Gould. I had read *Voyage of the Beagle* as well as Darwin's *Origin of Species* and *Descent of Man*[5] three times each by the time I graduated high school, as well as most of Gould's books, my favorites of which were Gould's lesser-known *Wonderful Life*,[6] on the Cambrian explosion, and his popular *Ever Since Darwin*.[7]

Meanwhile, my life at middle school, where drugs, gang violence, and students' knife fighting were regular realities, was becoming increasingly rough. Some of my classmates did not make it to high school but were gunned down, stabbed, expelled, or locked up. I stuck out, not only for my intellectual proclivities, but also as the only kid at school who took off for the Jewish holy days of Rosh Hashanah and Yom Kippur; Judaism became a part of my social identity. Even though I did not believe in God, I fasted on Yom Kippur and attended religious services with my dad. I particularly enjoyed our family celebrations of Passover, which had become my favorite religious tradition. These were the only religious services I attended as a child. I had been to synagogue many times, but it would take traveling to Central America near the end of high school for me to step into a Christian church (excluding Unitarian) for a religious ritual for the first time.

Martial Arts and Asian Traditions

In the fall of my seventh grade, things had become so bad at school that I was desperate to get out. My little brother and I moved in with our father, and from then on I was raised in a Jewish home, albeit not a strict one. My friends were all Jewish and preparing for their bar and bat mitzvahs. I wanted the same, so my father arranged

---

[4] Charles Darwin, *The Voyage of the Beagle* (1860; New York: Doubleday, 1962).

[5] Charles Darwin, *The Descent of Man and Selection in Relation to Sex* (London: John Murray, 1871).

[6] Stephen Jay Gould, *Wonderful Life: The Burgess Shale and the Nature of History* (New York: Norton, 1989).

[7] Stephen Jay Gould, *Ever Since Darwin: Reflections on Natural History* (New York: Norton, 1977).

for private Hebrew tutoring to prepare me for a future bar mitzvah sometime after I was thirteen. During this time I fell in love with the study of human evolution and of primatology (the study of apes and monkeys) as well as with the martial arts. I had already been training with specific techniques to defend myself daily and had been physically defending myself on a regular basis, but that was driven by fear more than affection.

It was in this context that I first was exposed to East Asian religious and philosophical traditions, mainly Buddhism and Taoism. I never took to the more mystical and apparent relativistic thought in these esoteric traditions because my mind was too shaped in modern science for that. Yet I loved the martial aspects, and by the eighth grade I was practicing four to six hours a day, seven days a week, and even helping out with instructing the adult classes in the evenings.

Jewish Family

My dad remarried before I entered high school, and we moved out to the Cleveland area where he had grown up. Since my stepmother was Jewish, and my stepbrother was approaching bar mitzvah age, we decided to share the occasion and each have a bar mitzvah[8] on the same day. My first year of high school thus included the intense after-school preparation for the bar mitzvah with private instruction. I also attended Hebrew school after school, but we were separated into age groups, so I was the only student in my class who had not yet had a bar mitzvah. There we studied more intense Jewish ethical debates, using *Pirke Avot*, the ethical teachings of the ancient rabbis, as our guide. It was a Conservative synagogue that would soon become what is called Reconstructionist.[9] Because my mother was

---

[8] A "bar mitzvah" is when a Jewish boy, typically at age thirteen, becomes a man, signified by his reading from the Torah at synagogue and providing a commentary, and often accompanied by a large festive celebration.

[9] There are four major divisions in contemporary Judaism: Orthodox, Reform, Conservative, and Reconstructionist. Orthodox Judaism is simply traditional Judaism. From the Orthodox perspective, only Orthodox Judaism is Judaism. The Reform movement (begun in early nineteenth-century Germany) within Judaism was a response to social pressures wherein it allowed Jews to live and dress in a way that did not make them stand out in society. The major theological differences stem from the Orthodox belief that the Talmud contains the oral

not Jewish, I would not be considered Jewish, since Judaism is traced matrilineally, but that was not an obstacle at this synagogue.

A Summer in Honduras

The bar mitzvah has historically been a coming-of-age type event; after the bar mitzvah, a Jewish boy was now able to join the men in wearing the tallit (prayer shawl) and in being called upon to read from Torah or to say the prayers prior to and after the rabbi read from Torah. For me, however, my first real taste of teenage independence was when I spent the summer prior to my senior year of high school in the rural mountains of Honduras. Spanish language and literature had joined ranks with my martial arts practice and study of evolution as one of my passions. I spent the summer before my senior year of high school living with a Catholic family in a remote village of Honduras. I was there with the Amigos de las Americas program, a volunteer organization, where I helped build latrines for families whose annual income was about fifty U.S. dollars a year.

Along with another volunteer, I joined a family of nine (including the grandmother) in a one-room house with a dirt floor and no electricity. We had to bathe in the local river, which was a bit of a hike in that mountainous region. I did not notice anything distinctly Catholic about the family with whom I lived, except that every few weeks they hitchhiked into town to attend Sunday Mass. I joined them in my time there. I noticed that only a handful of people received Holy Communion—although I did not know what any of this meant. I also listened to the homily with my skeptical ears. I remember distinctly hearing the priest preach about the importance of asking God for good crops and for their material sustenance.

---

teachings of Moses (thus Oral Torah), whereas the Reform movement believes the Talmud represents the attempt of the rabbis to adapt the Torah to the needs of the day and to continue that trend. The Conservative movement (originating in the late nineteenth century in the U.S.) began as a response to the Reform movement and the belief that it had given up too much of its heritage. Reconstructionist Judaism emerged from within Conservative Judaism in the mid-twentieth century as a way of keeping the traditions kept within Conservative Judaism but of continuing modernization and adapting to society in a way similar to that of Reform Judaism.

I remember thinking to myself, "this priest, in his nice clothes, is manipulating the people, giving them false hope in some God out there, when what they really need is to put away such childish fantasies. They need money and food, not fairy tales." Another experience I recall vividly was being afflicted with two parasitical infections at the same time: giardia and E. coli. I was in such pain and torment that I thought I might die. I'll spare you the details, but I did something then that I would soon forget, and it was a singular moment before I embraced Christianity: I prayed to God, in my own words. My prayer was simple and was the prayer of an agnostic. It went something like this, "God, if there is a God, please deliver me of this illness." My father, being a caring physician and dad, had packed me with just the right medicine to take if I had such-and-such a combination of symptoms. When I was able to take the medicine, I did, and my symptoms grew milder. I quickly forgot my prayer to God, and would not have attributed the ease and comfort, the healing, to God even had I remembered; I would have chalked it up to modern medicine, never realizing that my skeptical image of God having to work outside of the ordinary was a strawman. Most of the time, God works in our lives through the mundane and ordinary, as Christianity has always taught, even if this is not the image of God or of Christianity in the caricatures of skeptics.

One final event from high school deserves mention at this point. I recall arriving early to a math class my senior year of high school, and I pulled out a book on evolution that I carried with me as pleasure reading. A student nearby was reading a book as well, and I asked him what he was reading. It was a book affirming the historical reliability of the Bible. I would later remember the event and realize it was a book of Evangelical Christian apologetics, and the student, whom I would later meet again in college, was an Evangelical Protestant. I all but laughed in his face and said something rude, like "that's a bunch of nonsense", and went back to my own reading, feeling only slightly guilty as I noticed the student seemed a little crestfallen.

God Finding Jeffrey at College

I attended Miami University, nestled in rural Oxford, Ohio, founded in 1809. My choice of Miami was simple. It was close enough to home that I could take a four-and-a-half-hour drive north if anything urgent arose, but also far enough away that I would not have parents visiting every weekend. It was also where my maternal grandmother, her uncle (a once-famous scientist and inspiration for me), and both my mother and my stepfather had attended. Finally, given my interests at that time, I was intent on working with a famous primatologist who was a professor at Miami.

Campus Crusade for Christ

My first day on campus, I discovered that my freshman R.A. [resident advisor], Jason Shanks, lived in the dorm room next to mine. Jason was an Evangelical Protestant and confident in his Christian faith. He had narrowly lost the race for student-body president the previous year, and it was only because of this that he ended up as my R.A. During his time at Miami, Jason had been actively involved as a student leader in a primarily Protestant parachurch organization known then as Campus Crusade for Christ, founded in 1951 by Bill Bright, and now known as Cru. While we were at Miami, our Campus Crusade was the largest parachurch movement on any college campus in the world, boasting more than a thousand members in attendance at its weekly Thursday evening "Prime Time" meetings of praise and worship. Inspired by Christian intellectuals like C. S. Lewis, Jason gravitated toward apologetics, the rational defense of the Christian faith. At the time, perhaps the best-known figure associated with apologetics with Campus Crusade (as we called it back then) was a man named Biff Rocha.

Biff had been on full-time staff with Campus Crusade for a number of years, but at this point was on staff as a volunteer. He was famously brilliant on campus. He had attended Miami as an undergrad and was an A-student double majoring in English and political science, with enough credits to have added a third major in geology. After earning an M.A. in Communication, focusing on rhetoric, Biff eventually went on to earn a second M.A. and a Ph.D., both in Catholic theology, at the University of Dayton, where I joined him in both graduate and doctoral programs the year after him. Biff was one of the most gregarious individuals on Miami's campus; he seemed to know everyone. We would often avoid walking through the student center because it would take hours to get out because so many people would approach him to talk.

When people had questions relating to Christian apologetics, Biff was the person to whom they were most often sent. So, when Jason became intent on honing his apologetics skills, learning more about church history, etc., he sought out Biff. The two became fast friends. When Jason lost the presidential race, he decided he could have an impact on the university by leading a freshman Bible study in a dorm as an R. A. He spent the remainder of the spring semester and the entire summer fasting, praying, and studying with Biff for the future Bible study he would lead his final year at Miami. They read the Bible together and read through classic Bible commentaries, mainly by the Protestant Reformers, especially Luther and Calvin. They read works on church history, and some of the writings of the early Church Fathers. Jason knew that Biff was Catholic—one of only a handful of Campus Crusade staff members at the time to be Catholic—so he asked Biff to explain Catholicism to him.

An Introduction to Truth

When I met Jason, he was already starting his freshman Bible study, and he had continued to study Catholicism with Biff, as he was becoming increasingly convinced that the Catholic way of reading the Bible made more sense than what he had been taught as an Evangelical. I knew none of this, of course, at the time. But I do recall that Jason gave a public talk in the dorm on the question of whether truth was relative or absolute. My curiosity was piqued. Scientifically oriented as I was, I would have said that some matters of truth were clearly absolute, but, on the other hand, much of what people claim to be true, as with morality, was merely relative. I do not remember the exact arguments, but at some point, the matter of the Holocaust came up. This hit a nerve since I had relatives who had suffered in Nazi Germany; my "uncle" Glenn (his exact relationship was more complicated, both by blood and through marriage) was a concentration camp survivor.

Jason responded to me something along the lines of, "If all moral truths are relative, then such moral truth claims are no more true than matters of opinion."

"Yeah, that's how I see it", I replied. "It's like Hamlet said, 'there is nothing either good or bad, but thinking makes it so.'"

"So the Holocaust wasn't bad? It just displeases some and pleases others?"

He caught me. I was not sure how to respond to this. I knew in my bones that the Nazi attempt at exterminating Jews because they were Jews was evil. There were a host of other things I thought were evil too. Afterward, Jason invited me to his Bible study.

"But I don't believe in the Bible, or in God. I'm not a Christian."

"That's fine. You don't have to be a Christian to be in my study, but I'd love to have you in there."

"Let me think about it."

Freshman Bible Study

Well, I showed up, and the rest is history. Typically, such freshman studies were considered well attended if they had six students in them. Jason's became so well known and sought after that, by the end of the year, there were forty of us in the study. I will never forget my first day in that September Bible study. It was co-led by Biff, which was unusual, as staff members did not normally assist freshman Bible studies.

That Wednesday evening Biff was leading the discussion. There is one thing I will never forget from that first evening, which is perhaps my most memorable Bible study moment from the entire year—when Biff read from Saint Paul's First Letter to the Corinthians, "if Christ has not been raised, then our preaching is in vain and your faith is in vain" (15:14). By the end of that evening, I realized, for the first time, that not only do Christians believe in God, but they believe that Jesus was that God and, moreover, that the man Jesus not only died on a cross but was raised from the dead—and that that was what Easter celebrated! I had a lot of questions for Jason and Biff after everyone left the dorm study. I wanted to clarify these points about just what Christians believed about Jesus and the Bible. It was clear to me that Jason wanted me to be convinced of the Christian faith. Otherwise, why invite me to his Bible study? Our parting conversation that evening was something like this:

"You guys would like to convince me that Christianity is true?"

Jason unhesitatingly replied, "Of course!"

"Because we're convinced it's true", Biff added.

They said all this with the most sincere smiles, as if it were so obvious. So I added, "I'll keep showing up to the Bible study, but I won't ask any questions during the study."

"It's fine if you do. We'd love to field whatever questions you may have", Jason explained.

"No, I'd feel more comfortable waiting until after the study, after everyone has left. I don't want to derail the conversation, and I have no desire to cause these other students doubts about the faith they grew up in. But, if you're hoping to convince me this stuff is true, then I'll do my research and try to show you that God probably doesn't exist, the Bible's simply a collection of mythical stories that never happened, and Jesus never rose from the dead. How does that sound?"

My Quest to Disprove Christianity

They both chuckled, not in a demeaning or patronizing way, but in a cheerful, pleased way, as if they thought this would be a lot of fun. Jason began by handing me some books by Josh McDowell, a famous Evangelical apologist who was also on staff with Campus Crusade. Over the course of the semester, I devoured these books: *More Than a Carpenter*,[10] *The Resurrection Factor*,[11] *A Ready Defense*,[12] and volumes one and two of *Evidence that Demands a Verdict*.[13] There are a number of problems with some of McDowell's arguments, which I progressively learned, but they gave me my first real exposure to robust Christian apologetics, and I quickly began to realize not all Christians were as ignorant and illogical as I had thought. I began to see that I had my work cut out for me. As I got to know Jason and Biff, I was increasingly amazed by their intellects.

So my task consisted of reading not only the books Jason (and Biff) provided me but also many of the books and articles these sources

[10] Josh McDowell, *More Than a Carpenter* (Wheaton: Tyndale House, 1977).
[11] Josh McDowell, *The Resurrection Factor* (San Bernardino: Here's Life, 1981).
[12] Josh McDowell, *A Ready Defense* (Nashville: Thomas Nelson, 1993).
[13] Josh McDowell, *Evidence That Demands a Verdict: Historical Evidence for the Christian Faith*, vol. 1 (Nashville: Thomas Nelson, 1979) and vol. 2 (Nashville: Thomas Nelson, 1992).

referenced. I spoke with science professors—I was a declared zoology major at the time, although I quickly switched to psychology and then later switched to anthropology. I spoke with philosophy professors and historians. I spoke with local religious leaders on campus who would visit, from Jewish and other traditions. I always had questions for everyone. Most of my time was spent at the library, poring over scholarly journals and popular and scholarly books. I read not only popular works by Christian philosophers like J. P. Moreland and Peter Kreeft, but the works of skeptical philosophers like Antony Flew (who became a deist after this time, prior to his death over a decade later). I was taking a course in formal logic at the time, and I was increasingly frustrated by how illogical I was finding so many of the atheist and skeptical arguments I was reading, but with whose conclusions I naturally agreed, and yet how logical the Christians were—even if I was not yet persuaded by their arguments and I still doubted their evidence.

I spent every Wednesday evening after the Bible study grilling Jason and Biff with questions. It was not uncommon at all for us to spend all night in discussion. On more than one occasion, I had to rush out of their room, after nearly twelve hours of intense debate, to shower and head to my Thursday morning class. I also recall the times we continued our discussions late in the evening at the local Burger King. The staff would invariably come by, mopping the floor, saying, "Gentleman, I'm sorry, but I'm going to have to ask you to leave again. It's after four A.M. when we close. You're more than welcome to come back in two hours when we reopen."

Jason and Biff had a persuasive response to every argument I gave against God's existence, the Bible's trustworthiness, and Jesus' Resurrection, and, moreover, they had a persuasive answer to every question I asked. I could tell that by November Jason was getting a little frustrated, because I was exhausting the arguments—not their arguments, but my own. At one point he said something like, "What more evidence do you need? You know the arguments and the evidence better than any Christian I know!" He put his money where his mouth was; he and Biff got permission from the full-time staff of Campus Crusade to allow me to join a public open forum panel on the truth of Christianity. A Christian student and I would explain what Christians believe, what unites Christians, and then we would defend the claims.

"But I don't believe any of this", I protested.

"That's fine. But you know the arguments better than anyone. Use it as a testing ground. There will be philosophy grad students and others in attendance who might be able to help you find holes in Christianity that you haven't yet explored."

That sounded like a possibility, but I had read so much, it was difficult to imagine a smoking gun. The best I had, and it was not very persuasive, was the noncommittal, "maybe Christianity is not true." I had begun this quest as a sort of game with Jason and Biff. I never imagined at the time that, two months later, I would be in the position where I thought this was probably true! I'll never forget that open forum as long as I live. The skeptics in attendance had no solid arguments. At one point, one of the frustrated philosophy graduate students shot back at me, "you're only saying this because you're a Christian", to which I responded, "are you kidding me? I'm a Jewish agnostic who doesn't believe in God. I think all this stuff is nonsense, but I was hoping someone in the audience would be able to help me shoot Christianity down." I am confident that I left the room the most frustrated of everyone. Biff and Jason could not have been more pleased with how it went. I could not have been more disheartened.

I had been reading multiple articles, and sometimes multiple books, every single day since that first September Bible study. Having been a speed reader in high school helped, but my grades were hurting because I was skipping classes and assignments to conduct this extracurricular research. There were days when I spent sixteen or eighteen hours reading and taking notes. I was speaking with most of the intellectuals in my life. I was not able to converse with my grandfather on the topic because earlier that semester he had died of a massive heart attack while playing tennis. I was not really able to speak with my stepfather either; he was very ill with terminal cancer and would die early that next semester, just before his fiftieth birthday.

Reading Both Skeptics and Believers

Most of what I read from skeptics was of no help whatsoever. I read fairly widely and aimlessly, anything on the topics I could get my hands on. I had no filter or means of evaluating the quality of what I read other than the argumentation being laid out. I began to discover who the major scholarly critics of Christianity were (e.g., members of the infamous "Jesus Seminar") because of how often they were being responded to by Christian scholars. It was in vain that I sought out the arguments of the skeptics for help in tearing down Christianity, because their arguments were less persuasive than that of the Christians. I began to discover who the major Christian scholars were, again, by how many of their arguments were relied upon in popular works of apologetics like McDowell's—unfortunately, they were usually ignored by the skeptics.

I devoured the philosophical debates of atheist philosophers like Kai Nielsen and Flew with Christian philosophers like Moreland and William Lane Craig. Consistently, however, I found Craig's and Moreland's arguments to be more persuasive than Nielsen's and Flew's, even when I had some problems with Craig's and Moreland's arguments and when I agreed with Nielsen's and Flew's conclusions! It was incredibly frustrating. Peter Kreeft's works, especially his *Handbook of Christian Apologetics*,[14] coauthored with Father Ronald Tacelli, S.J., was most helpful because I could see the major Christian arguments and ignore the ones that were not that persuasive for me (like Saint Anselm's ontological argument) but really try to tackle the ones that were difficult. The cosmological arguments I found very challenging. Saint Thomas Aquinas' argument for the first mover was important as well as his argument from causation. Every effect has a cause. That made perfect sense to me; all of modern science is grounded on such an assumption. Yet there had to be a cause that is itself uncaused. Certainly, such arguments do not get you the Triune God of Christianity, but they sure helped make my more atheistic position problematic.

I saw how so much hung on Jesus' Resurrection. I had read quite a lot on the historical reliability of the Bible. Miami University's ancient historian Edwin Yamauchi had written extensively on this topic, and I read everything by Dr. Y, as we called him, that I could get my hands on. At the time, two of the more helpful of his books for me were his *Composition and Corroboration in Classical and Biblical*

---

[14] Peter Kreeft and Ronald K. Tacelli, *Handbook of Christian Apologetics* (Downers Grove, Ill.: InterVarsity Press, 1994).

Studies[15] and his *The Scriptures and Archaeology,*[16] both of which were dated even by then, but the main arguments of which I still believe hold true, namely, that the Bible is historically trustworthy. F. F. Bruce's classic, *The New Testament Documents: Are They Reliable?*[17] and Kenneth Kitchen's *Ancient Orient and Old Testament*[18] were also among the more helpful for me—Kitchen would later update and expand these arguments in his massive 2003 *On the Reliability of the Old Testament,*[19] which I think remains the best text on the topic to date.

All three of these scholars represent Evangelical traditions, and yet, they not only were serious scholars, but brought together persuasive arguments and evidence. They were all very careful in what they claimed and were never hesitant to criticize the arguments of others that would have supported their own positions. I found it quite common in more popular works of Christian apologetics that any argument or bit of evidence supporting the Christian claims would often be adopted quite uncritically. Yamauchi, Bruce, and Kitchen were not guilty of such things and disagreed with the arguments recycled in a number of popular works of apologetics. Also helpful for me were the popular and scholarly articles by these and other scholars. One example is Yamauchi's popular "Easter: Myth, Hallucination, or History?" which is now available free online on multiple sites.

The Bible as Trustworthy History

The evidence amassed in these volumes, as well as the arguments of the skeptics, taught me a few things. First, the overwhelming majority of the arguments against the historical trustworthiness of the Bible amounted to little more than arguments from silence or else arguments based on hypothetical compositional theories, which

---

[15] Edwin Yamauchi, *Composition and Corroboration in Classical and Biblical Studies* (Philadelphia: Presbyterian & Reformed, 1966).

[16] Edwin Yamauchi, *The Scriptures and Archaeology: Abraham to Daniel* (Portland: Western Conservative Baptist University, 1980).

[17] F. F. Bruce, *The New Testament Documents: Are They Reliable?* (1943; Leicester: InterVarsity Fellowship, 1953).

[18] K. A. Kitchen, *Ancient Orient and Old Testament* (Leicester: InterVarsity Press, 1966).

[19] K. A. Kitchen, *On the Reliability of the Old Testament* (Grand Rapids, Mich.: Eerdmans, 2003).

I was beginning to see unravel. It did not surprise me to find skeptical scholars advocate complex compositional theories that ended up supporting their skeptical positions. What surprised me more was finding secular Jewish scholars like Cyrus Gordon (Yamauchi's own teacher) and more mainstream scholars like Roger Norman Whybray (who also dated the Old Testament material skeptically late) utilize the same sorts of arguments against these positions as their Evangelical counterparts! What is more, I was finding their arguments persuasive! The little I read, e.g., from Gleason Archer's *A Survey of Old Testament Introduction*,[20] has since been increasingly confirmed in my later continued studies: the Pentateuch (Genesis through Deuteronomy) is replete with authentic background details that fit second-millennium Egypt—from where the Israelites emerged according to the biblical text—which supports the Bible's idea (but not that of contemporary more skeptical scholars) that these histories emerged from second-millennium Egypt and not first-millennium Babylon (as I have since found persuasively argued in, e.g., James Hoffmeier's *Israel in Egypt*[21] and his *Ancient Israel in Sinai*[22]).

As for the arguments from silence—"we don't find clear evidence of that in the archaeological record, therefore it didn't happen that way; the Bible is wrong"—Yamauchi's and Kitchen's classical explanations for this make sense, namely, as they both are so fond of pointing out in multiple works and in person, "the absence of archaeological evidence is not evidence of absence." Yamauchi's *The Stones and the Scriptures*[23] provides the best explanation of this, namely, that the archaeological record is by its very nature incredibly fragmentary, since of all that once existed, only a small fragment has survived, and only a small fragment of what has survived has been examined. We should not expect to find positive evidence for most things in such a context where all such evidence is inescapably fragmentary.

[20] Gleason L. Archer, *A Survey of Old Testament Introduction* (Chicago: Moody Bible Institute, 1994).

[21] James K. Hoffmeier, *Israel in Egypt: The Evidence for the Authenticity of the Exodus Tradition* (Oxford: Oxford University Press, 1997).

[22] James K. Hoffmeier, *Ancient Israel in Sinai: The Evidence for the Authenticity of the Wilderness Tradition* (Oxford: Oxford University Press, 2005).

[23] Edwin Yamauchi, *The Stones and the Scriptures: An Introduction to Biblical Archaeology* (Grand Rapids: Baker Book House, 1972).

But more powerful than this deft handling of the skeptical arguments, all of which these scholars addressed, were the positive lines
of evidence they brought forward. Unlike many of the apologists
who, like myself at the time, were limited to reading English or
a few modern European languages, these scholars were able to read a
wealth of the ancient documents in their original languages. Yamauchi, for example, had studied Akkadian, Egyptian, and Ugaritic,
along with Hebrew, Aramaic, Greek, and other ancient languages,
some of which he taught as an ancient history professor. Kitchen was
primarily an Egyptologist by training.

In fact, I was discovering that many of these Evangelical scholars were primarily trained in ancient languages and history, with
the Bible as an ancillary discipline for them, whereas most of the
skeptics were primarily Bible scholars who may or may not have
had much training in the relevant ancient languages (beyond, perhaps, the requisite knowledge of Greek and Hebrew). I quickly
came to the conclusion that the Bible appeared to be a collection of
the most historically reliable documents from ancient history. The
more comparable material was unearthed from the Bible's time and
place, the more the Bible dovetailed with the evidence, despite the
disappointed expectations of skeptics. Again and again, when such
comparable evidence was discovered, the biblical accounts were supported by external evidence.

The Reality of Jesus' Resurrection

This applied also to the New Testament and the historical events
surrounding the life of Jesus, just as it did to the Old Testament. I
even read the references to his crucifixion in the first-century Jewish
historian Josephus and in the first-century Roman historian Tacitus.
Neither Josephus nor Tacitus was a Christian apologist. Yet from
their writings, the basic contours of Jesus' life recorded in the New
Testament could be discerned: his wide following, his shameful death
by crucifixion, and the fact that his followers believed he lived on. As
I studied the events surrounding his death, his burial, the empty tomb,
and the eyewitness appearances, I could not find another explanation
that adequately accounted for all of the historical facts other than

the Resurrection, the answer the New Testament provides. I have written about this in my book for the Principium Institute, *Jesus' Resurrection: A Jewish Convert Examines the Evidence*. At the time, however, perhaps the most helpful book for me was William Lane Craig's scholarly tome *Assessing the New Testament Evidence for the Historicity of the Resurrection of Jesus*.[24]

Although more recently a few scholars had been denying the evidence of Jesus' burial and the empty tomb tradition, this flew in the face of all of the evidence. A more skeptical Jewish scholar of the New Testament, Geza Vermes, had conceded as much in his work *Jesus the Jew*, where he wrote, "In the end, when every argument has been considered and weighed, the only conclusion acceptable to the historian must be ... that the women who set out to pay their last respects to Jesus found to their consternation, not a body, but an empty tomb."[25] Why were Vermes and so many other skeptical scholars so ready to concede Jesus' burial and the empty tomb tradition?

The main reason was because all four Gospels, despite their different accounts, are united in depicting Jesus' women followers as the first witnesses of the empty tomb. The Gospels are clearly trying to convince their audience that Jesus, in fact, rose from the dead, and a Jewish audience could only have understood by that a bodily resurrection, hence the focus on the empty tomb. And yet, at the time, women's testimony was banned from both Jewish and Roman courtrooms. Their societies were so biased against women that no one would believe in the Resurrection—or just about anything—based on the evidence of women. Despite this, the Gospels depict the women as the first witnesses of the empty tomb.

The only explanation, as Vermes and others are forced to concede, is that it is because it is true that the women, in fact, were the first witnesses of the empty tomb. Had this not been the case, had the accounts been pure fiction, the fabricators would have placed Peter, James, John, or another of the more prominent male apostles as the first witnesses of the empty tomb, and yet, that is not what they did. Additionally, despite some skepticism about the burial of crucifixion victims, the

---

[24] William Lane Craig, *Assessing the New Testament Evidence for the Historicity of the Resurrection of Jesus* (Lewiston: Edwin Mellen Press, 1989).

[25] Geza Vermes, *Jesus the Jew* (1973; London: SCM Press, 1983), 41.

only archaeological evidence we have from crucifixion victims indicates that during Jesus' time, at least, Jewish victims of Roman crucifixion could be given proper burial, as evidenced by a Jewish man from
that time with a nail still stuck in his heel bone.

Thus, the major problem I encountered when examining the various theories concerning what happened to Jesus was the question of
mechanism and motive. How would someone steal Jesus' body, and
why would he do it? The "how" was an issue because there would
have been a large boulder sealing the tomb to keep out wild animals,
and also there was a guard of soldiers. How do we know the Gospels' account of the guard is accurate? I find Craig's argument here
persuasive, and that concerns the implied polemic in the Gospel texts
themselves.[26] Craig points out the logic of the argument:

> CHRISTIAN: "The Lord is risen!"
> JEW: "No, his disciples stole away his body."
> CHRISTIAN: "The guard at the tomb would have prevented any such
> theft."
> JEW: "No, his disciples stole away his body while the guard slept."
> CHRISTIAN: "The chief priests bribed the guard to say this."[27]

The response of the Jewish opponents in the Gospels is not something
the Gospel authors would fabricate. Since all of Jesus' most intimate
followers, as well as most of his early opponents, were Jewish, any
Jewish opposition would if possible have been erased by a fictional
Gospel writer. The only credible explanation for the depiction of
Jewish opposition, especially in light of early Christianity's Jewish
context, is that there was in fact opposition from these members of
the Jewish religious leadership. It would obviously have been more
persuasive to report, "and all the Jewish religious leaders recognized
and accepted Jesus as the Jewish Messiah." They could not write this,
because it did not happen.

The fact that the Gospels themselves provide what has historically
proven to be one of the most powerful arguments against Jesus' Resurrection, on the part of members of the Jewish opposition, namely,

---

[26] See, for example, Craig, *Assessing the New Testament Evidence*, and William Lane Craig,
"The Guard at the Tomb", *New Testament Studies* 30, no. 2 (1984): 273–81.
[27] Craig, *Assessing the New Testament Evidence*, 207.

that the disciples stole Jesus' body, can only be explained by recognizing that this was one of the real charges circulating at the time. Why else include this argument? Why provide ammunition to the opposition? Notice how the foundation of the Christian response, the guard at the tomb, was accepted by the opponents. Had there been no guard present, the opposition would not have come up with a story about the stealing of the body while the guard slept; rather, they simply would have denied that there was any guard present to begin with.

What Craig does when he covers this implied polemic is underscore how much both sides assume, how much they agree. They disagree on what happened to Jesus' body and on his Resurrection, but they both agree that Jesus was dead, that he was buried, that his tomb was in fact found empty, and that there was a guard protecting it. That is quite a lot. I realized that had one of those pieces of evidence, those data points, been the slightest bit controversial, you would have had historic protest, even before the nineteenth- and twentieth-century skeptics.

Equally difficult, or perhaps even more difficult, was the motive. Why would someone bother to steal Jesus' body? Those opposed to Christianity, had they stolen the body, could easily have ended the Christian movement by producing the stolen body as soon as the disciples went around proclaiming the risen Jesus and the empty tomb. And yet that clearly did not happen. Christianity, as had Judaism before it, preached a bodily resurrection, and the empty tomb was evidence of that bodily resurrection. Had the apostles stolen the body, they would have been in on the lie, and yet history shows that they all received torture for belief in the Resurrection, and all but John died for that belief. People die for things that are not true, and they suffer for such things, all the time. But people do not suffer torture and death for lies they know are not true.

Moreover, I had to deal with the matter of prophecy fulfillment. The most important Old Testament passage for me in this regard was the account of the suffering servant of the Lord from Isaiah 52:13—53:12, an entire Hebrew copy of which we have from more than two hundred years prior to Jesus' birth. I recognized that a common Jewish interpretation was that the singular servant was representative of the entire people of Israel, and yet the earliest Jewish interpretation, as evidenced, for example, in the Aramaic translation of Isaiah in the Targum, as well as in the Talmud, identified the figure as a future Messiah, which seemed to me to fit the evidence of the text better. Even the famous Jewish medieval sage Maimonides held that Isaiah 53 foretold the Messiah. I also had to explain the multiple accounts of his eyewitness appearances. They could not have been hallucinations, which are private and personal, since he appeared to multiple people at the same time. Such accounts eventually, after this time, convinced Vermes of the veracity of the post-Resurrection appearances in his later study of Jesus' Resurrection, even though he was unwilling to concede the Resurrection itself! What was I to do?

Accepting Jesus

The words of my stepfather kept coming back to me. Long before this investigation, in our many conversations about science and good reasoning, my stepfather had instilled in me the importance of following where the evidence led, attacking arguments, and never attacking conclusions. He said, "You don't want to attack the conclusions of an argument based on your opinion; any fool can have an opinion. You want to attack the arguments that led to the conclusion based on reason and the evidence." By the beginning of December, after these brief but intense months of research and struggle, I realized that what was holding me back from becoming a Christian was no longer evidence or reason, but rather that I was uncomfortable with the conclusion. I had an anti-supernatural bias. I began to recognize that my fears also held me back. What would all my Jewish friends and family think? I had not spoken with any of them about this process at all. Moreover, I had an uncomfortable emotional reaction to the name of Jesus. When I heard "God", my first thought was simply irrationality, but there was an emotional charge with "Jesus", probably due in part to having been beaten up as a kid by Christian classmates because I was Jewish. The difference for me between the very words "God" and "Jesus" was the difference between "assault" and "rape".

Late on the evening of December 4th, my Christian friend Donnie, from the Bible study, found me out in the hallway alone with my thoughts. He asked me what I was thinking about, and I explained how difficult a decision this was. He encouraged me gently, explaining quite wisely that we never know any of the really important things in life—whom we should marry, what career we should choose, how best to meet the needs of our future children— with 100 percent mathematical certitude; there is always faith involved, like when Indiana Jones had to step out on the invisible bridge in *Indiana Jones and the Last Crusade*. I do not remember everything Donnie left me with, but Indiana Jones had been my childhood hero. Several hours after he left, sometime between 5 and 5:30 A.M. on December 5th, I did what Evangelicals sometimes call "accepting Christ"; I prayed a spontaneous "sinner's prayer", thanking Jesus for dying for my sins and asking him to come into my life. I had lost my quest to disprove Jason and Biff. And yet somehow, though I did not fully realize it yet, I had ultimately emerged as a winner.

My First Answer to Prayer

I spent the next few hours praying to God. I had committed myself to Christianity, but I did not really know what that entailed. Our Bible study that semester had covered most of what a fresh-man study would cover in a year, but it was all very elementary material—the second semester we would read and study the entire New Testament. I knew, though, that I had so much to learn. I went to tell Jason and Biff what had happened, and they could not have been happier. Our friendship changed dramatically. They had lived with me in an apostolate of friendship. They not only bore with me patiently as I challenged Christianity but would take me out to dinner, invite me to social gatherings with their friends, etc. Now they began to model the Christian faith for me beyond the intellectual arguments, helping me learn what it meant to become a man of prayer and of Scripture, struggling to live as a Christian. Later that first evening, however, I heard that Donnie had been in a horrible car accident and was barely clinging to life as he had lost the majority of his blood and his body had rejected the initial blood transfusion. I joined a large gathering of Evangelicals to pray for Donnie, and when he survived, despite its looking impossible, I knew that had been an answer to our prayers.

Telling My Family

I spoke with my mother over the phone about this decision. Between the relatively recent death of her father and the imminent death of my stepfather, for whom she was caring, I do not think she was able to process everything, and I think she feared I had fallen in with some cult. I only had a few weeks before I was going home to see my dad, so I waited to tell him when we were face to face. He was certainly not happy, nor did he understand my decision. I had my notes with me, so I spent the first few days over the break distilling my notes into more than one hundred pages of a handwritten letter that covered the majority of the arguments that I had found persuasive. I later met with our rabbi, who had some very persuasive arguments against reading some of the Old Testament prophecies the way I thought they should be read (but not Isaiah 53), but I kept bringing the conversation back to Jesus' Resurrection, the foundational issue. What happened to Jesus' body? I emerged from that conversation confirmed in how solid the evidence for Jesus' Resurrection is, acknowledged by another Jewish scholar, Pinchas Lapide, who, despite being convinced as an historian of Jesus' Resurrection, never became a Christian.[28]

Looking back on this time from my vantage point now, more than twenty years later, I think the prayer and fasting Biff and Jason did for the future Bible study I would be in was far more decisive for my conversion than any of the intellectual components. I think that all of us in that freshman study benefited from their prayers: almost ten of us came to faith in Jesus for the first time, and three of us, including Jason, entered the Catholic Church. We've seen more than thirty of our friends and spouses from those next few years at Miami also enter the Catholic Church. The third Bible study member to become Catholic was Eric, who is now a priest for the Archdiocese of Cincinnati. All three of us entered at the Easter Vigil of the following

[28] Pinchas Lapide, *The Resurrection of Jesus: A Jewish Perspective* (Minneapolis: Augsburg Fortress, 1982).

year. Yes, the arguments were convincing, but our conversions were not simply the result of arguments.

Which Church?

I had so much to learn, even about just the basics of Christianity. I was now spending time in prayer and reading Scripture every day. From December to May of my freshman year, I read through every book of the Bible (including the deuterocanonical books absent from most Protestant Bibles) at least two times each. Already I saw the great diversity of Christianity and recognized that the different Christian communities, churches, and denominations disagreed on very important issues, including what one needs to actually get to heaven. None of my Evangelical friends encouraged me to get baptized, for example. Most of those I was encountering in the parachurch organizations seemed to encourage those who had been baptized as infants to get baptized as adults, but I had never been baptized, and since they saw it as merely a symbol, they never encouraged me to seek baptism.

Biff was Catholic, and Jason made it clear to me in private that he was rapidly becoming convinced of the truth of Catholicism as well. This intrigued me because these were the two most intelligent Christians I had thus far met. What sort of Christian should I be, and did it matter? I began attending a variety of different church services on Sundays, to get a sense of things, but most of them felt more like an abolishment of the Judaism I grew up with than a fulfillment. I attended the weekly Campus Crusade meeting, but again, I did not understand how this was the Christianity of the New Testament that I was reading, or a fulfillment of the Old Testament that I was poring over. When Biff took Jason and me to a Catholic Mass, we sat in the back and he explained everything that was going on. The Mass felt much more like a fulfillment of the Jewish liturgy, with the Eucharist taking the place of the Torah as the central part, than most of the Protestant services I had attended.

Studying the Denominations

I began reading popular, mainly Calvinist, theologians. I also began reading Catholics. I started reading through the papal encyclicals of

Pope Saint John Paul II, the reigning pontiff, and works of other theologians. One very helpful book was the newly published (in English) *Called to Communion*, by then Joseph Cardinal Ratzinger, now Pope Emeritus Benedict XVI.[29] Biff had a massive collection of Scott Hahn audio cassettes. I began listening to all of them, taking notes as I went, tracking down some of the sources Hahn mentioned throughout. The only books he had published by that time were *Rome Sweet Home*[30] and *A Father Who Keeps His Promises*,[31] both of which I read after making the decision to become Catholic. Most helpful for me, however, was his audio-cassette series walking through specific books of the Bible, such as Genesis, Exodus, the Gospel of Matthew, the Gospel of John, Acts, Romans, Hebrews, and the Book of Revelation.

The Historical Church Was the Catholic Church

I was rapidly moving toward Catholicism, so much so that by the spring break of my freshman year I was calling myself a "Catholic in desire". I spent each spring break with Campus Crusade on mission trips overseas: freshman year in Spain, sophomore and senior years in Macedonia, and junior year in Kosovo. I had the opportunity to get to know most of the full-time staff members, including the campus director, very well through these experiences. These were serious men and women of God who had been following Jesus for a number of years, many of whom were beginning to raise Christian families. I had begun studying church history intently, reading classic secondary sources like John Henry Newman as well as important contemporary scholars like Jaroslav Pelikan. Newman's *Essay on the Development of Christian Doctrine*[32] and Pelikan's *Emergence of the Catholic Tradition*[33]

[29] Joseph Cardinal Ratzinger, *Called to Communion: Understanding the Church Today*, trans. Adrian Walker (San Francisco: Ignatius Press, 1996).

[30] Scott and Kimberly Hahn, *Rome Sweet Home: Our Journey to Catholicism* (San Francisco: Ignatius Press, 1993).

[31] Scott Hahn, *A Father Who Keeps His Promises: God's Covenant Love in Scripture* (Cincinnati: Charis, 1998).

[32] John Henry Cardinal Newman, *An Essay on the Development of Christian Doctrine* (Notre Dame: University of Notre Dame Press, 1994).

[33] Jaroslav Pelikan, *The Christian Tradition: A History of the Development of Doctrine*, vol. 1, *The Emergence of the Catholic Tradition (100–600)* (Chicago: University of Chicago Press, 1971).

and *Reformation of Church and Dogma*[34] were particularly important for me. Pelikan's works were unique in that he wrote them while he was an ordained Lutheran minister, prior to his eventual conversion to Eastern Orthodoxy.

That summer after my freshman year, I read as much of the writings of the early Church Fathers in English as I could find online: the Apostolic Fathers, Saint Irenaeus, Saint Justin Martyr, Tertullian, and especially Saint Augustine. I also read mainly the biblical commentaries of the Reformers, like Luther and Calvin. Obviously, I did not read all of their works or commentaries, but I went to the commentaries of key books like Romans, Galatians, John, etc. As in summers past, I worked as a garbage man that summer, but when I was not working I was reading the writings of the Church Fathers or Protestant Reformers.

By the time the summer was over, I knew I had to be Catholic and thus I enrolled in RCIA. My readings in and on the early Church showed me that the early Church was essentially Catholic. They believed in the Real Presence of Jesus in the Eucharist, as Ignatius of Antioch, the early-second-century disciple of the apostle John who wrote John's Gospel, made clear. They venerated Mary; they had a hierarchical structure of bishops, priests, and deacons. The bishop of Rome was looked to, by both orthodox and heretic, as an authority figure, who was revered both East and West, at least in the earliest centuries.

Reformation Controversies

My study of the Reformation taught me two things. First, I began to see, despite the popular Protestant assumptions to the contrary that I encountered, how Catholic the Reformers actually were. Many of the large issues dividing Catholics and Protestants today, e.g., concerning Mary and the Eucharist, were more minor issues at the time. Their larger issues pertained to the role of tradition and salvation (e.g., by faith alone). Moreover, the Reformers were united in their acceptance of the perpetual virginity of Mary; in fact, Luther held a

---

[34] Jaroslav Pelikan, *The Christian Tradition: A History of the Development of Doctrine*, vol. 4, *Reformation of Church and Dogma (1300–1700)* (Chicago: University of Chicago Press, 1985).

quite high view of Mary, affirming all of the Catholic dogmas that were not even defined yet in his day. Luther and Calvin both understood baptism sacramentally, and Luther held a high sacramental view of the Eucharist, in contrast to much of the Evangelical Protestantism I was encountering.

The second thing I learned was that I disagreed with the Reformers in many of their biblical interpretations. Luther understood the faith that Saint Paul says justifies in Romans 3:28 as "faith alone" and, thus, added the word "alone" to his German translation of that passage. And yet, as he was fully aware, James teaches that works are what justify and not faith alone (Jas 2:24). The Evangelicals with whom I was in constant dialogue were adamant about the merely symbolic nature of the Lord's Supper, and yet I could not reconcile that with Jesus' teaching about the necessity of eating his Flesh and drinking his Blood in the Bread of Life discourse in John 6. When I was in RCIA my sophomore year, I would print out transcripts of some of Hahn's lectures that were posted online, especially his lecture on the "Fourth Cup", long before he had a book on that topic, and hand them to various Campus Crusade staff members and Bible study leaders.

At their encouragement, and not knowing what to do with me— since none of them had any arguments I found able to cast doubt on the Catholic interpretation of Scripture—I began to meet with Edwin Yamauchi, the famous historian whose works had helped me so much in my initial conversion to Christianity, who taught in the history department. Yamauchi and I have continued to keep up correspondence and exchange publications to the present day. He conceded much more than the full-time staff members would concede, including that Peter was the head of the apostles and clearly was the rock upon whom Jesus built his Church. Catholic teaching on the Eucharist and the papacy were the areas I became convinced were best attested in Scripture. Yamauchi had many resources for me to read, including his own coauthored church history book, *Two Kingdoms: The Church and Culture through the Ages*,[35] and yet, although I found his arguments persuasive for the historical reliability of the Bible in light of the broader

---

[35] Robert G. Clouse, Richard V. Pierard, and Edwin M. Yamauchi, *Two Kingdoms: The Church and Culture through the Ages* (Chicago: Moody Press, 1993).

context of the ancient Near East in which it was written—his main area of expertise—I found him far less persuasive in commenting on later church history.

This was something I noticed as I switched my majors to the majors with which I would graduate—I graduated with a double major in comparative religion and classical Greek, and minored in Jewish studies. I noticed how the more skeptical agnostic or atheist professors of history and religion seemed blind to their biases when it came to the foundations of Christianity and the history behind the Bible. Many of them were willing to accept almost any theory to get out of something supernatural. And yet, when these same historians and scholars approached Church history, they almost always took the "Catholic" side in interpretations that impinged upon Catholic-Protestant theological controversies. I found the exact opposite with Yamauchi, whom I found to be quite brilliant in commenting on the history behind the Bible and at the foundation of Christianity. And yet, when it came to something that seemed so clear to me, and so clear to agnostic scholars, like Ignatius of Antioch's affirmation of the Real Presence of Jesus in the Eucharist, he seemed unable to accept that interpretation of Ignatius.

My RCIA program taught me much about Catholicism as lived in the U.S. from a completely different vantage point. I had fallen in love with the Catholicism of the books. Now I was beginning to experience the Catholicism of the pews. I began attending Mass almost every day, even though I was not able to receive the Eucharist yet, something at the time I begrudged. God taught me patience, and I was able really to appreciate receiving the Eucharist after my baptism. I got to see how messy, complicated, and diverse the real Catholicism of Catholics is compared to the pristine Catholic theology of orthodox theologians. I did not like what I saw in people, but part of that, I think, is that I did not have an accurate view of myself. My weekly confessions since then have helped me to know myself better and, thus, have greater patience with others.

For me that Easter Vigil of 1999 was like a wedding, the RCIA having been an engagement. From that point forward, I was able to participate fully in the Church's rich sacramental life. I continued to study these matters, spending one summer at Campus Crusade staff training, where I sat in on, among other courses, a course on the Book of Romans. I challenged the professor with the Catholic view and was unable to find an intellectually satisfying response. All of my studies and dialogues since have continued to solidify my conclusion that the Catholic Church was the Church Jesus founded, as evidenced in the Bible, and that the sacraments are a primary means of our living our Christian relationship with God.

Vocation

I went on from Miami to earn my M.A. and Ph.D. in Catholic theology just down the road from Oxford, at the University of Dayton, which is a Catholic and Marianist university. Despite all my reading and conversations, I knew I still had much to learn about the faith, and I could not imagine a different career path than one that would allow me to continue studying the faith. At the University of Dayton, I was given the opportunity to study under professors who had been raised Catholic and really knew the lived experience of Catholicism in the U.S. During this time, I also began to grow in what my doctoral advisor, William Portier, would call "devotional knowledge". I was immersed—not only in a Catholic theology program but also in Catholic prayer life, finding my home within the Church.

While Biff was now my roommate and classmate at Dayton, our dear friend Jason's wedding date was set. It was the first year of my doctoral program and right before my first general exam, and Biff and I were both to serve as groomsmen in the wedding. On the drive to the wedding, Biff and I prayed Psalm 150 together, thus completing my 150 days of prayer for discernment of my vocation within the life of the Church. As we prepared for the wedding rehearsal at the back of the Church, I was introduced to a bridesmaid named Maria, who had been the freshman year roommate of Jason's fiancée. That first conversation revealed that, although she was now teaching at an elementary school in California, she had actually majored in theology and philosophy. It seemed we would have a lot to talk about at the wedding reception ... and we did. I made sure I left with her email address and planned to get in touch with her after I had taken my exam.

To make a long story short, we began formally dating with a long-distance relationship on November 1st. After much conversation and a few cross-country flights to see each other, we were engaged just a few months later, on February 9th. Maria moved to Dayton to begin the M.A. program in theology, and we were married on May 21st, 2005.

Marriage and Family

A shared passion for Catholic theology can go far in a marriage, but the challenges of beginning a family while doing doctoral work should not be underestimated! The stress of applying for jobs in a limited market, knowing that you have a family depending on you financially, certainly requires some faith. Yet somehow, by the grace of God and the assistance of Saint Joseph, I secured a job at Seton Hall University's Immaculate Conception Seminary School of Theology in 2009, and Maria was able to defend her doctoral dissertation several years later.

No doubt my eighteen-year-old self would be astonished at a peek into the future that included life as a professor at a Catholic seminary while raising a family with seven children. Now I find myself faced with different kinds of challenges, such as how best to raise our children in the faith, since I did not grow up Catholic myself. Most of all, I hope my children can come to recognize what I have realized since my conversion: God's providential mercies have been ever present in my life, although I was not really aware of them until after I began to recognize that he is and that he was calling me to be his friend, and more than a friend, his son.

The parts of my journey that stand out are mostly intellectual, but the reality is that my conversion is the result of the prayers of many people, some of whom I mention here, but above all, my conversion is the work of the Holy Spirit, who never gave up on me and who I know will never give up on me. Many of my obstacles were intellectual, and so the Lord led me to individuals he knew would be able to help remove those obstacles to my experiencing his love. Fundamentally, that is what all conversion is about, the love of God. Conversion is about God loving us into existence and his ever-patient wooing us until we recognize that the ultimate answer to our questions, the ultimate love after which our hearts long, is only to be found in him. Everyone's story is different, because each of us is different. And each conversion is really a love story, a story of how God was able to break through and rescue us, his beloved, from dungeons of sin and despair.

Chapter 8

JONAH THE CROWD-SURFER BECOMING AN EXEGETE OF THE BYZANTINE TRADITION

by

Rev. Andrew J. Summerson, S.Th.D.

For Josh

I crowd-surfed for the first time when I was sixteen. It was the summer of 2002 at an outdoor music festival, the Vans Warped Tour.
I spent the whole year training for this moment. I downloaded
MP3s, traded mix CDs, and memorized the lyrics of the bands in
the lineup. Leading up to the concert, I spent weekends at music
venues, either listening to local music and the occasional national act,
or imitating our heroes with my band, Desi in Vegas. I started that
band on an invitation from the drummer, Josh. We knew each other
from playing around in other groups and he wanted to take a stab
at playing together. What sealed the deal for me was not jamming
in the basement but singing in his car. Josh and I shared the same
soundtrack. While I grew up on grunge that my mother played on
the radio, when my own tastes developed, I found "emo": a sub-
genre that turned punk's loud, political protests in on itself. Instead
of screaming about cultural revolution, emo analyzed its musicians'
insecurities with the same intensity. The genre began in the D.C.
music scenes with bands like Rites of Spring and Embrace during

the 1980s.[1] I came of age around its third instantiation, listening to bands from New York and New Jersey, the most important of which to me was Saves the Day. Its lead singer, Chris Conley, suffers from Crohn's disease, and his physical pain served as conceits for his emotional distress: "'Cause I don't think that I have got the stomach to stomach calling you today."[2] His visceral metaphors introduced us to lyrics that went beyond the basic abstractions of bad teenage poetry. Saves the Day gave Josh and me images concrete enough to bite into while singing along with Conley's strained tenor. And we did so ... loudly. With Josh, I never felt insecure about shouting Saves the Day lyrics together. In the car, Josh and I could be candid with words, expressing our intimate secrets with someone else's scripture. With lyrics memorized, we would go to our heroes' shows, and they were waiting for us to join in, ceding the mic to the audience to sing the chorus. For a moment, I felt a part of something bigger than myself. The crowd was a body bigger than the sum of its parts, and its hands and arms were strong enough to lift me physically to the front of the stage, the source of energy. Screaming in the mosh pit before the band, I saw that crowd-surfing is a natural consequence of elated emotion. Taken up by the music, you could rely on the strength of others to lift you when you could not otherwise carry yourself.

That morning of the Warped Tour, I needed to feel light. Earlier that day, I had accompanied my grandmother to Lakewood Hospital to visit my aunt, who had just given birth to Caleb. Prior to this pregnancy, my aunt had aborted several children. My aunt's earliest abortion that I can remember happened when I was twelve. With the help of my mother, she stole my grandmother's credit card to do it. They both thought the credit card would fix the problem. They vowed to buy the family Christmas presents, then cut up the card and pay it off without grandma knowing. Instead, after the abortion, they maxed out the credit card with cash advances and jewelry. The scheme was exposed at the luncheon of the funeral of my great-uncle, my grandma's brother.

<hr/>

[1] See Andy Greenwald, *Nothing Feels Good: Punk Rock, Teenagers, and Emo* (New York: St. Martin's Press, 2003).
[2] Saves the Day, "See You", track 2 on *Stay What You Are*, Vagrant Records, 2001, compact disc.

My aunt's pregnancy with Caleb caught her by surprise and snagged her conscience. She kept him to term and put him up for open adoption. The adoptive parents were medical doctors living in Cleveland Heights, across the river from my West Side Cleveland home. It was a beautiful juxtaposition. My aunt, who could do little more than self-medicate with methadone, gave her child over to medical doctors who could care for him. He would live across the river and be given a chance at life instead of death. In an instant, his whole life was different, down to his name. They renamed him Jonah. Through the haze of my tears, I saw my cousin handed over into the arms of a miracle. Though grateful, I needed my own handing-over. Crowd-surfing did the trick that day, holding me steady when I could not carry myself.

Finding Baptism between the Bars

I owe my conversion to Byzantine Catholic Christianity to many hands, hands coming from the Church that reached out to me as a kid. My intellectual commitments would come later. I am a student of Byzantine theology—since we only reserve the title "theologian" for select saints[3]—because I made a decision to serve the Church that picked me up when I needed it most. My research aims to hand over the best version of that Church to others. As a young man, I experienced the hands of the Church's charity through her institutions. John Henry Cardinal Newman is right when he tells us that "Christianity ... has long since passed beyond the letter of documents and the reasonings of individual minds, and has become public property."[4] Christianity's first impression is sometimes best made with its monuments before its mental habits, as I saw in my own life growing up. At a time when the Byzantine Catholic Church in the United States had all but abandoned the educational apostolate,

---

[3] The Eastern Christian tradition uses the title of "theologian" for three saints in particular: John the Evangelist, Gregory Nazianzus, and Symeon the "New Theologian". The selective use of "theologian" indicates the difficulty of making true statements about God, the fruit of contemplative experience.

[4] John Henry Newman, "Introduction", in *An Essay on the Development of Christian Doctrine* (London: Longmans, Green, 1906), 2.

my home parish's staunch defense of its adjoined Catholic school kept the Church's hands outstretched to care for the community and caught me up in it. The patinaed twin domes of Saint Mary's Byzantine Catholic Church, with the kindly face of the Mother of God on its façade, broke above the normal roofline of continual bars and fortune-teller storefronts that lined State Road. Built with the same brick and mortar, all these venerable institutions tried to care for the same people, however imperfectly. My family never ducked into church, but they knew our name at the Sports Inn, where my aunt tended bar, or at the Grey Wolf Tavern, where my uncle would cash his check every Friday, not leaving before he gave them his tithe.

Church entered my life when I was ten. Gutted by white flight, the city of Cleveland's tax base was not strong enough to support an overbuilt and underperforming school system. After a few years of trying out public schools, my single mother decided it best to get "a decent Catholic education". All the neighborhood Catholic schools had waiting lists, except for Saint Mary's. In ways similar to the mosh pit, this place would have the strength and grace to carry me through my mess.

During my time, Saint Mary's was still staffed by the Sisters of Saint Basil the Great, a Byzantine Catholic order of nuns based in Uniontown, Pennsylvania. As a priest, I hear many people tell me stories of stern nuns who taught them with the business end of a ruler. In my case, the Sisters were gentle. Sister Agnes taught us how to pray, with her hands, both delicate and serious, clutching the rosary. We saw her with the other Sisters crouched in the church before the school day began, rosary in hand. She would later share this experience with us, leading a decade of the rosary at the beginning of every religion class, followed by a decade of the Jesus Prayer: "O Lord, Jesus Christ, Son of God, have mercy on me, a sinner." Before each rosary, Sister Agnes would invite us to say our prayer intentions aloud. My classmates and I were candid. Some prayed for their sister's addictions, others prayed for their sick dog. In the sixth grade, I prayed regularly that my mom would receive her child support check, which I had overheard was not coming. I was unaware that, in fact, it was coming, but overspent by the time it arrived. Sister Agnes took note and folded our intentions into her slight hands before she led us in prayer. The day before Christmas break, Sister Agnes asked me to come to her classroom. She presented me with a Christmas care package the parish had collected for needy families in the school. I walked home down State Road past the taverns and tarot card readers, unable to see over the top of the basket. This gift came from the Church. After this experience, I knew I wanted to belong to the source of that charity.

I later asked Sister Agnes what it took to become Byzantine Catholic. She took matters into her own hands. She made an appointment with the pastor and discussed the process with me. I was to go to liturgy every Sunday. Religion class during the school week would serve as baptismal preparation. Sister Agnes decided that it would be best that I be baptized during the school day, offering the other students a chance to witness the sacraments of one of their peers. On the last day of eighth grade, I received the Mysteries of Initiation, Baptism, Chrismation, and Eucharist.

At fourteen, my newfound Christianity was caught in the crosshairs of adolescent existential crises. I do not belittle this intense time. We sometimes forget that teenagers are painfully serious. They experience the full spectrum of emotions, before learning the adult art of delusion. John Hughes, whose melodramatic teen movies like *The Breakfast Club* babysat me as a child, gets it right. When movie critic Roger Ebert asked Hughes why he cast teens in such intense dramas, he replied: "People forget that when you're sixteen, you're probably more serious than you'll ever be again. You think seriously about the big questions."[5] All my big questions were wet with baptismal water. Questions like "Who am I?" collided with "What kind of Christian should I be?" I continued at a Roman Catholic high school and regularly participated in their active campus ministry. This kept Church in my frame of vision. Nevertheless, anxieties about love, longing, loss, and belonging found relief through the act of singing to or with a crowd. I never found an answer, but I did get some catharsis and clever ways to speak about it. Leading retreats and being a lead singer made priesthood a viable choice, which required me to be a

[5] "John Hughes: When you're 16, you're more serious than you'll ever be again", Roger Ebert.com, last accessed May 26, 2020, https://rogerebert.com/roger-ebert/john-hughes-when-youre-16-youre-more-serious-than-youll-ever-be-again.

front man of a different sort. I had little idea about what priestly life entailed, other than my perception that it was a way to be a "serious" Christian. As the only practicing Catholic in my family, I occasionally experienced Christianity intensely on retreats but had little familiarity with its daily rigors. I did, however, know what type of Christian I chose to be. I was Byzantine Catholic. I observed the external differences, such as how I made the Sign of the Cross, and the continuous singing of the liturgy. I knew I was odd. Vocational discernment during university gave me the space to explore the difference.

My Apophatic Way to the Liturgy

Until university, music consumed my life and left little time for interest in academics. I was able to coast along with a good GPA in high school, but I lived to play music on the weekends. In college, however, I brought the zeal and discipline I developed in practice spaces to the classroom. I majored in philosophy, English, and Catholic studies at the local Jesuit college, John Carroll University. There, I was able to engage Eastern Christian interests as I considered the priesthood. I enrolled in an Eastern Christianity class, where for the first time I learned about the Sunday experience I was supposed be having. We read John Paul II's apostolic letter *Orientale Lumen*, written to acquaint the wider Catholic Church with the riches of the Christian East. John Paul II dedicated much reflection to the "genius of Eastern liturgy", emphasizing its power to envelop all of our human senses into the fullness of the mystery of God. It is worth quoting in full:

> Within this framework, liturgical prayer in the East shows a great aptitude for involving the human person in his or her totality: the mystery is sung in the loftiness of its content, but also in the warmth of the sentiments it awakens in the heart of redeemed humanity. In the sacred act, even bodiliness is summoned to praise, and beauty, which in the East is one of the best loved names expressing the divine harmony and the model of humanity transfigured, appears everywhere: in the shape of the church, in the sounds, in the colors, in the lights, in the scents. The lengthy duration of the celebrations, the repeated invocations, everything expresses gradual identification with the mystery

celebrated with one's whole person. Thus the prayer of the Church already becomes participation in the heavenly liturgy, an anticipation of the final beatitude.[6]

Subjective experiences of the liturgy proved quite potent in the history of the Christian East. It led to the baptism of the entire kingdom of the Kievan Rus in A.D. 988. As the story goes, its ruler, Saint Vladimir the Great, sent emissaries to find a religion fit for his kingdom. On their return from Constantinople to Rus, Saint Vladimir's envoys convinced him to accept baptism in the Byzantine tradition on behalf of the nation precisely because of their experience of the liturgy: "We knew not whether we were in heaven or on earth. For on earth there is no such splendor or such beauty, and we are at a loss how to describe it. We only know that God dwells there among men.... For we cannot forget that beauty."[7]

Reading these texts, I noticed the dissonance between these commentaries and the experience of my own parish. Byzantine theology is said to prioritize the apophatic, preferring to speak of the mystery of God by way of negation. My liturgical experience growing up was apophatic, demonstrating little of John Paul's maximalist vision or Saint Vladimir's emissaries' glowing reports. At Saint Mary's, deferred maintenance deteriorated the plaster and left it chipped and cracked along the wall. The choir struggled to maintain the repertoire of its founder and robbed the worshippers of any regular congregational singing, a hallmark of the Eastern Catholic Churches. The cantor, who stood in for the choir, preferred to solo and collapsed the entire eight-tone system of chant into one of her own devising. The priest prided himself on being short, both for "the sake of the people's" attention span, but also so he could go back to the rectory for a smoke. I was baptized into that experience. I can see now how the impotency of this scene is outmatched by the excess of providence. As Jean Corbon, himself an exegete of the Byzantine liturgy, writes: "In the celebration of the sacraments, just as in our life in the Spirit,

---

[6] John Paul II, apostolic letter *Orientale Lumen* (May 2, 1995), http://www.vatican.va /content/john-paul-ii/en/apost_letters/1995/documents/hf_jp-ii_apl_19950502_orientale -lumen.html, section 11.

[7] *The Russian Primary Chronicle*, trans. S. H. Cross and O. P. Sherbowitz-Wetzor (Cambridge, Mass.: Mediaeval Academy of America, 1953), 111.

there is an inverse proportion between spectacle and authenticity, between appearance and effectiveness. In his masterpieces the Father uses a minimum of show and a maximum of omnipotence."[8] The fissure between the church I read about and the church I lived did not deter me but urged me on to exploration. By this time, I recognized that, however imperfectly, the Byzantine Catholic Church lulled me into Christianity, not with her aesthetic trappings, but with the loving hands of her members. As such, the Church deserved a fair shot. So I went on pilgrimage to give it one.

In Search of Heaven on Earth in Chicago

> I fell in love again
> All things go, all things go
> Drove to Chicago
> All things know, all things know.
>
> —Sufjan Stevens, "Chicago"

In college, I listened to too much Sufjan Stevens. The indie rock musician's God-haunted lyrics reveal Christianity as an elemental tool in artistic composition. Stevens comments as much, saying, "It's not so much that faith influences us as it lives in us. In every circumstance (giving a speech or tying my shoes), I am living and moving and being."[9] In his song "Chicago", Stevens makes a simple road trip to the Windy City sound like a religious experience: "You came to take us / All things go, all things go / To recreate us / All things grow, all things grow."[10] Songs like this made a pilgrimage to Chicago seem irresistible. My sophomore year was the first of several college trips

---

[8] Jean Corbon, *The Wellspring of Worship*, trans. M.J. O'Connell (San Francisco: Ignatius Press, 2005), 139. Corbon's work is a living example of this juxtaposition. The French-born Melkite priest served in Beirut. Desiring an Eastern Catholic voice, the Commission on the Catechism of the Catholic Church selected him to compose the fourth section on prayer. This contemplative masterpiece was written during an intense period of war in Beirut, where he frequently had to retreat to the basement during bombings. See Cassian Folsom, "The Holy Spirit and the Church in History", *Homiletic and Pastoral Review* 96, no. 7 (April 1996): 15–23.

[9] David Roark, "How Sufjan Stevens Subverts the Stigma of Christian Music", *The Atlantic*, March 29, 2015.

[10] Sufjan Stevens, "Chicago", track 9 on *Come on Feel the Illinoise!*, Asthmatic Kitty Records, 2005, compact disc.

to Chicago. For the first time, I stopped at Annunciation Byzantine Catholic Parish. Its pastor, Father Thomas Loya, combined four floundering communities into one healthy, robust church in Homer Glen, Illinois. A commercial artist by training, Father Loya filled the church, floor to ceiling, with his own iconography. Depicting brightly colored scenes of salvation history and transfigured saints in a seamless whole, it had an impressive effect. On the southern wall, Father Loya's depiction of Christ's "Harrowing of Hell" imitates the famous image found in the Church of the Holy Savior in Chora, modern-day Istanbul. It features a muscular Christ in dazzling white with the broken bars and locks of Hades strewn at his feet, lifting up Adam and Eve to new life. Christ seems poised to burst forth from the wall into the crowd. This is intentional. Father Loya's icons are meant to inspire iconic worship among the congregation, uniting on earth with what is in heaven. When I entered the church for the first time, it was standing room only, with parishioners flowing out into the vestibule. The cantors in the back erupted in waves of sound that caught you in the undertow. The cantors and the acoustics urged you to throw your voice into the ether. It would bounce around the dome and join the one, full-throated voice of the Body of Christ.

At Annunciation, I found a liturgy that lived up to the legends I was reading in my Eastern Christianity class. Also, for the first time I found a Church that matched the emotional pitch of the music scene where I spent my weekends. In clubs and in cars, music ripped me open from the inside out and called me out of myself. I would not call it heaven on earth, but it did put me in touch with something ineffable, if only ephemeral. The worship at Annunciation Church did something more. It united temporal emotions with eternal longings, my own heart with God's inner life. The Byzantine Catholic tradition, at its best, enjoys an intense, congregational form of worship, in contrast to other practitioners of the Byzantine rite, who by and large restrict singing to a small coterie of professionals. The populist impulse of the Byzantine Catholic Church can be dated to one energetic priest working in the Austro-Hungarian Empire 150 years ago, named Father Papp.[11] With his own

[11] Simon Marincak, "Notes on Congregational Singing in the Eparchy of Mukacevo", in *Unity and Variety in Orthodox Music: Theory and Practice Proceedings of the Fourth International Conference on Orthodox Church Music University of Eastern Finland Joensuu, Finland, 6–12 June 2011*, ed. Ivan Moody and Maria Takala-Roszczenko Jyväskylä (Finland: The International Society for Orthodox Church Music, 2010), 63–71.

money, the priest underwrote the cost of printing service books that contained all the texts of Vespers, Matins, and Divine Liturgy for Sundays and the Twelve Feasts to feed his people with prayers. By the twentieth century, congregational singing was bred-in-the-bone in the traditional homeland of the Byzantine Catholic Church, modern-day western Ukraine. The practice of congregational singing caught the attention of Orthodox musicologist Johann von Gardner,[12] who, remarking on his experience, wrote the following:

> In Carpatho-Russia, in all village churches, congregational chant-ing at all the services in their entirety has been practiced exclusively, including the hymns of the "proper", utilizing the full range of tones and melodies. The people chant from the Great Anthology [Velikii Zbornik], which contains all the necessary texts, which are quite diverse ... [and] were well known to all, even to school children.... The impression produced was one of extraordinary power.[13]

Gardner used these observations to urge greater congregational partici-pation in his own Russian Orthodox Church, where liturgical responses during his time were largely performed by a choir, with the excep-tion of the Creed and the Our Father and perhaps the hymn "Having Beheld the Resurrection of Christ", sung during the all-night-vigil service.[14] Gardner was impressed that the people "were unconsciously memorizing the texts", as they sang the services, chanting large chunks of the service from memory, without the aid of the book at all.[15] What Gardner witnessed was more than an example of worship lost to the annals of liturgical history, but a fulfillment of what David Fagerberg calls "Theologia prima", the primal encounter of theology, which, in turn, is internalized by the worshipper and cultivates his worldview.[16]

---

[12] His major studies are *Russian Church Singing*, vols. 1 & 2, ed. V. Morosan (Crestwood, N.Y.: 1980 and 2000).

[13] Johann von Gardner, "Several Observations on Congregational Chanting during the Divine Services", in *Readings in Russian Religious Culture*, vol. 4, *Russian Liturgical Music Revival in the Diaspora*, ed. M. Ledkovsky and V. von Tsurikov (Jordanville, N.Y.: St. Vladi-mir's Seminary Press, 2012), 264.

[14] For his views, see Johann von Gardner, "Still More on Congregational Chanting of the Divine Services", in *Russian Liturgical Music Revival in the Diaspora*, 272–77.

[15] Gardner, "Several Observations on Congregational Chanting during the Divine Ser-vices", 264.

[16] David Fagerberg, *Theologia Prima: What Is Liturgical Theology?*, 2nd ed. (Chicago: Hillen-brand Books, 2004).

Adding the Fathers to My Mix

With its hymns and prayers forged in the first millennium, the Byzantine tradition discloses the theological vision of the Church Fathers,
which, drawing from the Second Vatican Council, is an essential part
of divine revelation entrusted to the Eastern Churches as a gift to the
entire Church.[17] When gathered for worship, Eastern Catholics sing
a theology owed to the springtime of emergent Christianity. This
fact conditioned my choice to do a doctorate in patristic theology
at the Pontifical Patristic Institute "Augustinianum" in Rome, after
I finished my theological studies at the Pontifical Gregorian University and the Pontifical Russian College in preparation for priesthood. If I was going to be an effective interpreter of the language of
the Byzantine tradition for others, I wanted to master its grammar. The
Augustinanum offered the ideal place to get an industrial-strength
dose of the Fathers of the Church. The Augustinanum provided
space and time to study the writers of the first millennium in their
original languages, to immerse myself in Church history, and to
explore the art and archaeology of the early Church. Professors
made these figures come alive and we engaged with their ideas,
as they interpreted the Word of God and laid the foundation
of theology.

The Byzantine liturgy is remixed psalmody and patristic commentary, a pastiche of Scripture woven together to present one single
song of salvation that we are to take and make our own. The music
I listened to growing up gave me words to narrate my interior life
and offered a momentary sense of relief in the evenings at shows,
fickle and fleeting. Bright Eyes nails this feeling in "Lua". The song
is full of enjoyable evenings—at parties, in love, and on drugs—but
makes a full stop at the end: "What is so simple in the moonlight,
by the morning never is."[18] The words of the liturgy I prayed provided similar concrete vehicles on which I could hang my dreams,
desires, and failures, but these words were not escapes. Instead, they
brought them before the only One who could do something about

[17] Vatican Council II, Decree on the Catholic Churches of the Eastern Rite *Orientalium Ecclesiarium* (November 21, 1964), http://www.vatican.va/archive/hist_councils/ii_vatican_council/documents/ vat-ii_decree_19641121_orientalium-ecclesiarum_en.html, section 1.

[18] Bright Eyes, "Lua", track 4 on *I'm Wide Awake, It's Morning*, Saddle Creek Records, 2005, compact disc.

it. My vocational and intellectual interests developed with a view to handing these words over to others to articulate their guttural need for transformation. As I discovered through study, the connection I sensed between the worlds I loved—Father Loya's electric liturgy that I sang along with and the emo music I belted in Josh's car—was not of my own fanciful invention. The psalms give us a grammar to emote properly, a vernacular with which to enter into divine discourse. Precisely through their singing, the psalms open up a space to meet God and be moved and molded by him.

One of the earliest prescriptions on Christian prayer is Athanasius of Alexandria's *Letter to Marcellinus*, which reflects on the use of the psalms. For Athanasius, the psalms are a garden (Greek: παράδεισος), a new Eden, where God and man meet in the music of poetry. Among the garden's fruits is the summary of all of Scripture: the law, the writings, but especially the prophecies, Christologically understood.[19] Christ is present in almost every line of the Psalter, from his conception to the Last Judgment and everything in between.[20] Along with Christ, we find in the psalms all the emotions of the human soul: "For I believe that the whole of human existence, both the dispositions of the soul and the movements of the thoughts, have been measured out and encompassed in those very words of the Psalter. And nothing beyond these is found among men."[21] Athanasius tells us that we unlock this garden precisely by singing. The "broad voice" of the worshipper cracks open the compressed words of Scripture, turning the text into a space where he can dwell. Singing the psalms tunes our soul into "a living Psalter", molding us into a well-calibrated instrument of God's praise: "Thus, as in music there is a stringed instrument, so the human being becoming himself a psalter (αὐτὸς ὁ ἄνθρωπος ψαλτήριον γενόμενος) and devoting himself wholly to the

---

[19] *Ep. Marcell.* 3, translated in Athanasius, *The Life of Antony and the Letter to Marcellinus*, trans. R. C. Gregg (Mahwah: Paulist Press, 1980) (translation modified): "Yet the Book of Psalms is like a garden (παράδεισος) containing things of all these kinds [the Torah, the Writings, and the Prophets], and it sets them to music, but also exhibits its own properties (τὰ ἴδια) that it gives in song along with them."

[20] "The pronouncements of the Prophets are declared in nearly every psalm. About the visitation of the savior and that he will make his journey as one who is God." *Ep. Marcell.* 5 (translation modified).

[21] *Ep. Marcell.* 30.

spirit, may obey the spirit in all his members and movements, and serve the will of God."²² The first-person voice of the Psalmist aims to transform us, by uniting our voice to God the Word heard in every psalm.

Like Athanasius, Augustine sees Christ throughout the Psalter, specifically his Body, both its Head and its members, the Church. For Augustine, singing the Psalter makes the "wondrous exchange" of the Word-made-flesh happen anew: Christ's divinity is united to our wounded humanity. The psalms wed our voice to God's. Augustine affirms that Paul's "great mystery" (cf. Eph 5:31–32) is at play: "If two in one flesh, why not two in one voice? Therefore let Christ speak, because the church speaks in Christ, and Christ speaks in the church, both body in the head and head in the Body."²³ The psalms need to cut deep to effect such a healing. Augustine's reminder to his congregation in North Africa is left for us to hear: "If the Psalm prays, you pray; if it groans, you groan."²⁴ Incorporation into the Body of Christ means lending our own groanings to the Lord himself. For this reason, the psalms are keen to reveal vulnerable flesh for what it is, not unlike the coarse conceits Saves the Day sang about in the car with Josh: the psalms expose our bones through our gaunt skin (Ps 22:17), a human heart melted like wax (Ps 22:14), a body broken out in fever (Ps 38:7). The psalms know pain at its most torturous, but they do not just leave us wallowing in lament. The psalms speak of God's care and protection for our fragile bodies. He bottles our tears up and writes them in his book (Ps 56:8). Though our bones may grow weary, God guards them from breaking (Ps 34:20).

Drawing from this patristic meditation, Byzantine prayer life organizes the psalms throughout the day, giving us divine words written by human hands to narrate our way through our emotions. At the beginning of Matins, separation from God consumes us, burying us in isolation: "I am reckoned as one in the tomb; I have reached the end

---

²² Ep. Marcell. 24 (translation modified). "It is fitting for the Divine Scripture to praise God not in compressed speech alone, but also in the voice that is richly broadened (ἀλλὰ καὶ τῇ κατὰ πλάτος φωνῇ τὸν Θεὸν ὑμνεῖν)." Ep. Marcell. 27.

²³ Enn. in Ps. 30[2]. I am indebted to Michael C. McCarthy, S.J., "An Ecclesiology of Groaning", in The Harp of Prophecy, ed. B.E. Daley and P. Kolbet (South Bend, Ind.: University of Notre Dame Press, 2015), 227–56, here 237.

²⁴ Enn. Ps. 30[4], 3.1. Cf. McCarthy, "An Ecclesiology of Groaning", 229.

of my strength" (Ps 88:4). The thrust of these beginning Matins psalms moves from alienation to hope for communion, culminating in the daily refrain of Psalm 118, which functions as a sort of theme song of Byzantine morning prayer: "The Lord is God and has revealed himself to us, blessed is he who comes in the name of the Lord" (v. 27). In the original Greek, the liturgy uses this psalm to play on the verb *epiphanisen*, an "epiphany", meaning both to reveal and to shed light upon. The daily chanting of this psalm as the sun rises calls to mind Christ, who comes to earth as the Light of the world to dispel the darkness.

Left to our own devices, we may content ourselves to sing of alienation without resolution. In the verses of the psalms, we are accompanied in our estrangement and transformed. In Psalm 51, chanted no fewer than four times a day in the Byzantine office, the Psalmist reveals his remorse for his sinfulness with intense immediacy. Our faults linger for more than the moment of our realization. They consume us to the point where we imagine ourselves muddled in sin from our conception: "O see, into sins I was born, a sinner was I conceived" (v. 5). The psalm, however, narrates a way out. We ask for rescue to turn our sorrow into a song of promise: "O Rescue me, God, my helper, and my tongue will ring out your goodness; O Lord, open my lips and my mouth will declare your praise" (v. 14–15). The Psalmist also presents exaltation at its most acute. At Vespers, the beginning of the Byzantine liturgical day, we stand before the creation as God sees it, singing Psalm 104. Echoing the affirmation of created goodness in Genesis, the Psalmist exclaims, "How many are your works, O Lord, in wisdom you have made them all!" (v. 24). At the end of Matins, we sing the psalms of praise, where we share the hasty exuberance of the Psalmist, who clears out the orchestra pit and asks that we take every instrument at hand to finish the triumphant coda, "Let everything that lives or that breathes give praise to the Lord" (Ps 150:6).

Christ the Sea Monster: Liturgy and the Transformation of the Self

"No sign shall be given to [this generation] except the sign of Jonah.
Just as Jonah became a sign to the men of Nineveh,
so will the Son of man be to this generation."

—Luke 11:29–30

Byzantines, however, do more than psalmody: they sing their theology. Its hymnography is characteristically theocentric. We tell
God what he has done, confirming our belief that he continues to
do likewise: "Although you descended into the grave, O Immortal One, you destroyed Hades' power. You arose as a victor, O
Christ God. You exclaimed to the myrrh-bearing women: Rejoice!
You gave peace to your apostles and granted resurrection to the
fallen."[25] To find the "I" voice, we need to turn to the canons of
Matins, where some of the best poetry is kept waiting for worshippers.[26] The best example is the hymnographic treatment of Jonah,
where we hear ancient hymnody at the most existential: "Seeing
the ocean of life surge with waves of temptations, rushing toward
your calm harbor, I scream: Raise my life from destruction, most
merciful one!"[27] God seems distant, though Jonah gasps for a more
intimate experience of the Savior, one experienced in wrestling
with waves: "The extreme abyss of sins encircles me, and my breath
fails me, but extend your exalted hand, O Master. As Peter, so save
me, O Water-walker."[28]

The hymns dedicated to Jonah make clear a key Gospel theme:
Jesus makes friends with failures. In associating himself with Jonah,
Jesus associates himself with the worst prophet who ever lived (Mt
12:38–41; 16:4; Lk 11:29–32). When God tells Jonah to go "up" to
Nineveh, Jonah defies with descent. He goes down to Joppa, down
to Tarshish, down to the bottom of the boat, sinks down to sleep,
flings himself down to the belly of the sea into the bowels of Leviathan, the antithesis of God's upward command. At the bottom of the
sea, Jonah generates prophecy for the first time. From the humid hull
of the whale, he sings confidently of a salvation that has not yet come.
So assured, he speaks of it in the past tense: "I called to the LORD, out
of my distress, and he answered me; out of the belly of Sheol I cried,
and you heard my voice" (Jon 2:1).

---

[25] Kontakion of Pascha, Tone 8.

[26] One of the features of Byzantine Matins is the canon, a unit of liturgical poetry that
draws from biblical odes of the Old and New Testament: Ex 15:1–19; Deut 32:1–43; 1 Sam
2:1–10; Hab 3:2–19; Is 26:9–20; Jon 2:3–10; Dan 3:26–56; 3:57–88; Lk 1:46–55; 1:68–79.
For an introduction to the structure of Byzantine services, books, and the liturgical year, see
Job Getcha, *The Typicon Decoded*, trans. P. Meyendorff (Crestwood, N.Y.: SVS Press, 2012).

[27] Sunday, Tone 6, Ode 6, Irmos.

[28] Sunday, Tone 3, Ode 6, Irmos.

Jonah's tragedy resparks his prophetic vocation. The Byzantine tradition likewise understands Jonah's time in Leviathan as providential. The canon at Matins for the feast of the Nativity paints a similar picture. Most strikingly, the hymn compares the sea monster to Christ: "The sea monster spat forth Jonah like a newborn infant from his bowels just as it received him. And the Word, who dwelt in the virgin and took flesh, came forth guarding her incorrupt, for himself not being subject to decay, he preserved unharmed the one who bore him."[29] The hymn compares the sea monster and the Word, both subjects of the sentence, who are unified in their mission to preserve: Jonah is kept intact, and the Mother of God remains inviolate. The sea monster bears the extra burden of birthing Jonah. This hymn echoes an interpretive strategy we see as early as Irenaeus, who sees Jonah's episode as the formative experience for humanity's recreation: "For as He patiently suffered Jonah to be swallowed by the whale, not that he should be swallowed up and perish altogether, but that, having been cast out again, he might be the more subject to God, and might glorify Him the more who had conferred upon him such an unhoped-for deliverance, and might bring the Ninevites to lasting repentance."[30] Together with Irenaeus, the Byzantine liturgy interprets the sign of Jonah more broadly than as a one-to-one correspondence to Christ's burial and Resurrection. The entire mystery of Christ takes up Jonah, swallows him alive, and turns his stubborn, resistant flesh into a well-calibrated instrument of prophecy. In the same way, the liturgical economy of the Church aims to consume us in order to refashion us to bear "all the fulness of God", so that our lives can be "hidden with Christ in God" (Eph 3:19; Col 3:3). Byzantine liturgy works out this wondrous exchange through its words. In the case of Jonah and his first-person monologue, we find the place for our heart's inarticulate stirrings. Uniting our voice to Jonah's begins the process of reforming our fallen flesh.

A Tender Limb of the Christ's Body

My voice was my way in to the Body of Christ. But we cannot unite our voice to the Church's song unless we are first heard. The

---

[29] Feast of the Nativity, Ode 6, Irmos.

[30] *Adv. Haer.* 3.20.1, in *Ante-Nicene Fathers*, ed. Alexander Roberts and James Donaldson, vol. 1 (1885; Peabody, Mass.: Hendrickson, 1995), 449.

Basilian Sisters heard my basic needs long before I could articulate eloquent prayers and, with their encouragement, invited me in with their concern. The Sisters continued this work after my baptism and, at their invitation, I was thrown into the bigger Byzantine world, which rooted me more deeply in the Church. Sister Celeste, another Basilian Sister, was a pivotal player in this regard. Our youth minister at the parish and school, she was an easily loveable and zealous leader.[31] The summer after my baptism, I went to the Basilian motherhouse in Uniontown, Pennsylvania, to attend the first-ever National Byzantine Youth Rally, the largest of its kind in the United States. After four days of having the unusual experience of Byzantine Catholic kids feeling like they are part of a crowd, I wanted to return to Uniontown as soon as possible. I had my chance Labor Day weekend when the Sisters held their annual Marian pilgrimage. By myself, I got on a chartered bus from a nearby parish and went to pray. At the pilgrimage, I saw Sister Celeste, who told me she had been given another assignment and was not coming back. I was crushed. She did, however, give me the option to drive back with her to Cleveland, where she had to pick up her belongings. This bought me an extra day at the pilgrimage and a chance to say a proper goodbye, so I obliged.

I have spent a lot of time in cars singing along to Saves the Day's energetic anthem "Shoulder to the Wheel". Conley opens the song by pleading, "And I say just go, please Dave, just drive, get us as far as far can be, get us away from tonight."[32] This song was the soundtrack to the rides I would hitch with friends or later with my own car to escape, to sing, along to blasting speakers and the whistling wind through the windows at 65 on the highway. Those car rides remain some of my most vivid memories. However, the most consequential car ride of my life was this ride back from Uniontown, back to Cleveland—my home—with Sister Celeste. On the highway back from Uniontown, spontaneously and without any goading, I opened up to Sister Celeste about my home in the car. My aunt's life was not the only part of my family in a mess; my own

---

[31] Sister Celeste, now renamed Mother Theodora, has founded Christ the Bridegroom Monastery, which attempts to provide a form of traditional, female Eastern Catholic monasticism. See www.christthebridegroom.org.

[32] Saves the Day, "Shoulder to the Wheel", track 2 on Through Being Cool, Vagrant Records, 2005, compact disc.

was as well. Earlier that year, my mom had just run off and left me with my grandmother.

A painfully serious teenager, I spent my time searching for the right lyrics that sang at the right volume to match my emotional pitch, while searching out experiences that could move me away from what I was living for a while. The lyrics I spent my days memorizing and metabolizing did much, but they never listened back. The difference between these songs I sang and the psalms I pray now is that a song may or may not be meant for us, but God's words *are* meant for us. They are divinely written scripts, ready for us to fill with intention. Without the words of the liturgy and its remixed psalmody, my playlist was only partial. The playlist I played in my car could name my emotions with their deserved intensity. Admittedly, this gave me momentary relief, but little in the way of redemption. With the words of the liturgy added to the mix, I could add my problems to providence, narrating my story in light of a much bigger picture—a picture with the God of Christian revelation in it.

With the radio tuned down, now in the car, I could calmly tell my story to Sister Celeste, who as a Sister lived by "every word that proceeds from the mouth of God" (Dt 8:6; Mt 4:4). Praying the psalms day in and day out, she is a well-calibrated instrument of God, a living Psalter. When I told Sister Celeste about my sorrows, her listening ear and few words taught me with her presence the place to sing them properly. As soon as I began, she just turned the radio down. She returned her steady hands to the wheel and let me talk. Sister Celeste listened. When she did, it was like the whole Church was in the car tuning in to what I was saying, assuring me, that in Christ we never nurse our sufferings in our chest alone, but with Christ his Body, both in sacrament and in his people, we can be bruised, but never broken. "Many are the afflictions of the righteous; but the LORD delivers him out of them all. He keeps all his bones; not one of them is broken" (Ps 34:10).

In the Decemberists' "Red Right Ankle", singer Colin Meloy describes lovers so tightly bound by "muscle, bones, and sinews tangled" that one cannot exist without the other: "And how it whispered, 'Oh, adhere to me, for we are bound by symmetry. And whatever differences our lives have been, we together make a limb.'

This is the story of your red right ankle."[33] God's a different kind of lover. He is not co-dependent on us. He does not need us as limbs. Rather, he desires us to be a part of his Body. One of the principal elements of Byzantine art and architecture is the Pantocrator image of Christ. It is traditionally inscribed on the inside of the [central] domes, where he presides over the liturgy celebrated in the nave and lived in our lives, with his blessing hand outstretched. In his position above us, he is, as the title suggests, "the Almighty One". The Pantocrator image cuts off Christ at the waist; Christ's feet are firmly on the floor, found in the members of his Body. The Church is tangled up as Christ's muscle, bones, and sinews—his tender limbs bend the heavens to make God present on earth as he is in heaven. This connection is meant, not for a moment, but for eternity. Maximus the Confessor, a doctor of the Incarnation, tells us as much: "For the Word of God—who is God—wills always and in all things to effect the mystery of his embodiment."[34] The Church connects us to Christ's mission, that "God may be everything to every one" (1 Cor 15:28). Whatever differences we observe between our life and God's life, God bridges that gap. He seeks us out as his extremities, to warm our cold, vulnerable flesh with all the fullness of God (cf. Eph 3:19). God's hands reach out to us because he needs more hands. How else shall his yoke be easy and burden light if we do not pitch in and carry each other's crosses?

The trouble with concerts is that the crowd cannot hold its surfers up for the whole show. Eventually it grows weary. The concert will end, and, despite the promised finale, the band will pack it up. The mosh pit will dissolve and life will go on beyond the concert halls. Even on the longest road trips, the car will run out of gas, and soon there will be no juice in the battery to run the radio. The Divine Liturgy, however, is eternal. Through worship, we are configured to God's hands, his sign of blessing for the world. Those eternal hands of support give hope to Jonahs like me.

---

[33] The Decemberists, "Red Right Ankle", track 8 on *Her Majesty*, Kill Rock Stars records, 2003, compact disc.

[34] *Amb.* 7 (*PG* 91:1084D).

Chapter 9

AN UNCONVERSION

by

Matthew Thomas

For Roger Revell

This is the story of how I was led by my Evangelical faith into the Catholic Church. It is titled "An Unconversion", since to convert implies a turn from one thing to another, whereas in my case I arrived at Catholicism precisely by holding fast to the principles that guided my faith as an Evangelical. This did not make it an easy process, of course, since it required me to give up once and for all my Protestant impulse to individually choose what was right from Christianity, an impulse that had long been the main competitor with Evangelical faith in my life. The Evangelical side won out and led me into the Church's happy pastures that I now enjoy. Having received blessings beyond what I imagined possible within the Church has proved to be the ultimate vindication of Evangelicalism in my life, and I could no more turn from it than I could from Christ himself.

But to make sense, all this requires a start from the beginning. I was born in the mid-eighties to parents who both loved me very much, but were unmarried and not practicing any religious faith, and when I was two my mother took me and left my dad. We spent most of the next seven years on the run, moving from town to town and house to house as my mom tried to find stability and happiness. We moved down the California coast until ending up in a ghost town called Dulzura, near the Mexican border, and from there ran away to New Mexico, where we lived until the end of third grade. We rarely stayed anywhere longer than six months, and my first five semesters of elementary school were spent at five different schools.

On the occasions when my dad would get partial custody of me, he would bring me to Sunday school at the Presbyterian church where his mother went, though these instances were fairly scattered. The more prominent religious influence in my life came from my mother, who by this point was overtly anti-Christian. She made a point of refusing to celebrate Christmas, and in New Mexico she began to practice various forms of occult spirituality. In third grade, I remember her once telling me that she was a witch, and, upon seeing the concern on my face, she added: "Don't worry; I'm one of the good witches." (Note to parents: if you are a witch, this information may be better left unshared with children.)

Along with this antipathy to Christianity, my mother's life was characterized by a deep brokenness, which was compounded by mental illness and substance abuse issues. She had become a lesbian by this point, and though she deeply desired to be a person of peace— as one illustration, she never let me play with toy guns growing up—I remember her ending up in violent conflicts with her lesbian friends and having to intervene to bring her back to her senses. When I reconnected with one of these friends years later, the late lesbian activist Yolanda Retter, she summarized those years in this way: "You were living in hell."

On the last day of third grade, my mother put me on a plane to spend part of the summer with my dad in California. When I was there, a friend of mine who went to an Evangelical church nearby invited me to a weeklong church camp, and it was here that I first heard the Christian message. Though I had been told to distrust it, the light of the Gospel, and the way it was reflected in the lives of the people there, was as clear as day. It was like someone turning on a light in a room that had long been left dark; and, being in a room that had been especially dark for a particularly long time, I found it easier to appreciate the brightness of the light than most. I knew in my heart that what I was hearing was true, and I prayed to receive God into my life and placed my trust in him. I was terrified of what my mom would think if she found out, but even more than this, I was convinced that this was the cure for the brokenness in her heart and the thing that would make her truly happy.

But the encounter I anticipated never came. I never boarded the return flight to New Mexico, as the courts, worried by my mom's downward spiral, took custody from her and granted it to my dad instead, and I would not see her again until midway through high school.

As a young new Christian, I mostly practiced my faith through prayer and reading the Bible, which I read through in elementary school. Though I bounced between different youth groups, I did not have a strong church community and struggled to connect at youth programs I would attend. Coming from my background, to be a Christian seemed like a matter of life or death, and I could not figure out why we would come to church and spend nearly the whole time playing dodgeball and eating ice cream. The most influential group of Christians for me was my best friend's family, who were part of a small church that would meet in their house. Though I would later find out that some of their beliefs were unorthodox—as one example, they did not believe in the Trinity, though I did not know what that was anyway—what they did believe they put fully into practice. The result was the fullest embodiment of Christianity that I knew, and their family provided an example for me to follow when churches elsewhere left me fairly rudderless.

At this point in the story, it may be helpful to give a definition of Evangelicalism as I understood it. To be an Evangelical simply meant to believe and practice Christianity, as it was expressed in the Bible and lived out in the early centuries of the church. The opposite of Evangelicalism was a pick-and-choose Christianity, where one adopted the things that appealed to him from the faith and left out the other parts. I had very little exposure to Catholicism, but my vague sense was that it was like Christianity, but with a bunch of man-made structures and traditions that the Church had added during the Middle Ages. Protestantism and the Reformation were just getting rid of these medieval add-ons and going back to the pure faith as it had been practiced in the early centuries.

Now, I had come to know God through Evangelicals, and my faith continued to be sustained by Scripture and prayer over the next years, even as I lacked a consistent church home. Through middle and high school, however, a number of theological questions were raised in my mind to which I struggled to find good answers, and these—combined with my own sinful desires, to be sure—often left me on the border between faith and unbelief. One prominent example was the relation between faith and works: I would hear it said that if I prayed a certain prayer and professed to believe a certain thing, then I would go to heaven when I died and be there forever, and nothing I could do would cause me to lose this. But when I would read the Bible, it seemed difficult to square this message with what I would read in the Old Testament, or with Jesus' words in the Gospels, or even with Paul himself (the one who was reported to have said it!). What is more, though I struggled to reconcile the idea with the Bible, it did leave open a significant loophole: it meant that I could do whatever I wanted, without having to suffer any eternal consequences for it.

As real as these struggles were, however, I could never completely leave my faith behind, because of the evidence that God had made present to me internally. I knew that God had taken me from my upbringing and shaped me in a way that was very different from how my family background suggested I should turn out, and he had provided evidence in answering my prayers that I could not deny. And so, functionally, I became one of those pick-and-choose Christians— still claiming to be a Christian, but interpreting what was binding and not on my own and (whether knowingly or unknowingly) primarily living for myself. And looking back years later on the destruction that this caused, in my life and in other people's lives, I realized it would have been better if I had not been called a Christian at all.

Toward the end of high school, my best friend and I both had reawakened in us the desire to live for God, and (with many bumps in the road) the Evangelical impulse in me eventually won out. I went to Pepperdine University—chosen in part because I had never been to a Christian school before—and had the good fortune of having a college pastor at Malibu Presbyterian Church named Jeff, whose teaching encouraged me to seek to live every part of my life for God. At the end of freshman year, I went with him and some other students on a mission trip to Costa Rica, a majority Catholic country. We were doing some maintenance work there at an Evangelical seminary, and I still remember one of the professors—a missionary from the U.S.—making an offhand comment about how God was still working through the Catholic Church there. For some reason, the comment struck me. It is not that I would have asserted the opposite; it had just never occurred to me that God was working through the Catholic Church until this Evangelical professor said it.

Our return trip from Costa Rica hit bad weather, and I missed a flight and ended up staying over with a friend's family in Santa Barbara. In the guest room the next morning I saw a copy of *Mere Christianity* by C. S. Lewis, from whom I had seen scattered quotes in other books, and I started reading it. It would not be an overstatement to say that you can date my life "Before *Mere Christianity*" and "After *Mere Christianity*". When I read Lewis, I finally came across a presentation of Christianity that made cohesive sense of what I had encountered in Scripture growing up but that I had never quite heard the same way in the churches I knew. That summer, I devoured Lewis' writings, and though I had heard he was not technically an Evangelical (an Anglican, which was something like a Catholic), he articulated the spirit of the Evangelical Christianity I knew better than anyone I had come across. Rather than taking anything away, Lewis' presentation of what the Christian faith was, and how it was to be believed and obeyed, brought my relatively piecemeal theology and practice to a fullness I had never known before. He is to this day my guiding light, and if there are debts to be paid in heaven, my account with him will be the last to be settled.

The next year I lived in Lyon, France, as part of a study-abroad program, and stayed with a practicing Catholic family, the Taverniers, who received me as one of their own. Though much of it was foreign to me, I was impressed by my experiences of going to Mass with them. The idea of becoming Catholic never crossed my mind, but the professor's comment in Costa Rica and reading Lewis had prepared me to appreciate what I found there, and in the homilies from the priests, I could clearly recognize the shared faith in Christ that we held.

When I came back to finish college, much of my time was taken up with my mom, with whom I had reconnected in high school and who now lived in Phoenix. Her physical and mental conditions often left her in need of support, and this provided the opportunity to call and visit her often. We would sometimes end up talking about religious things, and though her old antagonism toward Christianity had not left, she was so proud of me, and she recognized something in my life to which she had always aspired. On one visit, we were talking at night, and she said something that remains the most compelling testimony to God's power that I have heard. "When the courts took you away from me," she said, "I was always afraid you were going to turn out like your dad. But you didn't", she continued, "and I've never been able to figure out why. But now I understand. It's because your dad didn't raise you; Jesus raised you."

My mom passed away my senior year of college, after finally becoming reconciled with her family and the faith she had left as a teenager, and after graduation I went to work at Harbor House Ministries, an after-school program in inner-city Oakland where I had volunteered the summer before. This was my dream job, as it offered a chance to work with young people who were often raised in challenging circumstances that paralleled my own experiences, and to share the hope that God had placed in my life at a young age. As part of the program, I would teach a devotion for the youth each day, which was usually a verse or two of the Bible filtered through C. S. Lewis. Reading Lewis eventually led me into Chesterton, who was a tremendous inspiration for me and perhaps the first Christian writer I had read who openly opposed the Reformation. These were usually areas where I was less enthusiastic about Reformation theology anyway, but for the first time, the faint idea that one could actually become Catholic occurred to me through reading Chesterton, and I recall the thought crossing my mind that if this ever were to happen to me, I would be sure to blame him.

As I started studying Scripture more for these devotions each day, I came across another Anglican—N. T. Wright—who helped me to work through old puzzles I had never been able to solve. I had downloaded a class called *Romans in a Week* that he had given at a place called Regent College, and at one point he was talking about the relation between faith and works (and how Luther had gotten a number of things wrong). "Faith", he said, was actually the same word in Greek as "faithfulness", which meant that a conventional "believing" versus "doing" dichotomy cannot have been what Paul was talking about; rather, Paul's dichotomy was between fidelity to God—like Abraham's—versus practicing the Mosaic Law. Wright's explanation of Paul made far more sense of Scripture to me than the ones I had encountered growing up and resolved a tension that had undermined my faith from a young age. When I read critiques of Wright's ideas, they were largely along the lines of the critiques of Lewis I had heard: that what he was saying was not in line with the Reformers, that these ideas are indistinguishable from Catholic ones, etc. "So much better for the Catholics", I thought.

Working with young people in Oakland and witnessing God touch their lives, as he had mine, gave me more joy than anything I had ever done, and bonded us together into an unlikely family that still constitutes many of my closest day-to-day ties. I honestly thought this was what I would spend my whole life doing, but after a few years our organization experienced a leadership change that took us in a different direction, and I could see the writing on the wall with respect to my future there. This left me without a clear next step, but having listened to Wright's Regent course a number of times and having mentors who had attended the school, I first visited and then moved to Vancouver to enroll in summer 2010.

Regent is a uniquely excellent place, and distinct in being an inter-denominational Evangelical school, meaning that it seeks to draw positively upon the entirety of the historic Christian tradition (instead of focusing more narrowly upon a particular denomination). My first semester, I had the fortune of taking Systematic Theology with J.I. Packer, the Anglican theologian who had been one of the major voices behind *Evangelicals and Catholics Together*.[1] Having listened to N.T. Wright's *Romans in a Week* a number of times, I decided to focus the research paper for Packer's class on the competing books on the doctrine of justification from Wright and the Reformed pastor John Piper. I was persuaded by the study that Wright's vision was the more biblically faithful one, and Piper's critique that Wright's view would "be co-opted as confirmation of the Catholic way" only made me more curious what this way actually was.[2]

In this first year, I also followed a tip from a friend to check out an Anglican church in the area, Saint John's, which was also where Dr. Packer attended. I knew very little about Anglicanism, besides

---

[1] See "Evangelicals and Catholics Together: The Christian Mission in the Third Millennium", *First Things*, May 1994, https://www.firstthings.com/article/1994/05/evangelicals-catholics-together-the-christian-mission-in-the-third-millennium.

[2] N.T. Wright, *Justification: God's Plan and Paul's Vision* (London: SPCK Publishing, 2009); John Piper, *The Future of Justification: A Response to N.T. Wright* (Wheaton, Ill.: Crossway Books, 2007), 183.

that it was like Catholicism (but different in ways that were not clear to me, so that it was still technically Protestant), and that C. S. Lewis and N. T. Wright were Anglicans. This was more than enough for me to give it a try, and so I started attending the church and, in particular, the Holy Communion service at 7:30 A.M. to which Packer went. Since I was from a primarily low-church background (and had most recently been a part of house churches), this was a significant departure from what I was used to, but something about it resonated with me powerfully. I remember a phone conversation I had with a friend back home telling him about it: while the liturgical structures were foreign to me, rather than being confining (as I had expected them to be), they actually somehow enabled me to pray more freely. This Holy Communion service was focused on the Eucharist, about which I knew very little but which gave me a more profound sense of Christ's sacrifice for me than I had previously experienced at church. (It also made sense of parts of *Mere Christianity* that I had sort of passed over, as where Lewis talks about how the Christ-life comes to us through "Holy Communion", whatever that meant.) My friend and I were both fairly cynical from our church experiences, but I remember telling him that having church centered around the Eucharist like this actually felt like something worth showing up for on Sundays.

This year also gave me the first time to read Luther and Calvin in a focused way, and what I found was deeply unsettling. Growing up, my understanding was that the Reformation was essentially getting rid of unhelpful medieval add-ons, and though I had come across things that troubled me in Luther's and Calvin's theologies before, I still assumed they were generally on the right side. But when I studied Luther's, I found that his tendency to pick and choose from the Christian tradition reminded me precisely of that approach to Christianity which I had found so destructive in my earlier life. I recoiled at how he used Scripture to commend destroying the Jewish people in *On the Jews and Their Lies*[3] and was astonished at how he molded

---

[3] See Luther's seven recommendations in *On the Jews and Their Lies*: to burn down their synagogues and schools, raze their houses, destroy their prayer books, kill their teachers, forbid them safe travel, confiscate all their money, and make them slave laborers. Learning that the Nazis distributed Luther's treatise during their own genocide against the Jewish people only made these words more horrific. For the entire treatise, see Martin Luther, "On the Jews and Their Lies, 1543", in *Luther's Works*, vol. 47, *The Christian in Society IV*, trans. Martin H. Bertram, ed. Jaroslav Pelikan, Helmut Lehmann, et al. (Philadelphia: Fortress Press, 1955–1986), 121–306.

the Bible to fit his theology, removing disapproved books from the New Testament and adding "alone" to Paul's "faith" in Romans supposedly to elucidate his message.[4] When it came to the doctrine I had been studying, justification, I was amazed by his ease in dismissing the entire history of interpretation in favor of his own. As he wrote in the preface to his Romans commentary, "Unless you understand these words in this way, you will never understand either this letter of Saint Paul or any book of the Scriptures. Be on guard, therefore, against any teacher who uses these words differently, no matter who he be, whether Jerome, Augustine, Ambrose, Origen or anyone else as great as or greater than they."[5] (Though Calvin's contradictions of what I thought were basic Christian principles seemed less severe, I still marveled at how on the question of free will, he dismissed all the Church Fathers—save for Augustine—as "so confused, vacillating, and contradictory on this subject, that no certainty can be obtained from their writings", and then proceeded to correct Augustine as well!)[6]

One of the episodes of *The Simpsons* that I remembered best from growing up was "Lisa the Iconoclast", where Lisa does research on the supposedly noble founder of their town, Jebediah Springfield, only to discover that he was actually a murderous pirate. At the moment she is about to reveal the truth about Jebediah to Springfield's citizens, she sees the unity and goodwill brought to the townspeople by the myth of Jebediah and then loses her nerve at the last second, announcing her findings as "Jebediah was ... great." I remembered this episode because of how much it bothered me, on what I thought were Christian grounds—how does a lie profit anyone in the end? Yet here I was, studying a figure whom we upheld as a symbol of goodwill and unity, and finding that the real person actually violated the principles that made me an Evangelical in the first place. I remember explaining this to my classmates in a Greek tutorial one day: Martin Luther was Jebediah Springfield, and I was Lisa Simpson. What would I do?

[4] For Luther's justification of his translation, see his 1530 "Open Letter on Translating", which is in the public domain: https://www.bible-researcher.com/luther01.html.

[5] Martin Luther, "Preface to the Letter of St. Paul to the Romans", in *Luther's Works*, vol. 35, *Word and Sacrament I*, trans. Martin H. Bertram, ed. Jaroslav Pelikan, Helmut Lehmann, et al. (Philadelphia: Fortress Press, 1955–1986), 372.

[6] *Institutes* II.2.4; cf. II.4.3. See John Calvin, *Institutes of the Christian Religion*, trans. Henry Beveridge (Edinburgh: T&T Clark, 1863), 226.

My Evangelical struggles with Protestantism only increased from there. After writing a paper in my second semester that looked at how the early Church Fathers understood Pauline "works of the law" in comparison with the "old" and "new" perspectives on Paul (which would go on to become my dissertation), I decided to start reading the early Fathers from the beginning that summer.[7] As an Evangelical, I had always held a high view of the Church in the early centuries (vaguely before Constantine), though I had never actually read the early Fathers; I had just assumed that the Reformers were only restoring us back to the Church of this period and that what I found there would be more or less what I was doing today. And what I found was indeed very inspiring and in many ways akin to my own faith and practice; but I also encountered much that struck me as distinctly Catholic, which I had thought were inventions of the Middle Ages. So, for example, the *Didache* taught about the Eucharist as a sacrifice.[8] *The First Letter of Clement* attested to apostolic succession[9] and praised the example of someone named Judith along with Esther, who I figured out was part of the larger Catholic Old Testament.[10] Ignatius talked about the Eucharist as truly Christ's Body and the medicine of immortality and about the necessity of being in unity under the Church's bishops.[11] The *Martyrdom of Polycarp* attested to how the bishop's burned bones were preserved as relics, more precious than jewels or gold.[12] Justin Martyr described how

[7] The "new perspective" on Paul refers to the movement in Pauline studies, usually regarded as beginning with E. P. Sanders' *Paul and Palestinian Judaism* in 1977, which views the traditional Protestant understanding of Paul (the "old perspective") as anachronistic and in large part a projection of the Reformers' debates with the late-medieval Church onto Paul and his Jewish interlocutors. On the question of what Paul means by "works of the law", the Reformed theologian J. V. Fesko gives a helpful shorthand summary of the debate: "According to some New Perspective scholars, 'works of the law' refer to Sabbath observance, food laws, and circumcision—those things that identified Jews. According to the Old Perspective, 'works of the law' represents the Judaizers' attempt to secure salvation through moral effort." See J. V. Fesko, "Old and New Perspectives on Paul: A Third Way?" *The Gospel Coalition*, January 6, 2016, https://www.thegospelcoalition.org/reviews/old-and-new-perspectives-on-paul-a-third-way/.

[8] *Didache* 14.

[9] *1 Clement* 44.

[10] Ibid., 55.

[11] *Smyrneans* 6; *Ephesians* 20. For Ignatius on bishops and unity, see nearly any page of his epistles.

[12] *Martyrdom of Polycarp* 18.

Christians were regenerated by baptism[13] and laid out in detail the worship of early Christians, which sounded very much like the Holy Communion service I had been attending, and even more like the Catholic Mass.[14] These teachings and practices seemed uncontroversial in early Christianity, and while they were generally compatible with Anglicanism—indeed, some reminded me of the particularly Catholic-sounding points in Lewis—they were largely unfamiliar to my native low-church brand of Evangelicalism.

Now such differences may seem trivial, but it is difficult to overstate the importance that these discrepancies between the early Church and my own theology and practice held for me. For example, if you had asked me on what authority the canon of Scripture rested (since it could not be found in the Bible itself), my answer would have been that it was the agreed consensus of this early Church; while Jesus might not have dropped a list of books from his pocket at the Ascension, he did promise that the Holy Spirit would guide the Church into all truth. (Lewis had said as much: "The basis of our Faith is not the Bible taken by itself but the agreed affirmation of all Christendom: to which we owe the Bible itself.")[15] We might debate about how far this extends, but if we were not to listen to the disciples of the apostles, and if we did not think God's spirit was guiding the Church of the martyrs, then it was difficult to imagine anyone to whom Christ's promises would apply (and certainly not to a non-martyr such as myself!). Moreover, it was precisely the pick-and-choose game that was antithetical to the Evangelical spirit as I had experienced it: Christianity was not something to be judged according to one's tastes, but to be received and obeyed.

These issues were compounded by new difficulties as an aspiring Anglican. Back in California, I thought I would see if there were any Anglican churches around that would be similar to what I had found at Saint John's. When I searched around my area, I was surprised that there were so many of them—they were called Episcopalian churches, and I had never heard of someone going to one. When

---

[13] *1 Apology* 61.

[14] Ibid., 65–67.

[15] C. S. Lewis, "Letter to Janet Wise, 5th October, 1955", in *Collected Letters*, vol. 3, ed. Walter Hooper (London: HarperCollins, 2006), 653.

I looked at the church websites, it was immediately clear that these churches were very different from Saint John's and much more of the pick-and-choose variety of Christianity than the C. S. Lewis one. Of course, having repented of this kind of Christianity for a real Evangelical submission to Christ, I was not searching for anything besides historic Christian orthodoxy.

When I returned to Regent, I focused in more on the question of the New Testament canon, since this was the one piece of tradition that we all as Evangelicals seemed to regard as incontrovertible. (Interestingly, this did not extend to other pieces of common tradition like the Nicene Creed, which one of our professors famously regarded as suspiciously comprised of nonbiblical categories. While I did not agree with this position, I did respect it as consistent with the Protestant impulse to question critically all tradition, no matter how sacred.) One of our professors whom I most respected, when describing the biblical canon, frankly stated that here "there is no ground for us to stand on besides Tradition—with a capital T." For me, this prompted the question: How do we get a capital-T Tradition? The usual answer was that this came by the consensus of the early Church: but as I had come to recognize, the early Church's consensus was not something we regarded as binding elsewhere, whether it was on apostolic succession, the Eucharist, or the nature of baptism. These matters were attested early and occasioned little controversy within the Church, whereas the canon was settled later and was a matter of debate for centuries. If early consensus was the standard, how could I insist upon the lesser as inviolable and disregard the greater?

I do not wish to dramatize the seriousness of these crises here, but it is difficult to overstate how severely these questions affected me. I remember at this time having a recurring nightmare—a nightmare that must be hilarious to non-theologians, but to me was sheer terror—which went like this. I would be thinking about the question of authority, and particularly as it related to the Bible. "What is the authority on which the New Testament canon rests?" "Well, that of tradition, of course." "But aren't the traditions of the Church not necessarily reliable?" "Yes, tradition isn't necessarily reliable." "So then the contents of the New Testament, which are conveyed by tradition, aren't necessarily reliable either?" "Yes … that would seem to be the case." Around this point I would wake up in a cold sweat, like I was being chased by a zombie in a horror movie who was about to feast on my brains, except that here it was my soul on the menu. The only way I could get myself back to sleep was like this: I would remind myself that, according to the New Testament, while there are bad "tradition[s] of men" (Mk 7:8), there are also good traditions from the apostles that they convey as essential (2 Thess 2:15). The key was not to reject all tradition but, rather, to identify and hold fast to the traditions that the Spirit had committed to the Church.

There was one other way out of these quandaries, of course, which was what I found many other Protestants doing: to say simply that the early Church had it wrong and I had it right. And indeed, this temptation faced me as I studied early Christianity. When the Fathers said something with which I agreed, I would treat them as the most venerable of writers; but when they said something with which I disagreed—say on the nature of baptism—I would suddenly turn into Bart Ehrman, questioning whether they could really know anything about apostolic Christianity and, finally, whether anybody could know anything at all. This turn to a more radically individualistic Protestantism was a real option, but it would also be a real turn: a turn back to the kind of Christianity that places myself as the ultimate authority, where I identify which parts are true and false. But I remembered my own tendency toward self-deception, the destruction such a paradigm had caused, and how my heart was only fully converted when I committed my whole life to following all of God's revelation, not just some part. This was the faith that had transformed my life, that had convicted my mom of God's goodness, that had created an unlikely family in Oakland by his redeeming power. This faith might lead me to places that were uncomfortable; but true Evangelical faith never promises anything otherwise. I would not turn away from it.

This semester I also started dating a very cute girl whom I had met the previous year in Hebrew class, Leeanne Reid. She was from a small Mennonite town in Alberta, so far north that Santa Claus walked over to the house to deliver the presents on Christmas. She had survived cancer when she was in high school and was now studying to become an Anglican priest (having come to Anglicanism via Pentecostalism). She also had a striking perspective on the Reformation. When she was in Bible college her parents had split up, and years later the various family members were still dealing with the consequences. When we were talking about it one day, she stopped and said: "This is why I hate the Reformation so much; because it's a divorce, and a divorce just makes things worse for everybody."

Still searching for a set of consistent principles related to the canon, I decided next semester to try to write a history paper on why modern Evangelicals followed Luther's judgment on the Old Testament canon (relegating the "apocryphal" books to an appendix), but not on the New Testament canon (where Luther had given the same treatment to Hebrews, James, Jude, and Revelation). Though I found lots of interesting material (including modern Lutheran Bibles that still followed Luther's NT canon!), I could not find anything close to an answer to my question. With the paper deadline fast approaching, I switched the topic to a question I had noted with puzzlement the previous year: Why did the children of William Wilberforce, the great Evangelical abolitionist who was a hero of mine, become Catholic?

In choosing this topic, I inadvertently transgressed a rule I had set for myself, which was to avoid reading about John Henry Newman. I had come across in passing the story of this influential Anglican theologian who had shocked his church by becoming Catholic, and because I was hoping to avoid becoming Catholic (which seemed very complicated and uncomfortable), I figured I would do my best to avoid Newman as well. The trouble was that Wilberforce's sons had been under Newman's influence at Oxford, which meant that now I would be under it, too. As I read the accounts of how the theological foundations of their Anglicanism had crumbled and given way to a Catholic one, I was unable to avoid connecting their theological crises with our own in the diocese of New Westminster, where the Anglican church I attended, Saint John's, had been kicked out of our building for refusing to follow the diocese's new progressive policies on same-sex marriages (among other things), and was now meeting at an Adventist church. While Newman and the Wilberforces were at a loss as to how their church's principles could be upheld when baptismal regeneration was not doctrinally enforced, our church was facing an entire diocese that had denied its inherited moral teaching and punished those who refused to come along.

By a remarkable coincidence, I found that our library actually held an archive of materials from the Wilberforce family, and I was able to gain access to it. I had no idea what I was looking for, and so I opened a drawer and picked up a book at random, hoping to find something useful for the paper. In a second remarkable coincidence, the section to which I opened in the book was actually a letter from Henry Wilberforce, William's son, who was writing to his former Anglican congregation explaining the reasons why he had become Catholic. As Henry explained, the problem was not with Anglicanism in particular, but with Protestantism in general, which inevitably made inherited Christian doctrine relative to the views of the individual. I stood in our archives and read the following from Wilberforce:

All the Protestant sects have been set up by men who, from time to time, thought that they could make a new Church, better than the old Church which had been from the beginning, and more like what they think from Scripture the Church ought to be. For this reason, the people who made these sects called themselves *Reformers.* A reformer means a man who changes things from worse to better. These men were not content with the old Church, which had been from the beginning; they said, "We will make a change; we will have a new Church, which shall be a deal better"; and, indeed, they tried their hands at it. Each one of these reformers wished everybody else to be content with his own new Church. As soon as he had made his reformation he said, "Now we have had quite change enough: let everything stay just as it is now. We need no more reformation." But other people said, "No; why should not I make a reformation as well as another? I can make things better than they have made them." For this very reason all the chief reformers were always fighting with each other, because each man wanted his reformation and not another people's to be the reformation. And in this way it is that among Protestants one new Church and sect keeps springing up after another even to this very day. It will always be so in all Protestant bodies. The Church-of-England man reformed the Catholic Church, and the Presbyterian reformed the Church of England, and the Independent reformed the Presbyterian, and the Baptist reformed the Independent, and the Quaker reformed the Baptist, and now we have reformed Quakers, till it seems like soon enough we shall have pretty near as many sects as there are people. But in the middle of all these sects there is one old Church, which has gone on for 1850 years—hundreds of years before any of them were thought of, and before the men who made them were born.[16]

[16] Henry William Wilberforce, "Reasons for Submitting to the Catholic Church: A Farewell Letter to the Parishioners of East Farleigh, Kent", in *Miscellaneous Works, Wilberforce Period*, vol. 17a (London, 1851), 13–14.

As I read about how the crises of authority in the Anglican church left the Wilberforce sons on the brink of losing their faith altogether, I wondered how they would have reacted to the crises in our own context, where the moral and doctrinal degeneration had progressed farther than anyone then could have imagined. These considerations were all particularly concerning to me as the significant other of an Anglican priest-in-training; if my own Anglicanism was not able to remain firm, how could I act as a support for hers?

Seeking guidance, I met with one of my mentors and asked if he could give me advice on how to avoid becoming Catholic. I did not want to be Catholic, I explained, but wanted to be like Lewis—someone who may have been basically Catholic in theology, but still technically Protestant, so that he was still able to share the riches of the broader Christian tradition with Evangelicals like me. Who knows if *Mere Christianity* would have been on the bookshelf in that guest room if it had been written by a Catholic? And where would I have been without it?

My mentor flatly rejected my request. "I'm afraid I can't help you, because what you're doing is putting practical concerns before truth, and you can't do this and still remain a Christian." This was not the answer I came for. "But I don't want to be a Catholic! I'm from a crazy mix of Protestant backgrounds, but I'm grateful for them, and one of the only things that unites us is that we aren't Catholic. This is the world I'm from, and I don't want to leave it." My mentor was not impressed. He reiterated that I needed to let truth dictate my decisions if I was going to be a Christian and said I should start actually attending Mass and RCIA (the Rite of Christian Initiation for Adults—basically confirmation classes for big kids).

I was not close to being ready to explore being confirmed in the Catholic Church, nor was I even ready to stop attending my technically Protestant (though Catholic-flavored) Anglican one. But I did recognize that seeing what the Catholic Church was like in real life was an essential part of discerning whether her claims were true or false, and so a couple friends and I made a compromise: we would go to the early Holy Communion service at Saint John's Adventist/Anglican, go eat breakfast together, and then attend Mass at the local Catholic church afterward.

I will not forget the experience I had that first Sunday. After Saint John's and breakfast, we went to Our Lady of Perpetual Help, and

I recall being astonished by two things. First was how Scripture-centered it was: it seemed like nearly every part of the liturgy was drawn from one place in Scripture or another, so that our worship was taking God's words and offering them back in praise. The second was how Christ-centered it was: everything was focused on Jesus and his sacrifice, not the pastor or the church and their programs, and somehow having the priest acting *in persona Christi* helped me to look past him to Christ himself.

I noticed another thing once I stepped out of the building, something that was missing. What was it, I thought to myself? "My cynicism!" Where had my cynicism gone? As long as I could remember, I could recall there being a lawyer in my head during any church sermon, cross-examining the pastor regarding the various claims he was making. It was not something I conjured up, but more like a defense mechanism that had developed over years and years of hearing people try to persuade me of their individual opinions from the pulpit. And it was gone. I had no idea where it went, or why it had suddenly forgotten to enter this particular church with me, but it was an absence that I could not remember feeling before. And it was glorious.

I remember processing this whole experience afterward with Scott, one of my friends who had come along, who had been similarly affected by the whole thing. While neither of us necessarily wanted to face the scary prospect of actually becoming Catholic, we were both struck by an undeniable power that day. Whatever the claims of the Catholic Church and whatever our relation to her, what was clear was that attending this service brought about an increase of faith, hope, and love for God in us; and that seemed a pretty good reason to go to church.

The summer that followed (2012), I followed a professor's recommendation and read Louis Bouyer's *The Spirit and Forms of Protestantism*, which I checked out from the Regent library.[17] (As it turned out, the copy had actually belonged to none other than J.I. Packer and was full of his annotations!) At this point, Luther was still Jebediah Springfield in my mind, and my studies of Calvin did not rank him a great deal higher. It was a surprise, then, that these two figures would

---

[17] See Ignatius Press' recent reprint: Louis Bouyer, *The Spirit and Forms of Protestantism* (San Francisco: Ignatius Press, 2017).

be redeemed for me by a Catholic priest. The thesis of Bouyer's book was that, for whatever their faults, the central, positive principles of the Reformers are simply good Catholic ones, and if one does not affirm them, he is not just a bad Protestant; he is a bad Catholic. The trouble is not with the positive statements that are associated with each figure—think particularly of the priority of God's grace and sovereignty in our salvation—but, rather, the negative denials that are associated with them, which are often rooted in philosophical disagreements regarding how divine and human agency relate to one another. According to Bouyer, not only were these denials not necessary for the Reformers' affirmations, but they actually ended up producing counterreactions in the succeeding generations of their movements that were far worse than the original problems they sought to address. For Bouyer, this problem was only exacerbated by the Protestant appeal to individual interpretation, which rendered subsequent errors impossible to correct in a unified way.

For me, Bouyer's book was a kind of holy grail, as it forced me to appreciate the genuinely Catholic aims of the Reformers, while also explaining why the history of subsequent Protestantism went in directions so far removed from their intentions. It also got me thinking about the broader relationship between Evangelicalism and Catholicism, which started to clarify in my mind as I tried to explain it for my little sister. (Lauren is my half-sister on my dad's side and is eleven years younger than I, but she is my closest friend in the universe, and her judgment on things is second to none. As such, the true test of any idea was whether it made sense to her.) I cannot recall how we got on the subject, but the analogy that suddenly hit me was that Evangelicalism and Catholicism were kind of like comic books and Shakespeare; they were both telling the Christian story, but in different genres. Evangelicalism had the immediacy of a comic book: everything was simplified, and it engaged you in the way it seemed to jump off the page—"POW!"—"BLAM!"—so that you could easily see yourself in the story. It was easy to understand and easy to share. By contrast, growing up Catholic could kind of be like growing up with Shakespeare—I could think of examples from people I knew— where one has a general sense that some great something is present, but without good instruction it is not easily intelligible, nor is it as easy to see yourself in the story. And for someone who grows up with

Shakespeare and never really gets it, it makes sense how encountering the comic-book version could be like seeing the story for the first time, and even prompt one to disavow Shakespeare as totally lame.

But the relationship works in both ways. Comic books, for all their virtues, are indeed simplified versions of a story and, thus, have a limited amount of depth. This can produce a corresponding lack of depth in the reader's understanding in the long term if the comic book is not supplemented from elsewhere. And here is where Shakespeare comes in: it is precisely the person who is most devoted to the comic book that will be best equipped to understand the Shakespeare version—and when he does, he recognizes he has encountered a kind of depth and genius that a lifetime's devotion cannot exhaust. This does not require him to disavow the comic-book version in any way, and, if anything, the opposite is true; it is precisely the comic-book version that has enabled him to understand the Shakespeare one so well.

I thought through this analogy with my experiences, and it fit like a glove. The Catholics I knew who had become Evangelicals were those for whom the Catholic faith had never made sense; as happens when Shakespeare is read to children, it had gone in one ear and out the other. The Evangelicals I had encountered who became Catholics were precisely those who took their faith the most seriously and found in the Catholic Church the full telling of a story to which they had already committed their lives. And most importantly, this analogy really seemed to make sense to my sister, a key confirmation that perhaps I was on the right track.

That summer my girlfriend, Leeanne, was back in northern Alberta, where she worked doing road construction as a packer driver. She had been wrestling with various Anglican issues as well: the church where she had been training was part of the same breakaway group as Saint John's, where I had been attending, and although there was much she appreciated there, she also did not sense that they offered clear answers for the underlying questions of authority and orthodoxy that had caused the official Anglican church to go off the rails. She had also started praying the rosary and began going to Catholic churches around the province on Sundays. Besides generally really liking it, what stood out to her in these churches was the dignity with which women were treated. When she had become Anglican, she originally chose this instead of Catholicism because there seemed to be a higher value placed on women there (after all, they could become priests!).

However, the reality never seemed to live up to the ideal, and the more orthodox churches seemed to be precisely those least comfortable with her ordination. But in these Catholic churches, though there were no women priests, what she encountered in parish after parish was the kind of respect and appreciation for women for which she had always searched in churches but had never found in the same way. By the time the summer ended, she had decided she wanted to step down from her ordination training and to enroll in RCIA.

When I returned to Regent that fall, my friends and I recommenced attending the Anglican and Catholic services, and in September I was encouraged to drop my defenses against the Church by a surprising source. At Saint John's we had a class held after Holy Communion called "Learner's Exchange", where one of our many educated parishioners would teach on some theological topic. This Sunday the teacher was J. I. Packer, whose copy of Bouyer's book I had just finished reading and who was at that point the most distinctly Reformed theological influence in my life. His talk was titled, "The Future of Our Unruly Family", and the topic was on what sort of future he envisioned for Anglicans (which, as exiled Anglicans meeting at an Adventist church, was particularly pressing for us). Packer went through some of the historic problems with Anglicanism that reminded me of what Newman and the Wilberforces had described, detailing the various splits from Anglicanism that had happened since the Reformation and describing how no authority was left to hold its bishops accountable once they withdrew from Rome, leaving them free to do whatever they wished. His first recommendation for what qualities should characterize Anglicans in the future was "conservationist", an approach that values the past but judges one's heritage by Scripture and drops the parts that do not align with Scripture. He continued:

> What sorts of things am I thinking of? Well, just about everything that is reactionary against Rome. Evangelicalism has been burdened over the decades by anti-Romanism, as if everything that Rome is for we need to be against. That is a mindset which I think should be dropped, explicitly dropped—that isn't part of the heritage that is to be conserved.[18]

---

[18] See "The Future of Our Unruly Family", *St. John's Vancouver, Learner's Exchange*, September 16, 2012, https://stjohnsvancouver.sermons.io/sermons/the-future-of-our-unruly-family.

This was not the kind of thing I expected to be hearing from as convinced a Calvinist as J. I. Packer! And even as one who had come to appreciate the Catholic tradition, I knew he still described a part of me: I still retained a piece of anti-Romanism inside me, one that desired to maintain my own autonomy, and I took what he said to heart.

This fall I also had one of my closest friends move in as a roommate, Barney Aspray, who also shares an essay in this volume. He and I had been wrestling through similar questions over the past two years, and one of the first things he did was give me a copy of Joseph Pearce's *C. S. Lewis and the Catholic Church*.[19] Pearce's thesis was that if C. S. Lewis were alive today, he would be a Catholic, and though he did not claim to write without bias (since Pearce himself was Catholic), I found much of the book's evidence and the overall conclusion to be compelling. While Lewis' Catholic leanings had long been familiar to me, I had not considered what might have forced his hand with respect to Anglicanism. As one example, Lewis had written in "Priestesses in the Church" about how ordaining women priests would reverse all the sacramental imagery regarding Christ and his bride, the Church, and thus turn it into a different religion from Christianity altogether. However, while Lewis wrote in 1948 that such a proposal to "cut ourselves off from the Christian past" was "very unlikely to be seriously considered by the authorities", seeing as how "the Church of England would be torn to shreds by the operation", this all indeed came to pass in the decades following Lewis' death; and in the process, Anglicans who had been close to Lewis, like his secretary, Walter Hooper, eventually were received into the Catholic Church.[20]

The divergent paths of the Protestant and Evangelical impulses were brought into clearest relief for me in a class on modern Protestant thought, which I took in my last semester. The course had the reputation for turning one into either an atheist or a Catholic—as Lewis himself said modern Protestant theology would do in *Fern Seed and Elephants*—and it did not disappoint.[21] In reading figures like

---

[19] Joseph Pearce, *C. S. Lewis and the Catholic Church* (San Francisco: Ignatius Press, 2003).

[20] C. S. Lewis, "Priestesses in the Church?" in *God and the Dock*, ed. Walter Hooper (Grand Rapids, Mich.: Eerdmans, 1972), 235.

[21] C. S. Lewis, *Fern-Seed and Elephants: And Other Essays on Christianity*, ed. Walter Hooper (Glasgow: Collins, 1977).

Kant, Hegel, Schleiermacher, and Bultmann, we encountered the logic of Protestantism devouring more and more of traditional Christian orthodoxy with its new reforms, and struggled to find ways that we as Evangelicals could respond without appealing to the broader Christian tradition. This culminated in a special session of the class at a nearby pub, where the question on debate was whether there was some consistent Protestant standard by which one could say Schleiermacher was outside of Christian bounds. When Schleiermacher's side of the debate had won, so that (at least on Protestant grounds) his deconstructed version of Christianity was just as valid as our own, a professor attending posed the question: "So when are you all signing up for RCIA?"

That spring I had been accepted into the doctoral program in theology at Oxford, which meant that Leeanne and I needed to make a decision about getting married rather quickly, since I would be on another continent in the fall. At Easter that year she completed RCIA and was received into the Catholic Church, and so we tentatively started looking around for Catholic churches in California where we could get married. Even with these things coming together, however, I was still in an absolute fog about the decision, and all my prayers had not availed to bring clarity in one direction or the other. To make things even more confusing, I had had a ring made along the lines of what I knew she wanted—in the event that God gave me the green light—but when I picked it up, it had been made completely wrong and would take a whole month to redo.

I was as at a loss what to do and running out of time. The only idea I had left had come from a woman who started talking to us after Mass one afternoon at Saint Leo's, a church in Oakland we had visited. She had asked what our story was, and I filled her in about us potentially getting married there (though only Leeanne was Catholic, we did not know if we were actually getting married, etc.). She turned and spoke directly to me, with a surprising sense of conviction and authority, and said that if there was something I needed, I should ask Mary, because Jesus loves to listen to his mother.

I had not had someone address me like this outside a charismatic church before, and while I theoretically believed there was something to the idea of the saints interceding for us, it was not something with which I had any personal experience. Nor did I have enthusiasm for the idea. I had tried praying the rosary once before (and was mostly bored), and Mary's role was the part of Catholic doctrine with which I was least comfortable. But I was also at the end of my rope and the end of our calendar: the program in England started at the beginning of October, and we could not wait much longer for a decision. And so I started praying the rosary each day—first asking God to forgive me if doing so was idolatrous, then explaining that this was the last thing I could think of—and asking Mary to intercede for me, that I would receive clarity from her Son for what I should do.

And the strangest thing happened: it worked. Having asked God to give me peace with the decision for the past year, for some reason this peace only arrived in the three weeks I prayed the rosary. It all seemed impossible, like Indiana Jones standing on the invisible bridge after the leap from the lion's head; but there I was, standing on firm ground and finally able to get to the other side. At the end of these three weeks, the second ring came back perfect, and I drove up to Canada the next day to propose to Leeanne. I still did not know precisely how Mary and the communion of the saints worked, but I knew something more important—that somehow, in God's providence, they did work.

Leeanne and I were married at Saint Leo's in September and a few weeks later moved to Oxford, where we found remarkable communities at the Catholic Chaplaincy, Blackfriars, and the Oxford Oratory. I was now persuaded of the large majority of Catholic teaching and had undeniable personal experiences to go along with it, but the biggest factor that kept me from being received into the Church were the people in whose lives I carried a measure of pastoral responsibility, most of whom had little experience with the Catholic Church and regarded her as foreign to their own faith. This had slowly changed over the preceding years—for example, my sister had gone from telling me Catholic churches were weird and scary to thinking they were cool—but being married in a Catholic church by a Catholic priest was still perplexing to most of my friends and family. In Oxford, I still tried attending Anglican services from time to time and still loved many individual people and elements of the liturgy. However, these experiences did not reinspire confidence that it was possible to escape Protestantism's tendency to relativize doctrine (it turns out exchanging Henry VIII for the pope is not without long-term consequences), and the general drift away from historic Christianity was no less evident than what I had found back in North America. There was no better illustration of this than the University Church of Saint Mary the Virgin, the most prominent seat of preaching in the city. This had been the center of the Oxford Movement under New-man and the church where Lewis had preached my favorite sermon, "The Weight of Glory", in 1941. When I arrived, I found that the priest chosen to be vicar here was an atheist (!), who sold his book in the gift shop: *Christian Atheist: Belonging without Believing.*[22] What-ever fears Lewis may have had about Anglicanism, I did not think he could have foreseen anything quite like this.

As I continued studying, the positive draw to the Church found its fullest expression in Saint Irenaeus, a second-century Father whom I had been taught to revere as a guardian of orthodoxy by Evangelicals and who was the subject of one of the chapters of my dissertation. There was indeed much to love as an Evangelical: Irenaeus com-pellingly explained orthodox Christology in contrast with hereti-cal alternatives and provided a powerful early witness to the New Testament Scriptures and their authority within the Church. But he also provided much more: Irenaeus explained in detail how we truly become parts of Christ's Body by partaking of his Real Presence in the Eucharist and was the earliest figure to explain the active role Mary played in man's salvation as the counterpart of Eve. And while he was praised by Evangelicals—rightly, I should add—for dissuad-ing Pope Victor from excommunicating the churches of the East over the date of Easter, he also gave the clearest articulation of the Roman Church's leadership within early Christianity. If one wished to correct the errors of heretics, they need only be referred to "the very ancient, and universally known Church founded and organized at Rome by the two most glorious apostles, Peter and Paul", since "it is a matter of necessity that every Church should agree with this Church, on account of its pre-eminent authority."[23] My Evangelical

---

[22] The fact that holding to God's existence was optional for such a position was most fully problematized for me by E. B. Pusey, the prominent Anglican theologian during the Oxford Movement, who had preached in 1851: "To regard doctrines of the faith once delivered to the saints, as 'open questions,' would be to declare them no matters of faith at all." See E. B. Pusey, *The Rule of Faith, as Maintained by the Fathers and the Church of England* (Oxford: John Henry Parker, 1851), 64.

[23] Irenaeus, *Against Heresies* 3.3.2; cf. *Ante-Nicene Fathers*, vol. 1, ed. Alexander Roberts and James Donaldson (1885; Peabody, Mass.: Hendrickson, 1995), 415.

teachers were right about Irenaeus, I thought; we just had not known what he actually taught.

Being in Oxford also gave us the chance to connect with Walter Hooper, Lewis' old secretary and literary trustee, who had become Catholic in the late 1980s. I had first heard Hooper speak at the Catholic chaplaincy in town and was struck by his sanctity: if you imagined someone who internalized everything that Lewis wrote, the result was Walter. A mutual friend, who knew how much I valued Lewis, put us in touch, and we first met at his home in North Oxford. Among many things, I asked him why he thought Lewis had not been received into the Catholic Church in his lifetime, and I was surprised to find that (on an infinitely larger scale) it was the same reason I was not Catholic, either. Walter explained how Lewis was trapped by his own success: his writings had unexpectedly placed him in a position of responsibility to guide his Christian readers across the world, most of whom were Protestants, and carried at least some measure of suspicion toward Catholicism. This caused him to avoid issues whenever possible that could be a potential stumbling block (though in his last book, *Letters to Malcom*, he did seek to put his cards on the table a bit more). Walter explained how for those who had continued in Lewis' path in the decades after he died, the reality was that they had not left Anglicanism, but that it had left them: he believed in mere Christianity and, as an Anglican priest himself, he could not honestly say that his church's leadership believed it anymore. Walter told me that since being received into the Catholic Church in 1989, he had been the happiest person in the world, and while he imagined there must be someone for whom this is not entirely the case, in most cases, it really is.

The last pieces of this story took place back in California over winter break, a year and some months after we had moved to Oxford and a few months after our daughter, Camille, had been born. One afternoon we were back at the Evangelical church—the one through which I had first become a Christian—where they now ran a coffee shop where I would go to work and see friends who pastored there. I had offered to carry Camille around the campus a bit so Leeanne could read, and I decided to pop my head into the main auditorium. As we stepped inside the cavernous room, I suddenly had a sensation come over me that I had not felt before. I had always thought of this room in strictly functional terms: it had a big stage that went up and down, there were steps you could run up toward the balcony, etc. For some reason, as I stood inside with my five-month-old daughter, the distinct sense hit me that this place was a sanctuary. There was something holy that happened here. Yes, there was no Eucharist; but the Word of God was preached here, individuals were baptized into Christ, and God's spirit moved to transform hearts. Though I had never heard the place described in this way (and had never thought of it myself), somehow through being in Catholic contexts, my eyes could now see how this place shared in sacred activity.

Another day, one of my pastor friends came over to talk with me; he was in a cynical sort of funk, much like what I had experienced when I went there. My friend was frustrated by the various holes in the church's theology, and I knew what he meant; it was like a puzzle with a few pieces missing. Growing up around there, it had become harder and harder for me to focus on the general picture they presented over time and not to fixate on the holes. This was precisely where my friend was; it seemed like the holes were the only thing he could see anymore, and I knew just how he felt.

But for some reason, now, the whole picture looked different. The beauty of Catholic theology is that it contains all the puzzle pieces: the picture it presents filled in the holes that seemed persistent in the Evangelical churches I had been around (often, but not always, related to ecclesiology and sacraments).[24] And having had this full picture engrained in me, I saw the holes in a completely different way. While my friend was in despair at them, I knew now from experience how these holes were filled in, and this knowledge made me able to see the essential rightness of their overall picture more clearly than I ever had. The irony of the scene was beautiful: an Evangelical pastor who could no longer seem to see anything good in Evangelicalism, and a former cynic whose long-term Catholic exposure had given him new eyes to see the Evangelical church's goodness, trying to talk him off the ledge!

---

[24] On the former, the biblical scholar Daniel Wallace (who writes my favorite Greek textbook) articulated many of the same concerns I felt in this excellent post: see "The Problem with Protestant Ecclesiology", *Daniel B. Walllace* (blog), March 18, 2012, https://danielb wallace.com/2012/03/18/the-problem-with-protestant-ecclesiology/.

This recognition—that through the Catholic Church, God had given me a heart and eyes to appreciate my Evangelical background more than I ever could before—was a work of his grace that made my response a matter of obedience or disobedience. When we returned to Oxford, I started meeting with a priest at Blackfriars and was received into the Church at Pentecost with the confirmation name of Irenaeus, precisely five years to the day I now write. It would require another essay of similar size to explain all that I love about being within the Church, but I am most thankful for how it has taken the gift of faith that Christ gave me at a young age and placed it in a context where it can grow into the fullness he intended for it. There is no one who expresses my experience better than the aged Saint John Henry Newman, who, after being Catholic for forty-one years, wrote to an Evangelical correspondent as follows: "What can I say but that those great and burning truths which I learned when a boy from Evangelical teaching, I have found impressed upon my heart with fresh and ever increasing force by the Holy Roman Church? That Church has added to the simple Evangelicalism of my first teachers, but it has obscured, diluted, enfeebled nothing of it."[25]

---

[25] John Henry Newman, "To G. T. Edwards, February 24th, 1887", in *The Life of John Henry Cardinal Newman, Based on His Private Journals and Correspondence*, vol. 2, ed. Wilfred Ward (London: Longmans, Green, 1912), 527, http://www.newmanreader.org/biography /ward/volume2/chapter35.html.

Chapter 10

CLIMBING THE WREKIN

by

Petroc Willey

I am currently a professor of catechetics in the Theology Department at Franciscan University in Steubenville, Ohio. Before moving to the United States in 2015, I taught catechetics in England, at Maryvale in Birmingham—the first Catholic home of Saint John Henry Newman, who named it "Saint Mary in the Valley" and eventually "Maryvale". Maryvale also has the privilege of being home to the national shrine of the Sacred Heart. Prior to my move there in 1992, I taught Christian ethics, with a focus on Catholic social teaching, at Plater College, Oxford.

My taking up of that Oxford position closely followed on my formal reception into the Catholic Church in the summer of 1985. For many years I had been reading and praying my way toward the Catholic Church, drawn especially by my experience of the Benedictine— and, particularly, Cistercian—tradition. In fact, I had lived in a lay Catholic Benedictine community, the Community of Saint Gregory, in a tiny village in rural Wales, for three years and had experienced firsthand there the wonderful balance of *ora et labora*. During my time there I was still an Anglican, though able to participate in the general life and the Divine Office of the community. That extended period, together with my interest in the monastic heritage of the West in its many forms, came in due course to flow over into my marriage with Katherine. A cradle Catholic, Katherine had also spent time in a lay—Carmelite—community. In our early years we wrote a joint book, *Become What You Are: The Call and Gift of Marriage*, which

239

explored ways of living a monastic spirituality in a setting of marriage and family life. Blessed now with four children, I can still read that early work and stand by all that was written there.

Finding myself now in a position teaching catechetics and evangelization seems to be a clear act of God's providence. I was born at the precise time when the Church was calling for a renewed universal mission. On January 25, 1959, Pope John XXIII made his famous announcement at a consistory held at the Basilica of Saint Paul Outside the Walls, calling for an ecumenical council.[1] I was born on the following day. My life, as I now see it, was marked by this call to evangelization and to catechesis, to enable the precious deposit of Christian doctrine to "shine forth"[2] and be made accessible to all people through a renewed commitment to mission.

The essential reason for my conversion to Catholicism may be stated in a way that risks sounding circular: I knew my need for conversion and my desire for it, and I found in Catholicism an explanation both of that need and of that desire.

In my early adult life I had the great good fortune to be introduced to the novels and stories of George MacDonald, a Scottish contemporary of Dickens and Scott and—in his own time—as well known. A Christian thinker and writer, he excelled especially in writing fairy stories, including unforgettable, novel-length fairy tales for adults. All of the stories deal, in some way or other, with the nature of and call to conversion. One particularly evocative tale is *The Golden Key*, of two children who are given a golden key and know that they must seek the lock that fits the key. A moment in that story beautifully sums up the growing longing that accompanies conversion, as the children gradually become aware of the greater happiness and good that await them and of which the key is the promise: "After sitting for a while, each, looking up, saw the other in tears: they were each longing after the country whence the shadows fell."[3] The story as a whole speaks to the essential nature of conversion: we come to a point in life where that which we have been given pushes us inexorably to

---

[1] John XXIII, *Homily*, January 25, 1959, *AAS* 5 (1959), 70–74.

[2] This phrase is found in the opening section of John Paul II's apostolic constitution *Fidei Depositum*, introducing the *Catechism of the Catholic Church* on October 11, 1992.

[3] George MacDonald, "The Golden Key", in *The Complete Fairy Tales of George MacDonald*, introduction by R. L. Green (New York: Schocken Books, 1977), 226.

begin to journey, to quest toward a goal, with the nature of that goal only identifiable as "that which will fit perfectly what I possess". The image of the key in the story may also evoke for us the notion of a *symbolon*—half of a broken object that would be brought by the bearer to fit to the missing half in order to verify the bearer's identity—an ancient Greek term that came to be adopted for the Christian Creeds. That identity of the key with the Symbol of the faith is one important conviction to which I have come over time.

MacDonald's tales also make clear the cost of the journey of conversion and its paschal shape: that the greater reality sought is found only through a death to self. His stories in fact, each in its own way, provide us in narrative form with the pure doctrine of the Lord on the call to conversion: "For whoever would save his life will lose it; and whoever loses his life for my sake and the gospel's will save it."[4]

MacDonald's writings were well known to Chesterton, who often speaks, in his own inimitable fashion, to this same point about the nature of conversion. In numerous ways he writes of the essential paradox that the Christian journey is one directed toward fullness of life, a fullness that can be found only in self-forgetfulness, in becoming smaller. Thus, in *Orthodoxy*, he exclaims, "How much larger your life would be if your self could become smaller in it.... How much happier you would be, how much more of you there would be, if the hammer of a higher God could smash your small cosmos, scattering the stars like spangles, and leave you in the open, free like other men to look up as well as down!"[5] In this particular passage, Chesterton offers his own golden key for how we might understand this paradox of becoming greater through becoming smaller. He writes of the person as a "small cosmos" that must be shattered in order to become something larger.

In his description of the human person as a small cosmos, he is drawing on those strands in the Christian tradition that identify each of us as a "microcosm", a little cosmos, a little whole that participates in a greater whole. I have found in this concept an anthropology and a metaphysics that make sense of the whole journey of conversion toward a richer and fuller participation in being. It is precisely

[4] Mark 8:35.
[5] G. K. Chesterton, *Orthodoxy* (San Francisco: Ignatius Press, 1999), 25.

because we are a small cosmos, gathering the elements of the wider cosmos around us, that we can in principle "look up as well as down" since we hold within ourselves, in our own way, the highest and the lowest elements in the universe. In and through the small part that we are, we have participatory knowledge of the whole.

It is this nature of the human person, then, that gives us reason to believe that we can have true knowledge of the world, that we can, as Adam, name the animals, can know subatomic particles, and can model human creations in art and architecture after the golden ratio uncovered in nature by Fibonnaci. We know earth because we are earth, fire because we are fire. Because we are a little cosmos, we can know something of what it is to be a bat[6] or a rabbit or a horse, and we can hope to share heaven with the angels. In this knowing of being, the mind is not cast in the role of spectator; rather, knowledge is an operation "within" reality.

The seventeenth-century poet George Herbert, in his poem "Man", expresses this classic Christian view of the person, as one who embraces all of the levels of created being, both the spiritual and the material:

> Man is all symmetry,
> Full of proportions, one limb to another,
> And all to all the world besides;
> Each part may call the farthest brother:
> For head with foot hath private amity,
> And both with moons and tides.
>
> Nothing hath got so far,
> But Man hath caught and kept it, as his prey;
> His eyes dismount the highest star:
> He is in little all the sphere.[7]

We are each a little cosmos—that is our greatness. It is what enables us to know and to love the world in which we live. We have an amity, a friendship, with moons and tides and with every portion and

---

[6] See Thomas Nagel's essay "What Is It Like to Be a Bat?" in *Mortal Questions* (Cambridge: Cambridge University Press, 1979), 165–80.

[7] George Herbert, "Man", in *The Works of George Herbert in Verse and Prose* (London: George Routledge, 1854), 90.

part of the universe. The universe is our home, a place whose order is mirrored within ourselves.[8]

Why, then, does Chesterton write of the *smashing* of the little cosmos that we might find something more? And how does this relate to the theme of conversion, to the Lord's leading of us to die that we might live? As a teenager, I made a significant rededication to the faith after reading the Gospel of Saint Luke in a single sitting, a reading in which I was inescapably faced with the shape of the Gospel presented by the Evangelist as a single journey of Jesus to Jerusalem, leading to his Passion, death, and Resurrection. The *point* of the journey was to seek that goal: "his face was set toward Jerusalem."[9] When I had closed the Bible after this reading, I knew that I had been confronted with the essential challenge of Christ in the Gospel and that I had to make a fundamental choice in regard to it. That challenge was the paradoxical truth of, "Truly, truly, I say to you, unless a grain of wheat falls into the earth and dies, it remains alone; but if it dies, it bears much fruit."[10]

I could not express at the time the connection between the seeking of greater life that was made possible by my nature as a little cosmos that could reach out, catch, and keep all things as my prey with the fact that all such catching was really more like a little death, but a *good* death. It was a call from Being to *be* caught, to *be* snared, to learn to give home and space and attention to all that is by dying to self and giving room and loving attention to all to which my nature fitted me, with which I shared in the friendship of being. MacDonald has a beautiful phrase that captures it well: "To everything glad I lent the hall of my being wherein to revel."[11]

---

[8] Chesterton also brings out the importance of understanding this ordering within ourselves that gives us the capacity to be co-creators with God. It is, he says, because we are a microcosm of the wider universe that we can be co-creators ourselves, holding all things in ourselves as a mirror holds things in its reflection. In *The Everlasting Man*, he writes: "a new thing had appeared in the cavernous night of nature, a mind that is like a mirror. It is like a mirror because it is truly a thing of reflection. It is like a mirror because in it alone all the other shapes can be seen like shining shadows in a vision.... The mirror is the only thing that can contain them all. Man is the microcosm." G. K. Chesterton, *The Everlasting Man*, in *Collected Works*, vol. 2 (San Francisco: Ignatius Press, 1986), 167.

[9] Luke 9:53.

[10] John 12:24.

[11] *Phantastes and Lilith* (London: Victor Gollancz, 1962), 412.

Later on I found that the Orkney poet Edwin Muir offers a similar insight in *The Question*, though in the paradoxical form of the committed search being completed in a *being found*:

> Will you, sometime, who have sought so long and seek
> Still in the slowly darkening hunting ground,
> Catch sight some ordinary month or week
> Of that strange quarry you scarcely thought you sought—
> Yourself, the gatherer gathered, the finder found,
> The buyer, who would buy all, in bounty bought—
> And perch in pride on the princely hand, at home,
> And there, the long hunt over, rest and roam?[12]

Muir holds out for us here a promise and a condition. The promise is that we will find ourselves at home, finally, on the princely hand. And there is just one condition: if we allow ourselves to be caught, gathered, bought. The Christian promise, ultimately, concerns, of course, eternal life with the Lord. It speaks to that final reality of our resting and roaming in the eternal kingdom. What I came to discover in the Church's understanding was that the secret of the journey of conversion was that of the self being enlarged through capture and, moreover, that this was the potential built into every encounter with being. The path of learning is to be caught by the truth, the goodness, and the beauty of being; it is what the Church calls the path of conversion, and God in his goodness makes this path and possibility available to us at every moment. It is perhaps for this reason that the Church describes conversion as "an uninterrupted task".[13]

Denominations, Loss and Gain

At this point, I would like to say something about the denominational aspect of my conversion. My journey has led me from a Baptist church in Canterbury, where I worshipped with my family, to the local Anglican village church, where I found a welcome and home after that transformational reading of the Gospel of Saint Luke and within whose communion I initially pursued a path to ordination, and then, by God's

---

[12] Edwin Muir, "The Question", in *Collected Poems* (London: Faber and Faber, 1960), 122.
[13] *Catechism of the Catholic Church*, no. 1428.

grace, to full communion with the Catholic Church around ten years later, on the Feast of Saint Petroc, June 4, 1985.

Since then, I have continued to change and seek, for conversion is not a once and for all affair, and I have found that there remains a need both for a continual rediscovery of original graces, as one seeks to be true to the moments of "first love" that led to or deepened one's conversion, and also to revisit one's deepest reasons for belief in light of the testing, the falls, and the challenges of the years.

Although raised in a Baptist setting, I was always very conscious of the ancient Christian heritage of England, especially as it was expressed in the landscape, with every village and small town being joined, via its church towers and spires, to the heavens, to a heavenly Lordship over the fields, over work, and over every local relationship. My story is one of deep indebtedness to many elements of this heritage and to those who led me to appreciate the Christian tradition, both in its local manifestations and more broadly. In the course of this ongoing and uninterrupted conversion, I have "become Catholic". But this is not to say that the reasons I have been discovering during this journey have been mainly denominational in character, i.e., reasons for being Catholic *rather than* Anglican or Baptist. In fact, the movement between denominations has been in some ways a painful experience—in the words of the title of John Henry Newman's story of a convert, an experience of both loss and gain.[14]

In my mid-twenties there was a sense of deep loss, for example, as I gradually separated myself from communities of faith in the Anglican communion. And this sense of loss, in part due to distinctive elements in the Anglican tradition that I had come to love, also involved dislocations in terms of my sense of identity in relation not only to English history and my immediate community but to the very geography in which I lived. One of the deepest causes of mourning I felt was the distancing of my life from the English village *church* and all it stands for in terms of ancient Christian tradition in that country. That particular sense of loss is not entirely rational, since these churches are, by and large, churches that date from the period of *Catholic* England, their archways, altars, and spires reaching back to Norman or Saxon periods predating the upheavals of the Reformation. There ought to

---

[14] J. H. Newman, *Loss and Gain: The Story of a Convert* (1848; San Francisco: Ignatius Press, 2012).

have been a corresponding sense of *gain* of these in my conversion. Yet I found—and, indeed, still find—that in general there was not; rather, only a constantly rekindled nostalgia. This may in part flow from the fact that so many of the Catholic liturgical features were deliberately destroyed—statues, crucifixes, the stone altars, usually the rood screen, and so on.

I may have been helped to keep moving despite the protracted sense of experienced loss by the location of my home: I was raised just outside the village of Chilham in Kent, on "Pilgrims Lane", a part of the ancient route that was followed by the medieval pilgrims making their way to the shrine of Saint Thomas à Becket in Canterbury. Growing up in that setting had always been a pertinent reminder to me that in the process of conversion there is a need to welcome a changing landscape for the sake of a destination worth reaching.

The felt losses as a whole, I found, then, to be a constant reminder to look forward to the One who is attracting us, drawing us beyond our immediate living spaces, and calling us to make the separations needed for the increasing levels of response within the call to conversion. All conversion involves responding to a call from what is recognized as a greater and wider reality but is not yet within reach, and necessitates the recognition that what is presently possessed is only partial—and now uncomfortably so, requiring a further step. It is Frost's sense of the need to move his pony on, of the "miles to go before I sleep"[15]—or, from the Apostle to the Gentiles, the "one thing" that is important to him: "forgetting what lies behind and straining forward to what lies ahead".[16]

I also discovered in Rilke, the Christian existentialist writer and poet, in the beautiful poem "Autumn", something expressed of the trust called for in letting go of certain limited but real goods, knowing them to be held by God:

> The leaves fall, fall as if from far away,
> like withered things from gardens deep in sky;
> they fall with gestures of renunciation.

[15] Robert Frost, "Stopping by Woods on a Snowy Evening", in *The Complete Poems* (London: Jonathan Cape, 1951), 250.
[16] Philippians 3:13.

And through the night the heavy earth falls too,
down from the stars, into the loneliness.

And we all fall. This hand must fall.
Look everywhere: it is the lot of all.

Yet there is one who holds us as we fall
eternally in his hands' tenderness.[17]

We experience loss. But no good is lost to God who is the All-Good. And in finding God, we find the One who holds all goods in his hands. One of the sustaining convictions in the ongoing process has been that one will find again what one thought lost, but find it in a richer and deeper way, and with a renewed and purer love. The Second Vatican Council Fathers put it this way: "For after we have obeyed the Lord, and in His Spirit nurtured on earth the values of human dignity, brotherhood and freedom, and indeed all the good fruits of our nature and enterprise, we will find them again, but freed of stain, burnished and transfigured."[18] Certainly, this is a promise concerning the afterlife. Nonetheless, even now, on the journey, one finds truths and delights in what one thought had been necessarily left behind, now received anew as aspects of a broader communion, with all of the wisdom that they bring to that. So, for example, in later years I have *re*discovered ongoing challenge and incisive commentary on the Christian life in the works of the veteran Protestant biblical commentator Oswald Chambers, as well as the quiet beauty of the English village church depicted in the poems of the Anglican George Herbert, vicar of the little parish of Bemerton in Wiltshire.

Meanwhile, the *gains* in conversion to Catholicism gradually became clear, even if the changes required brought with them a concomitant lack of comfort and even if the goods promised were not yet able to be embraced in their fullness. I sensed in Catholicism a powerful ability both to unify my own life and to offer a unified conception of the cosmos within which my own life would find a greater wholeness. Jesus' instructions to the disciples after the

[17] Rainer Maria Rilke, "Autumn", in *Selected Poems*, trans. C.F. MacIntyre (Berkeley and Los Angeles: University of California Press, 1968), 45.
[18] Vatican Council II, Pastoral Constitution of the Church in the Modern World *Gaudium et Spes*, December 7, 1965, no. 39.

miraculous feeding, to "gather up the fragments ... that nothing may
be lost",[19] has always struck me as the voice and character of Catholicism in general. The fragments would be of my own life, drawn
into harmony, as well as the overcoming of fragmentary concep-
tions of the universe. I found this overarching dogmatic principle in
Catholicism helpfully enunciated by the Jewish Catholic Karl Stern
as "the unutterable mystery of the 'and'": Catholicism always speaks
of unities—of God *and* his creatures, of God's plan *and* of man's free
will, of male *and* female, of Christ *and* the Church, and so on.[20] Once
I had grasped intellectually and existentially the importance of this
principle, the acceptance of Catholicism as the natural and obvious
Christian denomination was not difficult. The uniting of the historical nature of Catholicism to its deeply personal character; its universal
reach; its commitment to the union of faith and reason; its embrace of
nature within the renewal of grace; its overall synthetic instinct—all
of these elements fell into place, and I was able to see that Catholicism must be the natural repository of the work of a universal Creator
and Redeemer.[21]

The Destination and the Path

Catholicism promised unity, and a unity that would be finally without loss—and yet achieved only on a path of constant and increasing
letting oneself be "caught" by all God places in our way to know and
to love. It offered the key of self-understanding as a little cosmos,
at once supremely valued for its capacity to embrace being, and yet
needing constantly to be shattered in order to make that embrace.

[19] John 6:12.
[20] See Karl Stern, *The Flight from Woman* (New York: Farrar, Strauss and Giroux, 1965), 273.
[21] For an excellent discussion of the unity of Being, see Stephen R. L. Clark, *God, Religion and Reality*, 2nd ed. (Peterborough, N.H.: Angelico Press, 2017), 50–64. We can also consider what T. S. Eliot said of Dante's *Divine Comedy*: "The vital matter is that Dante's poem is a whole; that you must in the end come to understand every part in order to understand any part." T. S. Eliot, "Dante", in *Selected Essays 1917–1932* (New York: Harcourt, 1932), 219. He relates this character of the poem to the fact that it is rooted in Catholic belief: "That is the advantage of a coherent traditional system of dogma and morals like the Catholic: it stands apart, for understanding and assent even without belief, from the single individual who propounds it" (ibid).

In this section, I want to write a little more about the nature of that final vision and goal being held out to us, and then to unpack the way in which I understand God to be seeking to lead me to himself. I do not claim this as "my" personal journey in any exclusive sense, even though I recognize that God calls each person on his unique path. As I understand it, my experience presents the broad contours concerning the ways in which he draws *every* person into a further conversion for the sake of union with him.

I would like to begin with the importance of memory and its role in conversion. Memory is in one sense, of course, connected to the recognition of loss. Memory captures and holds that which we no longer have. But there is also, within the tradition, a way of understanding memory as our *access* point to the fullness of Being itself. Augustine's treatment in book 10 of the *Confessions* is probably the most famous discussion. In that autobiographical work, Augustine writes of how the "fields and roomy chambers of memory"[22] act as a spur pointing to a need to *move on* precisely in order to recapture and gather up what lies behind for the sake of the fullness to which God is calling us.

We can begin, as Augustine does in his discussion, with the simplest memories of sensory impressions. Such memories of sights, sounds, and smells can haunt us. Here is one that often comes unbidden for me: of a still summer day, sitting on a warm hillside, the air softly moving across the skin. The memory is vivid and intense in its simplicity: looking out over fields, copses, scattered farmhouses falling away beneath me, while a far-off sound of a car being started, unseen, is a reminder of the life that is out of sight, of the more-than-the-eye-can-capture.

When we find ourselves recalling such a scene but the memory of it quickly seems insufficient and becomes painful in the longing it inspires for its recreation, what is it that we really want? That particular *moment* is lost and gone. But as the memory comes to mind, I am momentarily back there, and an intense longing to relive this sweeps over me. What is it that I want? I surely want the particularity of that moment, that experience, that scene; but not by a repetition, not by becoming the child or adolescent I was then in a

---

[22] Augustine, *Confessions*, 10.12, trans. J. G. Pilkington, in *Nicene and Post-Nicene Fathers*, First Series, vol. I., ed. Philip Schaff (1886; Peabody, Mass.: Hendrickson, 1995), 145

forgetfulness of myself now—a simple reliving of it. I am seeking, rather, the grasp of that same view and hearing and experience by *myself now*, in the greater fullness that includes my older self, my taking the child and that past experience to myself now. And it is not only a memory that I am seeking; rather, the *full reality* of that moment, with the earth, the warmth, the car starting, the lives out of sight, the birdsong, the grass, with the whole being of what they are. I am yearning for the *reality* to which my memory points me, a reality inclusive of the original experience but more expansive, both because it is held by me *now* and also because I am seeking to include all of the reality to which that experience pointed.

Memory, then, points us not only to the past. We seek to recover certain things in memory because of their connection to the good and to the promise of greater fullness that the memories contain. One avenue down which Augustine leads us in his complex exploration of the mystery of memory is precisely the connection with the Good. What is in the memory is sought and retrieved in this way because it is a remembered good. It is brought to mind because of our desire to embrace the good, because of our desire for happiness. And the happiness that we seek in the storehouse of memory already points to a wider and fuller embrace of being and a more comprehensive unity of the self.

I would like to connect this thought to how Saint Anselm concludes his *Proslogion*, where he leads the reader in a meditation on what the fullness of joy in God must be, beyond what the heart can at the moment imagine or experience. Anselm reminds us that the character of our joy is to be finally "not such as we have experienced in created objects, but as different as the Creator from the creature".[23] We are ultimately to find our joy not just in the limited created goods around us—the hill, the sunlight, the birdsong—though any one of these can already captivate us, can send us into a silence of wonder and delight. We are to find our life and our joy in the Source of all created goods, in That than which none greater can be conceived. "And now, my soul, arouse and lift up all your understanding, and conceive, so far as you can, of what character and how great is that

---

[23] Anselm, *Proslogion*, trans. Sidney Norton Deane (Chicago: Open Court Publishing, 1903), chap. 24.

good! For, if individual goods are delectable, conceive in earnestness how delectable is that good which contains the pleasantness of all goods; and not such as we have experienced in created objects, but as different as the Creator from the creature."[24] Saint Anselm tries to assist us in contemplating what the nature of such a goal must be, together with the implications for our conversion so that we can enter into such a good. Let us think of each individual good or beautiful thing that is in our mind and then multiply and combine these as we wish, so that we would then be contemplating all of these goods *together*, with nothing in any one of them being lost. In a limited way, we know that we can, indeed, enjoy multiple goods together.

But consider now, he proposes, a different kind of multiplication: when we love and care for another person, his happiness becomes our happiness also. When we love another, our heart expands to include a joy in the joy of the other. Our *own* happiness is made the more complete by including the happiness of the one we love.

> Yet assuredly, if any other whom you did love altogether as yourself possessed the same blessedness, your joy would be doubled, because you would rejoice not less for him than for yourself. But, if two, or three, or many more, had the same joy, you would rejoice as much for each one as for yourself, if you did love each as yourself. Hence, in that perfect love of innumerable blessed angels and sainted men, where none shall love another less than himself, every one shall rejoice for each of the others as for himself.
>
> If, then, the heart of man will scarce contain his joy over his own so great good, how shall it contain so many and so great joys?[25]

We know from experience something of the joy of what this expansion of the heart entails. We know also of the daily struggles to allow our hearts to live according to this widening embrace. What must the journey of conversion be like, he is asking, finally to know and be known, love and be loved in the simplicity of God, the Source of *all* goods, the ultimate Good Who may be embraced as One? This point has implications, in turn, for how we ultimately think about ourselves: the call to joy of which Anselm wrote points not

---

[24] Ibid.
[25] Ibid., chap 25.

only to the end to which our ongoing conversion is shaped but also to the contour of our created being, the *capacity* with which we are endowed. We are made in the image and likeness of that Joy, created as *capax gaudium*.

In this journey toward the Catholic fullness promised, and to which we are directed to hope, God must *break open the heart* time after time in order to allow it to embrace more and more of the reality it seeks to comprehend. The passage of conversion is that of this ongoing breaking open of the heart, helping us to understand something of Christ's heart being pierced—for us—on the Cross in order to receive us into *his* life. It is perhaps for this reason that Pius XI described the Church's devotion to the Sacred Heart of Christ as "the sum of all religion",[26] since it is within that human heart of the Savior that we can come to know and love the Father and all creatures with the fullness of that joy to which we are called.

Having briefly considered the goal, with the assistance of Saint Anselm, let us now examine *how* God in practice leads us down this pathway, *how* he breaks open and expands the heart and mind, drawing us toward himself. In my own experience, I have found that this takes place, first of all, through his grounding of me firmly in a theoretical and practical realism. This realism has been the prerequisite for conversion at every stage. It is a realism not only about the objects of perception but, over and above this, about the transcendentals of being—the true, the good, and the beautiful.

Expanding the Heart: Realism and the Transcendentals

At its most basic, realism is the conviction that there is a world larger than our consciousness, a world that always transcends our thought, while remaining accessible to it. The foundational principle underlying conversion must, I think, be a commitment to realism in this sense, to the conviction that, beyond my ideas, feelings, and desires, my fondest beliefs and my most unvarying persuasions, there is a Reality that validates or calls them into question. Realism holds that I am not the source of the measurement of the True, of "What Is".

---

[26] Encyclical letter *Miserentissimus Redemptor* (May 8, 1928), AAS 20 (1928), no. 3.

Rather, everything I hold is necessarily to be measured against that which is True.

Not to accept this most foundational of all principles is to make conversion impossible. It is to leave the mind and the heart untouched, encased in the solitary self, infallible in the computations and value judgments it makes, for there is no Real against which it can be judged wrong. The self is busy in its own world, but it remains only a "small cosmos", incapable of expansion through being captured by that which lies outside of it. It brooks no demands that are not self-generated. Other parts of the broader Western tradition speak of the self as not having been "awoken". It lies asleep in its own world. Thus, as Heraclitus says: "To those who are awake, there is one ordered universe common (to all), whereas in sleep each man turns away (from this world) to one of his own."[27] If I am content to live in my own private world where I establish my own truth, what can "conversion" mean except that I simply *changed* my views or *altered* how I acted? What sense could be given to the notion of conversion as an improvement, a turning of oneself toward the good? When Newman said, "To live is to change, and to be perfect is to have changed often",[28] he was not speaking of change indifferently; rather, the "perfect" of which he spoke was the Truth *toward* which the change was directed; the change leading to perfection consisted in coming out of the shadows and reflections into Truth.[29]

One might think that the Christian tradition is inescapably realist. As an undergraduate, I was surprised therefore—though also somewhat attracted by—the non-realism of outlying Christian thinkers such as the Anglican priest Don Cupitt and those in the associated "Sea of Faith" movement.[30] In *Taking Leave of God*, Cupitt argues for a rejection of traditional metaphysics and objective theism in favor

---

[27] Heraclitus, frag. 22 B89, in Kathleen Freeman, *Ancilla to the Pre-Socratic Philosophers: A Complete Translation of the Fragments in Diels* (Cambridge, Mass.: Harvard University Press, 1970), 31.

[28] John Henry Newman, *An Essay on the Development of Christian Doctrine* (Westminster, Md.: Christian Classics, 1968), 1.1.7.

[29] The memorial at Newman's grave carries his motto, *Ex umbris et imaginibus in veritatem*.

[30] The Sea of Faith movement is named after a phrase in Matthew Arnold's poem "Dover Beach", comparing the retreat of faith in England to a receding tide. For details of this group, see https://www.sofn.org.uk/index.html.

of locating religious value and reality purely in human conscious-ness. Alongside this non-realism, Cupitt embraces the enlightenment view that holds self-determination to be the highest expression of human dignity. What Cupitt argues to be important is to shape one's own destiny in a mature and responsible way, to take responsibility for one's choices, but not necessarily to feel morally bound by that which one does not choose. Moral obligation arises only from con-sent; truth arises out of enlightened choice.

At the time, Cupitt appealed to the young student in me. I was drawn to this view that the only worthwhile life lies in being free of any obligations that are not self-chosen, while the authentic life con-sists in following the "rules of reason"—but without any reference to their being grounded in a Truth that could disturb my own per-ception of their validity. Thus, for Cupitt, "Modern people increas-ingly demand autonomy.... They are no longer satisfied with lives that are almost wholly determined by external limitations, powers and authorities. As they put it, they want to live their own lives, which means making one's own rules, steering a course through life of one's own choice, thinking for oneself, freely expressing oneself and choosing one's own destiny."[31] The overarching task of reli-gion, he claimed, is to support and encourage this movement toward autonomy, to "celebrate the triumph of universal, free and sovereign consciousness, emancipated from and lord over nature".[32]

This exaltation of consciousness combined with non-realism appeared at the time a tempting path. I could feel the lure of aban-doning obligations in favor of a self-identified destiny, with all the posturing of a "higher life" that could be associated with that.

In an early essay, "Tradition and Individual Talent", T. S. Eliot argues against this kind of individualistic non-realism. It is vital, he stressed, that poets know their relation to other artists in history. "No poet, no artist of any art, has his complete meaning alone."[33] The art-ist is aware that his work "must inevitably be judged by the standards of the past". For this reason, Eliot proposes, "the mind of Europe" is "a mind which he learns in time to be much more important than

[31] Don Cupitt, *Taking Leave of God* (London: SCM Press, 1980), 156.
[32] Ibid.
[33] T. S. Eliot, "Tradition and Individual Talent", in *Selected Essays, 1917–1932* (New York: Harcourt, Brace, 1932), 4.

his own".[34] There is something larger than the individual "talent" in relation to which the poet must position himself.

Eliot is surely correct in arguing that there is a sense in which I must always place myself within a living tradition, must test my ideas and thoughts against those of others. And if I want to say anything more significant than that I judge my work valuable according to my own judgments, or that my work can be construed good according to my own lights, then I necessarily accept a comparative, a rule, that is indebted to the tradition in which I stand.

Eliot wants to argue for something more than this, though. There is a *good* that is reached by this willing engagement with tradition and with the creativity and insights of others. The creation of art involves the recognition of a common humanity in which poetry can be understood not only as the expression of the individual with his particular emotions and sensibilities but as reaching to something higher: "emotion that has its life in the poem and not in the history of the poet.... And the poet cannot reach this impersonality without surrendering himself wholly to the work to be done."[35] The poet, in doing justice to his subject, seeks a self-surrender to that which is larger than himself. The poet, in order to be creative, must be captured by something wider and larger than himself, something that calls him to response and to obedience.

Realism requires of me that I recognize a "common world" into which I can and should "awake". It is not a common world empty of value. Rather, it is precisely the goodness, beauty, and truth of this world that awakens me. In practical and immediate terms, this is usually the world of my family and my friends, my colleagues, and those who live in my locality. And this may indeed be a sufficient grounding for conversion: it is enough to break from a solipsistic worldview so as to share a world in a local, natural, and social community. Gradually, of course, it may be perceived that the world against which I should seek to measure myself is a less parochial one. Perhaps, like Eliot, I then seek to take on "the mind of Europe", or I measure myself against different strands of tradition, or perhaps I seek to follow the practices and customs of the contemporary majority and adhere to the "common opinion" of this majority.

[34] Ibid., 5.
[35] Ibid., 11.

But the key point for conversion lies precisely in the conviction about realism concerning the good, the true, and the beautiful. In the end, expansions of the self in relation to measurements of the broader community are only valuable insofar as they are grounded in realism. For why should I care for a conversion to whichever particular social "world" or tradition I am describing unless its standards are right and its opinions true? Only if I allow a measure beyond that social world as well, by which *it* may be judged, can my "conversion" be more than simply a matter of "change". Conversion understood as improvement, as reform, implies moving toward the good and the true. In the end, there must be a measure that is not simply the measure of "our" agreement, whoever "we" may be. "Conversion" is a concept that implies "That Which Is" beyond my—and all of "our"—desires, thoughts, and beliefs.

One other point about Christian realism became important to me for understanding how my conversion could be not only desirable but possible. The Catholic realist tradition had helped me to see that I do not stand in relation to Being as active subject to a passive "objectivity". That which transcends my thought and against which all my thoughts must finally be measured is *necessarily* more than that which is established as true as the result of my own—or of "our"—seeking. If it were only this, then *I* (or *we*) would have established it as the truth. If, then, there is an ultimate Reality that is worthy of our obedience and to which we are called to make a submission of mind and life, it also makes no sense to conceive of this Being as nonpersonal, as an impersonal *telos* of our search but in no sense the Origin, Ground, and Sustainer of that same personal search. Rather, the ultimately Real is the ultimate Being: Father, Son, and Holy Spirit, three Persons, seeking and finding and drawing us, the One who establishes *us* in truth.

A particular point of gratitude for me in this journey of conversion has been the publication of the *Catechism of the Catholic Church*. As a synthesis of the patrimony of the faith, offering us the "cultural capital"[36] of Catholicism, it has, over the years, both consolidated my searching and honed and structured it. The *Catechism* has made sense of the fact that my conversion must be crowned by a *dogmatic formation*

---

[36] See Tracy Rowland, "The Catechism of the Catholic Church and the Culture of the Incarnation", in *Speaking the Truth in Love: The Catechism and the New Evangelization*, ed. Petroc Willey and Scott Sollom (Steubenville: Emmaus Academic, 2019), 220.

through which, in the words of Saint Paul, we become "obedient from the heart to the standard of teaching to which you were committed".[37] Because the Truth is by definition the most certain of all things, at its *deepest*, it reaches us in dogmatic form. The "standard of teaching" of which Saint Paul writes is synthesized in the Creed that Saint Ambrose describes as our "spiritual seal".[38] Our affirmation of this Creed results, in turn, in our being "sealed" with the Holy Spirit.[39] This sealing is what the *symbolon* had promised. The Truth *himself* now "seals" us and re-forms us. The *Catechism* has been promulgated by the Church in our day to make this formation and sealing in the Truth possible through calling us to conversion and the assent of faith.

Among the transcendentals, beauty is the lure that captures the heart for conversion, that breaks it open and allows the heart to expand. Beauty stands in a particular relationship to the other transcendentals since it is understood as the *radiance* of Being. The more perfect a being is, the more unity, truth, and goodness are present and, correspondingly, the more "radiance" or splendor. Thus, beauty is the splendor of unity, the splendor of goodness, and the splendor of truth. According to Saint Thomas, "unity" radiates as integrity, "goodness" radiates as proportion, and "truth" radiates as clarity.[40] The tradition, therefore, speaks of beauty as the entry point to the good, the true, and the one.

The principal effect of beauty is that it calls one to *attend to the wonder of being*. An early memory of intense beauty was that of listening to the opening of Sibelius' violin concerto. It was, I think, the *alien* quality of the lonely violin, evocative of frozen wastes, that called me out of myself and made me attentive to something that I knew only as profoundly *other* than myself. That experience was also deeply formative for me in setting me on a journey of discovery of classical music that profoundly shaped my life. Later on, I was to discover this character of austere and otherworldly sound even more powerfully

---

[37] Romans 6:17. At baptism we are handed over into this dogmatic teaching for our formation in the faith. See Congregation for the Doctrine of the Faith, instruction *Donum Veritatis: On the Ecclesial Vocation of the Theologian* (May 24, 1990), no. 1.

[38] Ambrose, *Expl. symb.* I: *PL* 17:1193.

[39] Cf. Ephesians 1:13.

[40] Saint Thomas speaks of beauty as having three components: "integrity or perfection, since those things, which are impaired, are by the very fact ugly; due proportion or harmony; and lastly, brightness, or clarity, whence things are beautiful which have a bright color" (*ST* I, q. 39, a. 8).

in Beethoven's String Quartet No. 14, written in his final years, an
offering from another world breaking into my own.[41]

It is not always an alien quality in beauty that calls us to attend. It
can be simply the power of an uninvited experience of radiance in
nature or in another person. An example from my adolescent years
is one that took place on a wet November evening in a narrow lane
in the heart of the Kentish countryside. The ground was recently sat-
urated; the golden horizon was cold with the promise of the coming
winter, giving rise to that distinctive autumnal combination of fading
sunlight and intense clarity. Suddenly, the all too familiar country
lane was filled with an intensity of *presence* that was unbearable in its
beauty. I vividly recall *begging* for its intensity to be lessened. My life
could not bear to receive such beauty.

That experience of suffused presence in nature is not uncommon,
and we find it memorably expressed in literature as different as the
poetic exaltation of Thomas Traherne, on seeing the dust in the street
sparkling as with precious gems,[42] and the homely setting of Mole
and Rat meeting Pan in the *Wind in the Willows*.[43] We can allow a
famous passage from Wordsworth to represent the point for us:

> And I have felt
> A presence that disturbs me with the joy
> Of elevated thoughts; a sense sublime
> Of something far more deeply interfused,
> Whose dwelling is the light of setting suns,
> And the round ocean and the living air,
> And the blue sky, and in the mind of man;

[41] For an insightful discussion of the spirituality of Beethoven's final quartets, see Burnett
James, *Beethoven and Human Destiny* (London: Phoenix House, 1960), 147–66.

[42] "The corn was orient and immortal wheat, which never should be reaped, nor was ever
sown. I thought it had stood from everlasting to everlasting. The dust and stones of the street
were as precious as gold: the gates were at first the end of the world. The green trees when
I saw them first through one of the gates transported and ravished me, their sweetness and
unusual beauty made my heart to leap, and almost mad with ecstasy, they were such strange
and wonderful things." In Thomas Traherne, *Centuries of Meditations* (Oxford: Oxford University Press, 1960), 3.3.

[43] See Kenneth Grahame, *Wind in the Willows* (New York: Scribner, 1953), 134–36, where
Mole "looked in the very eyes of the Friend and Helper.... All this he saw, for one moment
breathless and intense, vivid on the morning sky; and still, as he looked, he lived; and still, as
he lived, he wondered."

A motion and a spirit, that impels
All thinking things, all objects of all thought,
And rolls through all things.[44]

What is common to all forms of the Beautiful is that each experience captures the attention of the mind and at the same time breaks
open the heart. The experience of the "weight of glory" (C. S. Lewis'
phrase)[45] breaks us out of any lazily accepted presumption that we
determine the boundaries of meaning in the world, that the world
can be described and redescribed solely as we think fit. Beauty wakes
us from sleep and ruins forever any comfortable view that the world
is ours to control and shape.

The experience of beauty can also signal the joy that is promised
from this breaking of the heart for the sake of its expansion. It can do
this especially when the call of beauty is united to an experience of
communion with another. The experience of beauty in another person, calling us to love, is the most familiar form of this. The French
philosopher Simone Weil once wrote, "Among human beings, only
the existence of those we love is fully recognized."[46] Her assertion is
perhaps not as fanciful as it seems. How convinced are we that others
really have a life as vivid and as full as our own? As we drive home,
past the dazzling headlights, do we not catch ourselves wondering at
times at our own thought that "each of those drivers is a center of
consciousness every bit as real as my own. And for each of them I
am the mere passing of light across their windshield"? The existence
of others as personal consciousnesses occasionally surprises us, just as
their ongoing existence does when out of sight. Falling in love "may
be the moment when we are made to realize the real being of at least
one thing".[47] Coming to love another, we realize that we share a

---

[44] William Wordsworth, "Lines Composed a Few Miles above Tintern Abbey, on Revis-
iting the Banks of the Wye during a Tour, July 13, 1798", in *The Poetical Works of Wordsworth*
(London: Oxford University Press, 1936), 93–103.

[45] C. S. Lewis, "The Weight of Glory", in *Screwtape Proposes a Toast and Other Pieces*
(Glasgow: William Collins Sons, 1977), 94–110.

[46] Simone Weil, *Gravity and Grace* (New York: G. P. Putnam's Sons, 1952), 113. Elsewhere
she described the state of attention we should seek as one of control, of focus, with the mind
and will learning not so much to give orders to do things as rather stopping us from doing other
things. See her *Lectures on Philosophy* (Cambridge: Cambridge University Press, 1978), 205.

[47] Clark, *God, Religion and Reality*, 46.

world and at the same time seek to share in it more fully. If we allow the heart to expand, to break open, we capture being and are snared. The dazzling being of the beloved seen at that point is—according to some who write within the tradition—the person's worth in the eyes of God. The one in love has been lifted up to share in the gaze of God, sharing for that moment in the true vision of the One who holds all things in being by his gaze.[48]

The gaze of love, sharing in the vision of glory, is, of course, a long way from the point where one begins to share *truly* in that fire of love. That requires a path of life, requires vows and commitment and giving and receiving in sustained friendship. But the moment of awakening is nonetheless there. Through beauty, Being has broken through the defenses of the cushioned self.

These and other forms and experiences of beauty combine and recombine to draw us higher and higher, like the rising trills of *The Lark Ascending* in Vaughan Williams' captivating idyll of the English countryside. The sounds spiral up from the summer fields into the heavens. In every person, forms of beauty settle and coalesce, with experiences crisscrossing and reinforcing as the incomparable Beauty himself pulls us in and through his created forms as he draws us to contemplate him finally in beholding the face of Christ.[49]

Climbing the Wrekin

A recurring image I have for this ongoing journey of conversion is that of climbing the Wrekin, a hill rising out of the undulating Shropshire countryside and affording far-reaching views across the beautiful surroundings in all directions.[50]

---

[48] For discussions, see Charles Williams, *The Figure of Beatrice: A Study in Dante* (New York: Octagon Books, 1972), and Dorothy Sayers, "The Beatrician Vision in Dante and Other Poets", in *The Poetry of Search and the Poetry of Statement* (Eugene, Ore.: Wipf and Stock, 2006), 45–68.

[49] See Joseph Murphy, "The Fairest and the Formless: The Face of Christ as Criterion for Christian Beauty according to Joseph Ratzinger", in *Benedict XVI and Beauty in Sacred Art and Architecture*, ed. D. Vincent Twomy, S.V.D., and Janet E. Rutherford (Dublin: Four Courts Press, 2011), 37–53.

[50] It is a hill I would often climb with my family, rising 1330 feet out of the Shropshire plain, that might have conceivably been one of the inspirations for Tolkien in his descriptions of Weathertop.

I have found several points helpful about this image for my conversion journey. In the first place, it is a realistic reminder both of the gradual nature of conversion and of the effort involved in making the changes required in one's outlook and life. Pope Saint Gregory proffered wise advice to Abbot Mellitus as he sent him on mission to the English people in A.D. 601, counseling patience as he would seek to draw the new converts more deeply into the faith: "For it is certainly impossible to eradicate all errors from obstinate minds at one stroke, and whoever wishes to climb to a mountain top climbs gradually step by step, and not in one leap."[51]

In the second place, it highlights the importance of an ongoing assessment of one's position. As I climbed the Wrekin in the past, I would regularly pause and take stock of the view, looking back on my winding path, drinking in and reviewing the scenery. I have found that there is just such a continual stock-taking in the journey of faith, a testing of footholds as one navigates the upward path: Is this a safe route? What is the view from *here*? How well am I, after all, resourced for this? Above all, there is a constant seeking to gain a *view* of all that can be encompassed in one's journey so far.

And, finally, the image speaks to me of the goal: the uninterrupted prospect, the whole vista laid out before me, the countryside laid out before me in all its beauty. Wordsworth speaks of such a moment of glorious vision, climbing on a summer's night near Mount Snowden in Wales:

> I looked about, and lo!
> The Moon stood naked in the Heavens, at height
> Immense above my head, and on the shore
> I found myself of a huge sea of mist,
> Which, meek and silent, rested at my feet:
> A hundred hills their dusky backs upheaved
> All over this still Ocean....
> Meanwhile, the Moon look'd down upon this shew
> In single glory, and we stood, the mist
> Touching our very feet.[52]

[51] Cited in Bede, *A History of the English Church and People*, rev. ed. trans. Leo Sherley-Price (Harmondsworth: Penguin Books, 1968), 1.30.

[52] William Wordsworth, *The Prelude*, rev. ed. (London: Oxford University Press, 1960), bk. 13, 40–54.

The scene for Wordsworth appears as the "perfect image of a mighty Mind, / Of one that feeds upon infinity".[53] While he locates the occasion for this meditation within a night climb, the ascent following the gradual fall of evening, I prefer to see ongoing conversion as a climbing in the brightening morning, with the goal to be achieved as a final emergence into a glorious day, crisp and clear, in which the whole panorama will finally be before us.

That vision, *finally*, will be a truly catholic one. As we know, "catholic" means "according to the whole", and my journey into the Catholic Church and my ongoing searching have been inspired by a desire for a greater grasp of the whole, in terms of breadth and depth. I was drawn to the Church precisely *because* of her teaching that the life of faith is not a once and for all affair, but requires a journey to gain a truly catholic unity in oneself and in one's vision of things—a journey into greater fullness and, ultimately, joy, meeting new challenges, discovering further enrichment, needing deeper conversion. I knew from experience the distance that I had to travel for the sake of finding integrity and unity in myself, and I needed a Church that took seriously the time needed for *metanoia*, that spoke realistically about the challenge of the ascent, had well-worn directions for how to walk that path, had the grace to enable the journey, and could draw me on through the inevitable challenges and setbacks by providing *reasons* for believing that the prospect gained would provide the perfect satisfaction of the mind and of the heart—it would be both a vision and the sharing in a new way of seeing, "fair as the moon, bright as the sun, terrible as an army with banners".[54]

[53] Ibid., bk. 13, 69–70.
[54] Song of Solomon 6:10.